Ceramics of the World

Ceramics of the World

From 4000 B.C. to the Present

General Editors:

Lorenzo Camusso and Sandro Bortone

Harry N. Abrams, Inc., Publishers, New York

Page 2: Chün ware vase. Sung dynasty; 960–1279 A.D. *Height: 11 in (28 cm). Width: 5 in (12.8 cm). Washington, D.C., Freer Gallery of Art (no. 50.8).*

Designed by Luisa Pizzeghella
Translated by Geoffrey Culverwell
Index by Valerie Lewis Chandler, BA, ALAA
Produced by Fenice 2000 s.r.l., Milan

Text, captions, and illustrations based on:
La Ceramica Europea by Henri-Pierre Fourest (Kodansha-Mondadori);
La Ceramica dell'Estremo Oriente by John Ayers [Chinese Ceramics];
Madeleine Paul-David [Korean Ceramics], and Adolfo Tamburello
[Japanese Ceramics] (Kodansha-Mondadori);
La Ceramica Antica by John Boardman (Kodansha-Mondadori);
La Ceramica Islamica by Geza Fehervari (Kodansha-Mondadori)

North American Ceramics text by Barbara Perry; illustrations © Courtney
Frisse (264, 272–76, 278–79, 281); © Anthony Potter (282);
© Jacques Cael Cressaty (283); Anthony Cunha (280)

Library of Congress Cataloging-in-Publication Data
Camusso, Lorenzo.
    Ceramics of the world: from 4000 B.C. to the present/Lorenzo
  Camusso, Sandro Bortone.
        p.   cm.
    Includes bibliographical references and index.
    ISBN 0–8109–3175–3
    1. Pottery—History.   2. Porcelain—History.   I. Bortone. Sandro.
  II. Title.
  NK3780.C37 1992
  738'.09—dc20   91–29808
                                                          CIP

Published in 1992 by Harry N. Abrams, Incorporated, New York
A Times Mirror Company

Printed and bound in Italy by Arnoldo Mondadori Editore, Verona

Contents

Kiln, from Li tre libri dell'arte del vasaio
by Cipriano Piccolpasso. Pesaro, 1879.

Introduction

Ceramics are as old as civilization itself. A prehistoric population that had learned to work, mould and bake clay in order to create useful containers was a population that had advanced beyond the most primitive stage of life and begun physically to manipulate its natural environment by the creation of lasting artefacts. It is no coincidence that the earliest pottery shards have been found mainly in areas that were home to relatively advanced societies, which generally already practiced agriculture. In other words, the potter is not a figure known since palaeolithic times, but one who arrived fairly late on the scene.

And yet, in the popular imagination, few activities are linked more closely to the concept of primitive man than that of the potter, since the only evidence we have for the existence of innumerable ancient cultures are tantalizing fragments of pottery. In many areas, shards have for a very long time supplied varied and plentiful information about the sort of life led by early man. In many cases everything else has vanished, obliterated by time, while pottery, despite its very fragile nature, has paradoxically proved to be almost indestructible, at least as a source of archaeological information. It thus represents an almost immutable testimony to life.

A special correlation therefore appears to exist between man and ceramics. Even the terminology would seem to emphasize this, since the description of ceramic wares normally involves terms borrowed from human anatomy. When talking of vases, for example, we refer to the body, the foot, the shoulders, the neck, the lip and so on. What is more, the Latin word *testa*, which originally signified an earthen vessel or pot, during imperial times began to be used, first jokingly and then in normal conversation, as a synonym for *caput* (head or chief). And we read in Genesis that God "formed man out of the dust of the ground," as though he were an earthenware vessel or a terra-cotta figurine.

Rather like Minerva, who sprang perfectly formed from the head of Jupiter, ceramics seem to have been perfect from the beginning. The basics must all have been discovered at once, because the method of working ceramics has followed certain fundamental rules which have remained substantially unchanged for many thousands of years. First and foremost, there is the preparation of the paste, which allows the potter to eliminate impurities and achieve the desired homogeneity. Then comes the modelling, which decides the shape. Another stage is represented by the decoration, which provides the finishing touch and enhances the aesthetic quality of a piece. The final operation involves firing, which, through the correct regulation of the heat, imparts an irreversible degree of hardness to the piece. These were and continue to be the essential stages in the production of ceramics. Each stage, however, offers a variety of possible choices, which, with the passing of the centuries, have been notably extended through the experiments conducted by countless generations of craftsmen in different parts of the world. There are certain operations that must be carried out, but there are many different ways of progressing from one stage to the next.

Each process poses its own special problems and the various operations are not independent, but influence each other and interreact in a fairly complicated way: for example, different types of material call for different methods of firing and different temperatures, just as one particular type of firing may preclude the use of a certain type of decoration. In order to clarify what follows, it would seem appropriate to examine separately each of the different stages involved in the manufacture of ceramics and also make some preliminary remarks.

The first problem is clearly that of the availability of the necessary raw materials. If the paste is based on ordinary clay, then there will be very little difficulty, since abundant and easily accessible deposits occur in nature almost everywhere. This explains why examples of earthenware are found in nearly every part of the world. The situation is very different with regard to kaolin, the essential ingredient, along with felspar and quartz, of the paste needed to make porcelain, by far the finest and most highly prized form of ceramic. Kaolin is a special type of clay, with very few impurities, which retains its shape, even in very high temperatures, and turns a white colour after firing. Compared to other clays, it is less elastic and therefore less easy to model, but, by way of compensation, it also allows for superior results, in terms of both functionalism and aesthetics. A significant part of the history of ceramics was taken up by the centuries-long attempts in the Islamic world and then in the West to discover the formula of the porcelain produced in the Far East and to find acceptable substitutes for its mysterious and wondrous white paste.

The paste holds the key to malleability, making it possible to mould a piece and to ensure it retains its shape. Before this, however, the potter needs to cleanse the clay of any possible impurities that might detract from the result or, at least, create unforeseen effects during firing. Allowances must also be made for "shrinkage," since the clay will contract in the kiln and thus increase the risk of distortions and fractures. A good way of avoiding this is to add "degreasing" materials to the paste, such as ground terra cotta, which will act, so to speak, as a sort of invisible framework within the piece. Additions could be made to the paste for other reasons as well: the Athenian potters, for example, enhanced the natural reddish colour of the local clay by means of a special colouring agent.

The modelling was originally done solely by hand, in the case of both practical wares and also small figures such as those intended for ritual use. Soon, however, work was assisted by a variety of different aids, for cutting, incising, smoothing and polishing. A primitive form of the potter's wheel was introduced, driven either by the potter himself or by an assistant, and used for modelling circular shapes. The use of moulds, which allow for a speedier, more exact and more regular output, is also a very ancient practice. Sometimes the different sections of a piece were modelled separately and then assembled, using a layer of semi-liquid clay to bind them together.

One very ancient method of potting involves building up a series of clay coils, the diameters of which match the dimensions of the piece to be created, and then combining the different layers by applying pressure with the fingers. Formal regularity has not always been regarded as critical: Japanese master potters would distort, by hand, pieces that had been too perfectly formed with the help of mechanical devices.

The shapes obtained are left to dry for a first hardening, and it is sometimes at this stage that the pot-ter will proceed to smooth the piece, an act that will affect its aesthetic appearance, but which has, above all, the practical consequence of reducing the porosity of the clay; this is particularly important when the potter does not intend to give the piece any additional coating to make it impervious. As clay is exposed to the air it gradually becomes less and less pliable, and the piece will harden, but it can still be re-worked or have the finishing touches applied. Complete evaporation of the water then takes place in the kiln, and it is the firing which determines the process, at a certain point irreversible, of fixing the shape; thus the clay cannot be returned to its malleable state by being wetted. It is, therefore, the fire which finally separates the clay from the water and so creates the ceramic end product.

Baking was originally conducted in the open air and involved the direct exposure of the piece to the flame; the construction of kilns with a separate chamber was a further advance that allowed, amongst other things, control over the atmospheric conditions under which a piece was fired. The degree of oxygen in the atmosphere is important because it can radically alter the effects of the firing process and even determine differences in colour. It is also normal for a single piece to be subjected to successive firings, which may involve different temperatures, different times and different types of atmosphere, depending on the needs of the materials used and the sort of effects desired. The first baking of a clay piece, as yet uncovered and undecorated, is called the "biscuit fire." Generally, in order to strengthen a piece, high temperatures are used, while, in order to avoid damaging the colours added during decoration, lower temperatures have to be adopted, or even special devices such as saggars, cases made of fireproof clay that provide further protection for the pieces being baked in the kiln.

The earliest type of ceramic decoration took the form of a wide variety of different coatings, whose initial purpose was the purely functional one of imparting the correct degree of impermeability to a piece, while also fulfilling a no less important aesthetic role. Slips, often applied by dipping a piece during the drying process, represent a very ancient type of coating that has an essentially decorative function. Based on coloured clays, a slip does not in itself generally give the surface any degree of vitreosity: this calls for other materials. The shiny and semi-shiny black or red patina on vases from the Classical era (one thinks of Attic or Arezzo wares) may be described essentially as a slip that has been vitrified by special firing techniques.

In order to ensure that a piece is completely impervious various types of vitreous coating may be used. The earliest types were the Ancient Egyptian ones based on alkaline fluxes. Later, lead glazes were introduced and, later still, tin glazes which, rather than being transparent, were opaque white in colour and could therefore act as a substitute for the smooth surfaces of Chinese porcelain, which used a felspathic glaze. Another special glaze is that found on luster ware, which was developed by Islamic potters to create magnificent effects of metallic brilliance and iridescence. Strictly speaking, however, it was a decorative addition rather than a covering, since it was applied to wares that had already been glazed. Yet another type of glaze is salt glaze, used typically on certain German stoneware pieces and based on sodium and silica.

The most spectacular aspect of the story of ceramics, as well as the one that excites the greatest degree of interest, is that of their painted decoration; and the main aim of this book, both in its text and its plates, will be to illustrate this. It would be pointless, however, in a brief résumé such as this, to anticipate the extraordinary events that make up its history: rather, we should emphasize the fact that the decoration of ceramics has always involved techniques other than painting, techniques which have perhaps been unfairly neglected in the past.

Decoration may, in fact, be achieved through incisions, punchmarks, *sgraffito* work, inlays, carving, encrustation, stamping, reliefs, the addition of elements in the round, etc. Special effects can also be achieved just by exposing a piece directly to the flame or by purposely leaving impurities in the paste, as well as in countless other ways, such as, for example, deliberately ensuring that a dense craquelure will appear on the glaze or by using sandy clays that will create a specific textural effect.

Ceramics can thus provide, albeit within a relatively simple and singularly constant technical context, a highly fertile breeding ground for invention, offering a wide variety of possibilities.

This is true for all sorts of ware, on the basis of their raw materials and their eventual covering: it applies to earthenware, which by definition has a clay body, with either no covering or just a simple slip; faïence or majolica, which has a vitreous covering; stoneware, which, unlike earthenware, is made of a tough, non-porous paste; porcelain, which is obtained from a paste that is not only extremely tough, but also white; creamware, which is based on a porous paste obtained from a mixture of special white clays and siliceous earths that is then coated with a glaze.

Over the years ceramics have found many areas of application. The anthology presented in this book concentrates on one in particular, which also happens to be the most important one, that of domestic wares, but it also includes a look at the qualitative impact of glazed terra cotta, majolica and porcelain on, for example, architectonic decoration. This particular phenomenon is illustrated by means of a journey that begins in ancient Mesopotamia and then passes through areas such as Islamic Turkey and Moorish Spain, Renaissance Italy and modern France and Germany. There are also passing references to the minor plastic arts, in the form of statuettes and small groups, as can be seen in the pages devoted to Pharaonic Egypt, China, Korea, eighteenth-century Europe and others.

While the text provides a historical framework, the illustrations form a sort of ideal and highly select museum. Both elements are aimed at readers interested in obtaining a balanced, overall vision and also in gaining an initial familiarity with the subject. This perspective view is achieved by revisiting different times and different places in the history of ceramics, ranging from prehistory to the end of the eighteenth century, from North Africa to Japan and from England to Persia. One area of investigation that lies beyond these chronological bounds, since it also involves recent developments, is that of North American ceramics: this section aims, above all, to show how ceramics have not lost their vitality as industrial techniques gradually replace the traditional skills of the craftsman, but, on the contrary, have exploited the potential of new, free forms of artistic expression.

The Near East, Egypt and the Mediterranean

The invention of ceramics dates back to prehistory. It is worth pointing out, however, that in the light of recent archaeological research, the old theory that their emergence coincided with the dawn of the Neolithic era, when nomadism was abandoned in favour of agriculture, now appears overly simple. We now know that the production of ceramics does not represent one of the first manifestations of settled life, and it is in fact possible to detect highly evolved and clearly pre-ceramic developments in Neolithic society. As it is, even after the properties of clay had been discovered and attempts had been made to exploit them, a long time would elapse before the invention became widely used; apart from anything else, until the appearance of the first kiln, the manufacture of ceramics was in no position to assume a role of any real importance in the settled community. It should also be remembered that during the prehistoric era, at a time when man was grateful just to survive, progress was very slow and there was no pressing need for change. It is misleading to state, as once was the case, that the Nile basin and the Tigris and Euphrates valleys were the only areas in which the first attempts at making ceramics occurred. A combination of clever detective work and modern excavation techniques has meant that the maps indicating discoveries of very early vases now include areas such as the Balkans, Turkey, Syria and Palestine.

Ceramics made their first appearance in the seventh millennium, in the Near East. But by the time we encounter the Samarra civilization of northern Mesopotamia (5500–5000 B.C.), characterized by wares of great technical and aesthetic merit, we are already in the Chalcolithic era and the tools of the Stone Age are beginning to give way to the new metal

Jar. Glazed earthenware with painted decoration. Ziwiyeh, Iran; Iron Age, eighth–seventh century B.C. Height: 16¾ in (43 cm). New York, Metropolitan Museum of Art (no. 51.29.1).

Ceramic styles of the Ancient World

Interior of a bowl decorated with stylized, long-haired female figures surrounded by a ring of scorpions. From Samarra (Mesopotamia); fifth millennium B.C.

technology. Painted pottery had already been common for some time, but the decoration on Samarra wares contains figures of animals (page 16) and stylized humans, as well as geometric motifs. These images, which possess a strong sense of movement and portray aspects of wild and domestic life, seem to respond, in this humble material, to the same impulse that had long ago led man to decorate caves and rockfaces.

If we look further to the east, to Persia, an area which made an important and perhaps decisive contribution to the early development of ceramics, we discover equally attractive wares, again dating from the Chalcolithic era. The high-speed wheel was now facilitating the production of thrown pots with thin walls. The painted wares of the proto-Elamite culture of Susa display a deft and exuberant style, characterized by skilful black patterns and subtly evocative zoomorphic motifs (page 17). They reveal a high degree of artistic awareness of the decorative potential of certain natural shapes.

Egypt calls for certain preliminary observations. Even though, as in other areas, the earliest evidence has been obtained from Neolithic sites, it is clear that the production of ceramics began relatively late. What is more, during the centuries that followed these early beginnings, archaeology has proved that ceramics continued to play a relatively minor role when compared to other sectors, particularly given the large numbers of artefacts that have survived in the region. This may be attributed to the dearth of high-quality clay deposits or the fact that the wares produced from Nile mud were not always of a sort to inspire potters. It is, however, true that there are some remarkable examples of Egyptian ceramics, particularly from the earliest period. Where the pre-Dynastic era is concerned, one thinks of the beautiful, highly polished red vases of the Nagada period, often bearing an abstract decoration of white dots or stylized animal shapes (page 18). The particular hallmark of this decorative style is the rich variety of its motifs, some of which portray hunting scenes and dancers and anticipate later forms of Egyptian genre painting.

An examination of Egyptian and Near Eastern ceramics from later periods reveals a certain regression rather than any progress. There appears to be an overall lowering of quality, particularly marked when it comes to imaginative decoration. In Mesopotamia the fascinating ceramics of the pre-Dynastic or Early Dynastic periods are replaced by a different type of wares during the course of the third millennium. In the Larsa period (2000–1800 B.C.) the most common form of decoration is that of incised patterns (page 19), whose grooves in some cases contain a white filling or alternatively act as outlines for anthropomorphic or zoomorphic forms. In their shapes and style of decoration, these Babylonian ceramics appear to echo contemporary wares from the southern part of Persia (page 20). There were very few innovations as far as clay vessels are concerned, even in Egypt.

The position is very different in the case of Turkey, where excavations, which can no longer be called recent, have brought to light sites that are no less informative than their Mesopotamian counterparts when it comes to illustrating the settled life of prehistoric man, with very fine examples of painted pottery from as early as the sixth millennium B.C. Much later, during the second millennium B.C., at the beginning of the new Hittite empire, there emerged a special type of local pottery that had a definite

Small jar with side grips and bold, swirling decoration. From Hacilar (Anatolia); c. fifth millennium B.C. Oxford, Ashmolean Museum.

Bowl with a painted decoration of stylized plant and animal motifs, including panthers along the rim, and geometrical patterns. From Tepe Siyalk (Iran); fourth millennium B.C. Paris, Musée du Louvre.

influence on later ceramic developments, even in the West. The pottery in question consists of zoomorphic vases, in which imagination combines with functionalism (perhaps for ritual purposes) to create animal shapes in clay (page 21).

In Egypt, the real innovative contribution of the modeller is to be found elsewhere, when the processes of glazing and glass making were discovered, probably by chance. The basic materials are sand (silica) and sodium carbonate (natron), and it was used from very ancient times (fourth millennium B.C.) to make glass beads and trinkets, generally blue or green in colour because of the presence of copper oxides in the clay paste. During the cooling process, alkaline glazes of this sort are subject to considerable shrinkage, to such an extent, in fact, that they cannot easily be applied to the clay body, which itself contracts, albeit not to the same degree. They therefore had to be specially prepared for the purpose, as was done in later centuries. Glazing could, however, be applied to soft stones such as steatite, which hardens with heat, and it was also used to cover a substance obtained from pulverized quartz, which could be moulded or modelled by hand and also, with some difficulty, worked on the wheel. The lucidity of the colour and the luster of the surface possessed characteristics that were unknown to the rest of the ancient world, and many years were to pass before non-Egyptian craftsmen learned the technique. Another, similar compound, also typically Egyptian, was the so-called "blue frit," based on siliceous sand, soda, potash and copper, which was used specifically for small objects. Various colours could be obtained, but the main ones were green and blue, which were also the royal colours.

In the first half of the second millennium, during the Middle Kingdom, very lively, glazed pottery figurines of animals were made, but the most outstanding wares were those produced in the New Kingdom, which are in a very real sense miniature sculptures. One example of this is the pottery sphinx in glowing, turquoise-blue faïence depicting the Pharaoh Amenhotep III (1417–1379 B.C.) (page 22). In the area of small figures there were also the models used as grave goods, such as *ushabti*, which, although once made of wood or clay, now became increasingly made of faïence (page 23). These take the form of mummiform statuettes portraying slaves or workmen, which were buried with the departed and were designed to perform any manual labour that might be required of their master in the hereafter.

Towards the end of the Bronze Age, Persia again provides the main focus of attention, with a succession of important local cultures. The site of Marlik Tepe, for example, has yielded a series of anatomically crude, but singularly expressive human figures from the Iron Age (page 24), whilst a very attractive style of decoration, whose freshness and fluency recall much more ancient traditions, begins to appear on the ninth-century painted pottery discovered in a necropolis in Luristan, a mountainous area of south-western Persia (page 25).

During the seventh century the potters of Cyprus made some of the most exciting and decoratively satisfying wares ever produced during Antiquity. The island would in any case have deserved special mention in a book on ceramics, since the thousands of pots preserved in its soil represent an extremely rich and in some aspects unique, documentary source. The contribution in this case, however, relates to quality rather than quantity and it affects the history of art and not simply that of archaeology. It involves a

Vase decorated with diamond shapes, chequered design and coloured bands contained within double lines. From Susa (Iran); fourth millennium B.C. Paris, Musée du Louvre.

Jar with comb-shaped boats and name flag. Gerzean pottery. From Nagada (Egypt); c. 3200 B.C. Oxford, Ashmolean Museum.

new style, with two-colour effects achieved using red and black glazes, which, at its height, introduced the surprising element of large, finely stylized figures of animals that spread unchecked over the surface of wide-bodied pots (page 26). The painter had suddenly freed himself from all geometrical restrictions and opened the door to an outburst of fantasy. That it was an uncommon style of decoration is proved by the fact that it did not spread throughout the island, and there were naturally other craftsmen who, only a short distance away, continued to decorate vases by simply relying on the rich repertoire of the past. A certain independence of local precedents, in this case Hittite, can also be seen on a strange fragment of a pottery chest, generally considered to be of Phrygian origin (page 27). Here decoration has combined with narrative to portray action and depict a hunter on horseback holding a javelin which he is about to plunge into a stag.

At the beginning of the sixth century B.C., the Babylon of Nebuchadnezzar showed how ceramics could be used in monumental architecture. The Ishtar Gate, erected at the head of a processional way, was decorated with glazed bricks, arranged like a mosaic in order to create meter upon meter of rosettes and also rows of monsters, including a spectacular, snake-headed dragon (page 28). Glazed tiles had already been used in Egypt since the third millennium B.C.

In around the same period the flourishing and prolific ceramic workshops of Cyprus began to produce large figures with cylindrical bodies made on the potter's wheel, to which heads and limbs were then added. This technique only lasted for a short time in Greece, but it enjoyed a spectacular development on Cyprus, where some sanctuaries are filled with large

terra-cotta figures. A typical example of the work found in sites on the east side of the island, and dating from around the mid sixth century, is the roundish head, in which the features of a rather weak face are brought alive by the use of colour (page 29).

The unique place occupied by Greece in the history of ceramics calls for an individual survey of the output of the Aegean world, where, during the second millennium B.C., there was a complex and intensive network of contacts between the two main centers, the island of Crete, situated to the south of the dense Cycladic archipelago, and the Greek mainland.

The Cretan civilization, also called "Minoan" after Minos, the legendary king of the island's main city, Knossos, developed between the second and third millennium B.C. For a long time, it exercised a strong influence on the new, Greek-speaking, Indo-European immigrants who arrived in the southern Balkans at the beginning of the Middle Bronze Age. In other words, it became teacher to the progenitors of the Classical Greek civilization that would later flourish in these same lands. The Greeks of the Bronze Age are called "Helladic" or, more specifically, "Mycenaean" (a term used particularly when referring to art and culture) because Mycenae was their main military and political center during the Late Bronze Age. In around 1400 B.C. Crete, whose population continued to be non-Greek, fell under Mycenaean domination, after which it began to reflect the cultural trends of the invaders: it no longer exercised hegemony, but was subject to it.

Of the many styles that mark the history of Cretan ceramics during the second millennium B.C., a special place is occupied by the pottery of Vasiliki (2500–2200 B.C.), whose most distinctive feature is its decoration (page 30). This unusual and sophisti-

Large composite vase with red slip and incised decoration, probably designed for funerary rituals. From Vounos (Cyprus); c. 2100–2000 B.C. Nicosia, Cyprus Museum.

Large pitcher decorated with chevrons and zigzags contained within double horizontal lines. From Kültepe (Anatolia); c. 1800 B.C. Oxford, Ashmolean Museum.

cated decoration is composed of a pattern of blotches, believed to have been achieved by exposing specific areas of the pot's surface to the flame.

Even more famous, and quite rightly so, are the ceramics of Kamares, which belong to a later period (1900–1700 B.C.). These highly refined wares vary widely in type and, from the point of view of their modelling and the composition of their decoration, include some of the most beautiful vases ever made in the ancient world. Typically, they possess a pale decoration on a dark ground, in keeping with a local preference that had already revealed itself in earlier days, with the difference that the black ground is now provided by a thick, rich and often glowing covering on which white and red patterns are painted. The patterns at one stage were composed of circles, spirals and curvilinear designs, enriching, so to speak, the curves of the vase. Very soon, however, other, more elaborate patterns were introduced, many of them reminiscent of living forms, particularly floral and marine ones. Decorations with a great sense of movement appear (page 31), and the typically Cretan motif of the spiral began to spread over the bodies of the largest pots. Another distinctive characteristic was, in certain cases, the extreme thinness of the walls (the so-called "egg-shell" pottery), made possible by the introduction of the high-speed wheel.

Pottery from the early phase of the Cretan Late Bronze Age has particularly graceful lines, with the use of polychrome restricted mainly to dark on light decoration (page 33). The initial preference was for floral motifs, delicately interlacing buds and grasses, but it was not long before the marine elements of more ancient times were developed in a magnificently exuberant style, with breathtaking composi-

tions of tentacled sea creatures, nautilus and other shells, and rocks and fish scattered liberally over the entire surface. The same period also saw the development of new and different trends, for example that of dividing the vase's surface into decorative horizontal bands (page 32). The latter can, in a sense, be said to anticipate the Mycenaean taste, even though in the example illustrated the typically Cretan nature of the spiral motif attests to the continuance, if not the vitality, of local tradition.

Although Mycenaean pottery was strongly influenced by Minoan models, it did not absorb them passively. For example, it imposed a rigid sense of discipline on the island's decorative repertoire, both in the sense that it enclosed it in bands and panels and also in the way that it subjected it to a stylization that substantially masked and distorted the identity of its origins.

The Mycenaean potters also produced a number of very advanced shapes that seem to anticipate later Greek creations, in particular the beautiful, long-stemmed Epirote goblets, with their broad bowls and sober decoration, but at this point the exuberance of the naturalistic Cretan motifs, both marine and floral, is weakened, frozen in much more abstract and formal solutions (page 34). One pictorial style of clearly Mycenaean origin appears in coloured ceramics, particularly the characteristic "craters" made during the last two centuries of the Greek Bronze Age, which are decorated with human figures and war chariots (page 35). The figures have a strongly stylized quality, being usually composed just of outlines, and yet their presence represents one of those elements in Mycenaean ceramics that seem to form a link, beyond the imminent Dark Ages, with the future Geometric styles of Greece's revival.

Vase with marine decoration of large octopus amidst seaweed, corals and shells. Palaiokastron (Crete); c. 1550 B.C. Heraklion, Archaeological Museum.

Small sub-Mycenaean amphora with hand-traced decoration; c. eleventh–tenth century B.C. Athens, Kerameikos Museum.

*Below: Plate. Earthenware with painted decoration (Samarra ware). Mesopotamia;
Chalcolithic period, 5500–5000 B.C. Diameter: 11 in (27.6 cm). Height: 2¾ in (7 cm). Berlin,
Vorderasiatisches Museum (no. VA 13400).*

———————

*Opposite: Goblet. Earthenware with painted decoration (proto-Elamite ware). Susa, Iran;
Susa I, 4000–3500 B.C. Height: 11½ in (28.5 cm). Diameter of rim: 6½ in (16 cm). Diameter of
base: 3¼ in (8.2 cm). Paris, Musée du Louvre (no. Sb 3174).*

Outstanding amongst the very fine wares of the Samarra period are a comparatively rare group of deep plates. It was upon these that the Samarra artist painted his finest and most lively creations. In the cavetto of these plates are found designs which are full of action, usually based on a group repeated four times; the impression is one of swirling motion. It was mainly on these vessels that the Samarra painter departed from his often purely geometric decoration, and animal, fish and human figures were commonly used as elements of the design. In the present instance there are fish and schematic long-necked birds holding fish in their beaks. The central swastika was another common motif in the artist's repertoire.

Tall, elegant goblets, such as the one opposite, are a feature of the work of the early Elamite artists. They were masters of geometric and stylized animal designs, always perfectly matched to the vessel on which they occur. The dominant central panel shows a goat with exaggerated horns, the body formed of two triangular blocks to which legs, bearded head and tail have been added. Above is a narrow horizontal panel of running saluki dogs; whilst the top panel of closely grouped bird forms with exaggerated long necks matches the tall and elegant form of the vessel. In places the paint, normally a lustrous black, has fired to a brownish tinge. Hand-made and possibly finished on a tournette.

Goblet. Earthenware with painted decoration (Amratian White Line ware). Egypt; pre-Dynastic, Nagada I, 4000–3500 B.C. Height: 10 in (25.2 cm). Diameter of rim: 3½ in (9.3 cm). Oxford, Ashmolean Museum (no. 1644. 482.95)

The clay of this type of vessel is the same as that of much of the Badarian black-topped and plain red wares. Fine, sandy and well mixed, it usually fired buff through brown to reddish brown on inner and outer surfaces, with a thick grey core. The vessels were covered with a thin, hard, reddish-brown slip, burnished and polished. Decoration was in a thick creamy-white to yellowish-buff paint. The motifs were most commonly linear and geometric, but natural scenes including animal and human figures were popular. This example is one of the finest of the contemporary buff wares and depicts sheep, goat and possibly giraffe in a landscape which has been interpreted as a river flowing between hills. Hand-made.

*Ritual jar. Earthenware with incised
decoration. Mesopotamia; Larsa period,
2000–1800 B.C. Height: 10¾ in (27 cm).
Diameter of rim: 5 in (12.2 cm). Paris,
Musée du Louvre (no. AO 17000).*

The fine painted wares of the pre-
Dynastic and Early Dynastic periods in
Mesopotamia gave way, during the third
millennium B.C., to a series of dull plain
wares. On wheel-made vessels of very
fine clay, the favoured decoration was by
incision. This interesting vessel was
probably for ritual use, and the condition
of the base suggests that it has been
broken from a stand which supported it.
The winged and naked central figure
represents the goddess of fertility as
protector of all the species of earth, air
and water. The upper frieze of birds is
divided from the earth and water species
– bull, fish and turtle – by an incised
channel. A series of raised relief plaques
show the goddess in the same attitude as
the incised figure.

19

Below: Jar. Earthenware with incised decoration. Susa, Iran; Larsa period, 2000–1800 B.C. Height: 7½ in (19 cm). Paris, Musée du Louvre (no. Sb 2852).

Opposite: Lion vessel. Earthenware with painted decoration. Kara Huyuk, Anatolia; Old Hittite Empire, 1900–1700 B.C. Height: 8 in (20.5 cm). Length: 8 in (20.8 cm). Paris, Musée du Louvre (no. AM 1517).

The distinctive ceramic opposite was common on sites in southern Mesopotamia and at Susa during the early centuries of the second millennium B.C. Though found at Susa, this vessel may well be a product of a Mesopotamian workshop. A polychrome effect is achieved by the red paint and the white filling of the incisions. The shape is invariably a squat, cylindrical jar with a sharply demarcated neck, flaring rim and vertically pierced horizontal lugs on the shoulder. Much of the incised ornament is geometric, but animal and, more rarely, human figures appear in the designs. The present example is of particular interest as a possible illustration of an early Sumerian story of a dispute between a bird and fish in which the god Enki was to give his judgement in favour of the fish. The jars are sufficiently uniform to suggest that they may have had a specialized ritual function. The same motif appears on later painted ceramics in Palestine and Cyprus. Very fine clay, fired grey. Wheel-made.

The excellent figure of a lion above is one of a group of animal forms popular amongst the ceramic artists of the early Hittite Empire. They appear both in painted wares, as the present example, and in plain red polished pottery. The figure had practical use as a libation vessel: it was filled through the tall neck on the animal's back, the nostrils being pierced for pouring. It is made of very finely mixed clay with fine grits, fired dull orange. The body was covered with a white slip and highly burnished.

In this superb piece, arguably the finest of XVIIIth Dynasty faïence sculptures, the Pharaoh Amenhotep III is represented as a sphinx holding two offering bowls before him. The representation is of the ancient Egyptian god Harmahkis, "Horus on the horizon," a personification of the rising sun. Harmahkis was also regarded as a fount of wisdom and a symbol of resurrection. The earliest representation of the Pharaoh in this guise is the great rock sculpture of Kephren at Gizeh (about 2500 B.C.). Of a brilliant turquoise blue, the present figure is composed of "glassy faïence," with a very hard glaze and brilliant colour, developed during the XVIIIth Dynasty.

Egyptian belief in a life after death included the onerous duties of labouring in the fields of the gods. Particularly from the New Kingdom onwards it was the custom to bury, with the deceased, small figurines such as the ones opposite, whose business it was to act as servants of the deceased. The inscription on such figures, from the sixth chapter of the "Book of the Dead," included the exhortation, "Be ye ready always to plough and sow the fields, to fill the canals with water, and to carry sand from the east to the west." The figures occur in great numbers in wood, stone and metal, but probably the most common material in the New Kingdom was "faïence," usually a plain blue. The figures are not often of as great an artistic merit as those of the Lady Sati. Polychrome faïence for these figures was rare.

Opposite: Female figure. Terra cotta. Marlik Tepe, Iran; Iron Age, c. 1000 B.C. Height: 14¾ in (37.5 cm). Teheran, Iran Bastan Museum (no. 25140.1).

———

Below: Jug. Earthenware with painted decoration (Siyalk B ware). Tepe Siyalk, Iran; Early Iron Age, c. ninth century B.C. Height: 14¼ in (36 cm). London, British Museum (no. 129072).

The graves of the north-western area of Iran (Gilan) have produced an outstanding series of sculptured human and animal figurines. Excavations in the region of Amlash and Marlik Tepe, from which this female figure comes, are at last placing these outstanding products in a secure archaeological horizon. The ears are usually pierced and some figures have been found still with gold earrings attached. One curious feature of the human figures is that they are usually shown with six toes on each foot. Of well-mixed, reddish-brown clay, the figures were covered with a slip and highly polished and burnished.

This superb jug is one of an elaborate group of probably ritual vessels first recognized in the wealthy Indo-European graves of the "B" cemetery at Tepe Siyalk, in Luristan. The jugs were probably used for pouring the final libations at the time of burial. The clay is very fine and fired buff. The vessel was then covered with a thick creamy-buff slip, polished and decorated in a lustrous red to red–brown pigment. Geometric design was favoured, but a great many of the more elaborate jugs feature ibex and horses, as the present example. The ceramic artist filled open spaces with geometric patterns (*horror vacui*). Wheel-made.

Below: Jug. Earthenware with painted decoration (Bichrome IV ware). Cyprus; Cypro-Archaic period, about 700 B.C. Height: 8¾ in (22 cm). Diameter of base: 3 in (7.5 cm). Paris, Musée du Louvre (no. AM835).

—————

Opposite: Phrygian larnax. Earthenware with painted decoration. Anatolia; Iron Age, c. eighth century B.C. Height: 9 in (23 cm). Width: 7 in (18 cm). Oxford, Ashmolean Museum (no. 1922.1).

The highly stylized bird on the jug opposite is typical of the free-field style of ornament in the Cypro-Archaic period. The bird is shown flying towards a disc-like object which, it has been suggested, represents the sun. The filling-ornament of swastikas, running chevrons and dot-filled circles is normal for the fabric. The clay is fine and fired a creamy buff. The surface had been worked up into a thin self-slip or slurry. The painted ornament is in matt black and red. Wheel-made.

This particular frieze is from the end of a small pottery chest. In addition to such containers, the Phrygians of Central and Western Anatolia made considerable use of painted terra-cotta plaques as architectural features. In this example, the box had been covered with a thick matt white slip and on this a hunting scene was framed within a panel of alternating red and black lines. The hunter, seated side-saddle and with javelin poised, pursues a stag. The hunter's arms, face and legs are outlined in red, as are the horse's reins and bit. The horse's face and stag's body were reserved in the colour of the white slip. The action of the simple free-field drawing is in contrast to much of Phrygian formal ceramic decoration.

This is one of the many such animal reliefs which decorated the magnificent Ishtar Gate erected at the end of the inner city processional way of Babylon by Nebuchadnezzar (605–562 B.C.). The art of glazing pottery had been known in Mesopotamia from soon after 2000 B.C., and some of the earliest true copper/lead glazes have been found in Near Eastern archaeological sites from soon after that period. Perhaps the finest examples of all are these glazed mosaic brick creations of Babylon. Against a blue glaze background, the walls of the monumental gateway were decorated with lions (the symbols of Ishtar), bulls (the symbols of Adad) and, as with the present example, serpent-headed dragons (the symbols of Marduk).

There were two main schools of sculpture in Cyprus during the Cypro-Archaic II period, one typical of the eastern centers of the island, the other typical of the west. The example above clearly shows the major eastern features: broad, well-rounded modelling, giving an impression of a soft and somewhat flabby figure. The almond-shaped eyes, prominent thickened nose and small, but full, lips are again a hallmark of the style. The clay is fine and gritty and fired a pinkish brown. It was covered in a thick, creamy-matt slip with details accentuated with black, brown and reddish-brown pigment. The feathered eyebrows and the formalized rounded ringlets of shoulder-length hair are again a feature of the eastern style.

Vasiliki pottery, consciously sophisticated, appears in Crete around 2500 B.C. In its shapes there is probably some influence of metalwork. The mottling of the paint is often said to result from applying flame here and there on the surface as the firing ended, but this seems barely practicable. Perhaps the "paint" was varied in density and in the third stage of firing only the less dense areas re-oxidized.

Around 2200 B.C. Vasiliki ware was superseded by a ware with simple patterns in a white pigment applied to a ground of dark paint, and this around 2000 B.C. progressed with the introduction of the potter's wheel into what is called Kamares ware. Shapes are more varied, shades from red to yellow are added to the decoration, and the ornamental repertory is enriched with curvilinear and natural motifs. The design of the beaked jug opposite is oblique, giving an effect of torsion to the body of the pot.

Below: Storage jar. Found on the island of Pseira, off Crete; Cretan, Late Minoan IA – Pattern style; 1550–1500 B.C. Height: 38½ in (98 cm). Heraklion, Archaeological Museum (no. 5457).

—————

Opposite: Beaked jug. Found at Phaestos in Crete; Cretan, Late Minoan IA – Floral style; 1550–1500 B.C. Height: 11½ in (29 cm). Heraklion, Archaeological Museum (no. 3969).

The handles on this storage jar at top and bottom of the main field are of a type designed to take ropes for lifting, but here may be only ornamental. The decoration, now dark on the light ground of the clay, shows a new tendency towards dividing the surface into bands and some weariness in executing the traditional curvilinear motives.

In Late Minoan pottery the curvature of the profile became more sophisticated. On the beaked jug opposite it is concave on the neck, then after a ridge, which hardly interrupts it, convex, and towards the base again concave. The decoration – of reeds – shows exceptionally close observation of nature.

Below: Stemmed cup. Found at Ialysos in Rhodes; "Mycenaean," Late Helladic IIIA–B; c. 1300 B.C. Height: 6 in (15.7 cm). London, British Museum (no. 70.10–8.100).

Opposite: Mixing bowl ("crater"). Found at Marion in Cyprus; "Mycenaean," Late Helladic IIIA; 1400–1300 B.C. Height: 16½ in (42.2 cm). London, British Museum (no. 1925.11–1.3).

The shape of the stemmed cup evolved from the Ephyrean cup. In the cup opposite the units of the decoration are identifiable as shells, surviving from the old Marine style, but again the Mycenaean craftsman prefers to break down the field into horizontal bands. It may have been made in Rhodes and not in the Peloponnese, but the Mycenaean style is still remarkably uniform.

The crater, a new shape of the fourteenth century B.C., is often decorated with figures. Where these are human, they are usually in chariots. The style of the figures shows no interest in natural forms, though there is such an interest in other branches of Mycenaean art, and the filling ornament is still more remote from nature. The division of the body into bands is now characteristic.

Most of these chariot craters have been found in Cyprus, but analysis of the clay is said to argue for manufacture in the Peloponnese.

Greek Vases

When people think of Greek civilization, perhaps the first image that comes to mind is that of a temple such as the Parthenon or a famous statue, such as the Venus de Milo. It would, however, be just as appropriate to think of the splendid decorated vessels, countless examples of which are displayed in museums all over the world. As representations of the Hellenic world, ceramics are as valid as architecture or sculpture: they document its progress and bear witness to its attitudes and values. There may have been times when Greek vases were overvalued as works of art, but they are still undoubtedly of fundamental importance for our understanding of the Classical ethos. In their decoration, these vessels not only provide a rich source of images relating to myths, historical figures, characters from epic poetry and so on, but their shapes also provide us with a great deal of information on particular aspects of contemporary life, ranging from banqueting rituals to funerary rites. As to the importance of the manufacture and trade in ceramics in the economic life of the *poleis* of both the colonies and the mother country, it is worth recalling that in Athens the potters' workshops and studios occupied an entire quarter of the city, known as *Kerameikos*.

Nor do ceramics represent a secondary aspect of Greek civilization where chronology is concerned. In fact, they represent an early sign of cultural stirrings in the heart of a period that has come to be known as the Greek "Dark Ages." In around 1000 B.C., after the collapse of the Mycenaean civilization and a long period of decline, the ceramics produced in certain areas of central Greece betray signs of a surprising renaissance. The center of this new style, known as "proto-Geometric," was Attica.

At first sight, these new wares still seem to display

Volute crater. Red-figure. Attic, by the Niobid Painter. Found at Ruvo in southern Italy; c. 460 B.C. Height: 31¼ in (80 cm). Diameter: 18¾ in (48 cm). Naples, Museo Nazionale (no. 2421). The subject of this crater's large frieze is the fighting of the Greeks with the Amazons.

Styles and decoration of Greek vases

Proto-Geometric vase with broad bands of colour and concentric circles traced using a compass; c. tenth century B.C. Athens, Kerameikos Museum.

37

features derived from remote Mycenaean models. Particularly noticeable is the absence of naturalistic forms of decoration. However, this is not a case of straightforward, or even an attempt at stylization: these later vases reveal a conscious striving for perfection and a completely new capacity for abstraction. As examples of the Greek taste, or rather the Greek genius, they are most striking for their exceptionally well proportioned and harmonious form, rather than for their decoration. Their most prominent feature is the meticulous attention to detail: the glaze is flawless, the walls thin, the silhouette clear and precise, the firing extraordinarily accurate.

Decoration saw the reappearance of the old division of the surface into horizontal bands (a system that was to last for a number of centuries), but for a certain period any additions to this purely volumetric language continued to be very restrained (page 48). The vast majority of proto-Geometric vessels were covered in a simple black glaze, of a uniformity and brilliance never seen before. The potters responsible for the adoption of this particularly elegant form of covering remained faithful to it for many years, and only at a later stage was there any marked revival of interest in decoration.

The result of this search for new forms was a carefully chosen and coherent repertoire of geometrical patterns. Although the dominant motifs were initially circles and semi-circles, traced using a variable compass, later, from roughly 900 to 700 B.C., during what is considered to be the golden age of the Geometric period, the decorative language of pots became articulated in continuous and broken lines, triangles, lozenges, chevrons, swastikas, squares, chequers, "castellated" patterns and the typical meander (page 49). This network of lines finally ended up covering the entire surface, creating a sort of visual saturation (page 51). At a much later date the Geometric style also embraced stylized zoomorphic motifs and, finally, the subject that was to become the central element of both the art and thinking of ancient Greece, namely man.

Items from around the middle of the eighth century B.C., discovered in the Dipylon necropolis in Athens, provide visible proof of this significant development: the human figures lined up on the great craters and grave amphoras are not much more than simple outlines, but they occupy a prominent place within the overall decorative scheme, giving it a whole new rhythm and breathing new life into it. The scenes in which they are inserted are not restricted to a purely decorative role: they describe actual events, for example the burial of a woman accompanied by a procession of mourners (page 50). This feature, which had never been seen before, heralded the development of a narrative art destined to vastly strengthen the role of the vase as a vehicle for figurative communication.

Because of their remarkable size and their function as grave markers, vases such as the ones by the Dipylon Painter imply what could be called a "monumental" concept of ceramics, and this too was able to stimulate research into less schematic forms of figurative representation. The new interest in figures led vase painters to dedicate more time and space to depicting people and this inevitably meant that the use of decorative motifs became less and less extensive. Only in this way was it possible to achieve something more like an actual painting on a vessel rather than a decoration on a vessel that included a painting. In order to obtain a greater differentiation between these figures and make it possible to identify at least

Attic Geometric kantharos *with handles rising above the rim to which they are attached; c. ninth century B.C. Munich, Staatliche Antikensammlungen und Glyptothek.*

Ovoid aryballos *in proto-Corinthian style; end eighth–beginning seventh century B.C. Oxford, Ashmolean Museum.*

some of them in order to facilitate the portrayal of, say, an episode from mythology, greater detail was required than that implied by an outline. It became necessary, in other words, to paint figures using a different technique. One ancient solution, which had already been used during the Bronze Age, involved drawing shapes in silhouette and this now became one of the techniques adopted by Greek vase painters.

Connections with the East intensified and contacts with Crete, which had never been completely broken, were revived. The Phoenicians introduced Oriental bronzes and ivories into Greece, while Greek merchants in turn became regular visitors, in Cyprus and Syria, to the marketplaces of the Levant. Events such as the great colonization of the Anatolian coast, a process that had been underway for some time, also made a major contribution towards the establishment of a dense network of contacts and cultural exchanges in the Aegean area. It is these factors which explain the Oriental influence that appeared at this stage in the history of Greek ceramics. This influence manifested itself in two ways, in a broadening of the iconographical repertoire and in the adoption of incision as a means of adding detail to images. We will concentrate mainly on the former.

The Orientally derived elements introduced by Greek potters to their decorative range consisted of a number of floral and animal motifs and certain specific images such as the sphinx and the griffin (neither of which were unknown to Bronze Age artists, but which, were now reintroduced to Greek wares) or an animal that was regarded as a monster, the lion. These exotic creatures appear on vessels as figures that are to a certain degree geometricized, in deference to the local vernacular, but which also retain clearly naturalistic attributes, for example long, arching tails and large claws. The griffin proved so fascinating that its head and neck even appear as the upper section of a vessel, of Orientalizing taste (page 52). Its decoration, a combination of the new, curvilinear and cordon friezes and old-fashioned Geometric patterns, identifies it as a typically seventh-century B.C. product of the Greek Islands. These surviving elements of the Geometric style that had given rise to many local versions in its day should come as no surprise: they had still not completely disappeared even a hundred years later, as shown in certain Boeotian wares (page 53), which are still innovative and original.

It would be a mistake to identify Greek vessels solely with those of Athens, since there was more than one important center of Greek ceramic production. As early as the eighth century B.C., at a time when Athens was still producing pottery exclusively for her own citizens, the Cyclades and Corinth had established a flourishing trade in their wares with countries in both the eastern and western Mediterranean.

Orientalizing vessels, with predominantly zoomorphic friezes, had already been produced in Corinth for some time when, around 700 B.C., in order to achieve a better portrayal of figures, the technique of outlining contours with a brush was matched by the introduction of black, incised figures. The reason for this was that potters had studied the images on Oriental ivories and bronzes and had discovered that the best and simplest way of highlighting such details as hair, facial features or clothing, was to incise them. The most typical wares displaying this new technique are the relatively small *aryballoi*, designed to contain perfumed oils, but there are also

Mid proto-Attic amphora depicting Heracles killing the centaur Nessos; c. 675–650 B.C. New York, Metropolitan Museum.

Wine jug (oinochoe). Wild goat style. Eastern Greece (perhaps Rhodes); c. 625 B.C. Munich, Staatliche Antikensammlungen und Glyptothek.

larger ewers and cups that reveal the same method of definition in their decoration. In around the middle of the seventh century B.C. the black outlines, as well as being incised, sometimes with extraordinary skill, were also occasionally overpainted, generally in red, although yellow or white is also known. The ground is often of a uniformly pale colour, sprinkled with rosettes (page 55).

However, the success enjoyed by vessels of this type, combined with a rise in exports, had led to a certain decline in their decorative quality by the end of the century, giving the impression of a somewhat rushed form of mass production. In the mature Corinthian style the visual effect of the decoration, still based on Orientalizing animal friezes, becomes rather cluttered by the background being filled with dots, leaves and other incised details right up to the edge of the figures (page 54). There are fewer gaps and pauses, with the result that the images lose much of their clarity and rhythm.

As a general rule, it could be said that in Corinth the black-figure technique continued for a long time to be a typical means of painting in miniature on ceramics, whereas the decision to draw figures in silhouette, a choice that favoured the creation of larger figures on larger vessels, was particularly popular in Athens and the islands. As it is, Corinthian potters also produced larger-sized vessels, mainly bearing anthropomorphic decoration or mythological scenes, with animal friezes either relegated to a subordinate position or completely absent. The figures normally stand clearly out against the background and are enlivened by broad areas of red and white (page 56). Around 550 B.C., for reasons that are still unclear, the production of vessels with figurative decoration ceased completely in Corinth, but by that date the most notable black-figure wares had for some time been made in Athens.

The Athenians adopted the new style towards the end of the seventh century B.C., but this led neither to a rapid demise of the old tradition of outlining nor to their well established preference for large vessels. The Corinthian influence, which suggests that at least for a certain period there was a constant influx of craftsmen from the neighbouring Peloponnesian city into the workshops of *Kerameikos*, also revealed itself at a later date in the introduction of new types of vessels, such as the column crater.

Athens, however, never accepted outside influences in a purely passive way, and the black-figure technique itself underwent certain alterations. The Attic clay, with its reddish tinge, which Athenian potters always took care to emphasize by the addition of ocher, provided a very different base from the paler clay of Corinth. The lustrous black glaze that did not have a tendency to craze, was also of a higher quality. The Athenian painters were much more sparing with white and red, using them for touches with which to highlight specific details of the image, rather than to brighten broad surfaces. Athenian wares display such a logical and precise approach to volume and colour, and also to the use of the brush and other instruments, that not even the most complex examples seem excessive. Towards the end of the sixth century B.C. some vessels adopted a white ground for the black-figure decoration, perhaps in imitation of the white ground used in decorated wooden panels. As to the problem of how to give the necessary weight to the lines incised on large figures, this was soon resolved in the simplest way: by doubling them.

Where Corinthian and, in particular, Athenian

Corinthian pyxis with black-figure decoration containing incised detail; end seventh century B.C. New York, Metropolitan Museum.

Cycladic amphora decorated with the figure of a panther at the shoulder and with horizontal bands of linear decoration on the lower part of the body. From Thera; end seventh–beginning sixth century B.C. Athens, National Museum.

black-figure pottery is concerned, it now becomes easier for experts to identify individual figures amongst the painters. This is not because the latter commonly adopted the practice of painting their names on vessels, but because styles became more individualistic than in the past. Since very few potters or painters signed their work, these names have for the most part been coined by modern scholars.

In this way we have been introduced to an important artist, active in Athens at the end of the seventh century B.C., known as the Nessos Painter, who created large, black-figure vessels and whose name derives from a splendid grave amphora (page 57), the neck of which bears a black-figure decoration of Heracles killing the centaur Nessos. Battles to the death between mortals and monsters and between wild and domestic animals is a recurrent theme of his work. After around 570 B.C., during a period that saw the decline of the animal frieze, one of the most important decorators is the Amasis Painter, whose carefully balanced compositions possess a strong sense of immediacy thanks to the artist's skilful use of line and colour. In depicting female figures the painter sometimes remained faithful to the old technique of outline drawing, identifying areas of flesh mainly by painting them white against the dark silhouette. The subject of one wine amphora (page 58) is a meeting between Dionysus and two maenads. Heracles was a very popular hero, destined to become practically a symbol of the Athenian state, while Dionysus was the god, whose cult, introduced to Athens in the sixth century B.C., gave rise to official displays of drama that laid the foundations of Classical theater. The decoration of ceramics clearly reflected what was going on in the city, its mood and its cultural evolution.

Another major figure is Exekias, who was both a painter and a potter. His works, which possess a monumental solemnity, make him one of the most influential practitioners of the black-figure style during the second half of the sixth century B.C. In Athens, the Homeric epics played a particularly important role, and it is no coincidence that some vessels by Exekias, whose favourite decorative subject was the world of myths and heroes, give particular prominence to figures such as Achilles and Ajax (pages 59 and 60).

There is a very simple explanation as to how scholars are able to identify with certainty the scenes and figures painted on vases. The scenes can sometimes be interpreted because the figures are accompanied by inscriptions and sometimes because they are identified by certain characteristic details, such as the lionskin of Heracles, the trident of Poseidon and the thunderbolt of Zeus, but mainly because once the layout of a particular episode had been adopted it became widely accepted and remained substantially the same in the works of later artists. In other cases literary sources can be of assistance.

Athenian black-figure wares were not restricted just to large vessels, with cups representing a no less typical example of the genre. As time went by, artists tended to specialize and become either cup painters or vase painters, although the best ones, such as Exekias or the Amasis Painter, worked on both. The cups also came in many different types: some of them left a certain amount of room for figures, while others allowed only for a miniaturist style of painting. On the latter, the actual signature, whether of the painter or the potter, could sometimes become part of the decoration, with a similar role being assigned to dedicatory inscriptions, formulaic good wishes or even just

Etruscan amphora with incised decoration. Bucchero ware; c. sixth century B.C. Paris, Musée du Louvre.

Laconian black-figure kylix with a band of peacocks within double horizontal lines and with radiating decoration. From the necropolis at Taranto; sixth century B.C. Taranto, Museo Nazionale.

scatterings of random letters (page 61).

It would be wrong, however, to think that the scenes were derived solely from the rich source of material provided by mythology and the epics, since everyday life, with its usual chores and rituals, was also portrayed. The Antimenes Painter, active during the last quarter of the sixth century B.C., and one of those conservative artists who remained faithful to the black-figure technique after the red-figure technique had become firmly established, created a magnificent example of this genre in the form of a wine amphora bearing an airy scene of olive picking (page 63).

The black-figure wares produced outside Attica were on the whole a pale imitation of their Athenian equivalents, but this judgement cannot be extended to include the pottery produced in Sparta, for example, which is often very fine. This is particularly true of certain cups whose interiors are completely covered in figurative scenes (an Athenian painter would have tended to concentrate his efforts on a roundel roughly half the size of the diameter). Although the style of these cups is closer to the Corinthian than the Attic, it is markedly superior to the former. As for the images, it should be said that they do nothing to enforce the stereotype of an especially strict or austerely "Spartan" life at any stage in the city's history. The most famous and typical example of these Laconian cups, dating from around the mid sixth century B.C., was decorated by the Arkesilas Painter and bears a lively, animated scene from everyday life (page 62). As well as dominating the Italic market, Spartan wares also became firmly established in the East Greek world, at Samos.

Historically speaking, the East Greek world had developed in partial isolation. The Ionian seaboard had been repopulated by Hellenic peoples during the Dark Ages and many of the colonies had subsequently achieved a high degree of wealth and power. In ceramics, the prevailing style of painting had continued to be of the Geometric type until well into the seventh century B.C. The later style, found on wares produced in a number of cities, including Rhodes, has a more original quality. Very decorative, although not always immune from a certain monotony, it has a clearly Orientalizing character and is known as the "Wild Goat" style. By around 630 B.C. this style appears to have become firmly established. The vessels, for the most part pitchers, have bands of painted decoration depicting rows of grazing animals, with an in-filling of rather unusual ornamental designs. At the end of the century a particularly charming variant of the Wild Goat style appeared in Chios (page 64). During the sixth century there emerged an even more impressive style, at least in its best examples, called the "Fikellura" style after the necropolis at Rhodes where it was first identified, but which in reality must have evolved in the workshops of Miletus and Samos. It adopted the black-figure technique, but the figures were depicted in reserve, meaning without recourse to incision, but by leaving uncovered within the images certain lines or areas of the pale wash enveloping the vessels. The compositions are further reinforced by the fact that the figures are often painted on a free field (page 65).

The Western colonies, in Sicily and southern Italy, provided a good market for the best Greek wares, mainly Corinthian to begin with, but later Athenian. It was not long before the inhabitants of central Italy also became excellent customers and the Etruscan cities, which had already been converted to the Hellenic taste where ceramics were concerned, became

Vase for pouring (dinos) and pedestal with black-figure decoration by the Gorgon Painter showing Perseus pursued by the Gorgons. Attic. From Etruria; c. 590 B.C. Paris, Musée du Louvre.

Cup. Black-figure decoration. Eastern Greek (probably Rhodes). From Camirus, Rhodes; beginning or mid sixth century B.C. London, British Museum.

home for considerable numbers of Greek artists. From around the mid sixth century B.C. Etruria saw the development of important workshops producing black-figure vessels in a clearly East Greek style. But there was also a more ancient, indigenous type of pottery, one of whose most popular products was "bucchero" ware, which was black and burnished like Greek vessels of the Early Bronze Age, but also sometimes very finely modelled and decorated with impressed or moulded shapes (page 66). Items of Etruscan bucchero ware were even imported into Greece.

There is one type of Greek-derived pottery made in Etruria that deserves special mention: the Caeretan hydria. The vessels, which were discovered during excavations in the necropolis at Cerveteri (the ancient Caere), can be attributed to one or possibly two artists, Ionian either by birth or by training, who worked at the end of the sixth century B.C. (page 61). The shape is that of a water jar ("hydria"), while the decoration, characterized by the use of very bright colours, reflects a style unequalled in earlier black-figure wares, with a particularly inventive and original quality displayed in the portrayal of Greek myths. The shape of these hydrias, which are amongst the most decorative Archaic Greek wares, is undoubtedly East Greek, although nothing similar has yet been discovered in that area. This strange characteristic, allied to the very individual use of colour, can be explained by the fact that the artists in their native country were clearly not involved in vase painting, but rather in the painting of wooden panels or walls. Confirmation of this theory has been recently provided by the discovery at Saqqara in Egypt, a site visited frequently by the Greeks, of a small wooden panel bearing a painted decoration of human figures and animals in exactly the same style.

In around 530 B.C. there was an important turning-point in Archaic Greek pottery caused by the appearance in Athens of the first red-figure wares. Whereas previously figures had been painted in black on the red clay ground, the new technique involved covering the surface of the vases in a black glaze, leaving only the figures uncovered, which thus remained the same colour as the vessel's ground. Details were also treated differently: no longer rendered by means of scratched marks or by the addition of a few touches of red or white, they were portrayed with a brush and using the same black glaze that provided the ground.

This change had many consequences. The figures seem warmer and more prominent (page 68), possessing a more natural quality because the flesh tones are now reddish rather than black. On the other hand, there was the disadvantage of a background which, however impressive its luster, isolated the figures in space and did not assist in depicting them on different planes. With the new technique everything took on a new significance: for example, it altered the role of the so-called "relief line." This was a thin strand of raised black glaze on the surface of the vase that had been invented by artists working in the previous style in order to trace thin lines on the red ground. Now it was used to replace its engraved equivalent, either as a means of giving images a cleaner outline or to accentuate particular details within them.

The initiator of this new red-figure technique was the Andokides Painter, one of whose works, a wine jar, shows Athena visiting Heracles at dinner (page 69). The amphora in question very clearly exemplifies the link that normally exists between a vessel's function and its decoration. It is what is known as a "bilingual" vessel, in that its two faces show the same

Black-figure amphora in the Fikellura style with bands of half-moon motifs on the center of the body and figures of birds around the shoulder; second half sixth century B.C. Rhodes, Archaeological Museum.

Wine amphora with black-figure decoration by the Paris Painter of the Judgement of Paris. Etruscan. From Vulci; c. 540 B.C. Munich, Staatliche Antikensammlungen und Glyptothek.

scene, one portrayed using the old technique and the other using the new, with the red-figure style for the moment clearly echoing its black-figure counterpart. Were it not for the different sense of liveliness imparted by the colour, it could be said that the scene had been simply translated into red.

After the first experimental works, the new technique was applied for some time to cups and plates, a practice that evoked a very positive response from the market, particularly in far-off Etruria; for larger vessels, however, it was used only by a very small group of artists, the so-called "pioneers." Epiktetos, one of the finest cup painters, showed what excellent results could be achieved in the portrayal of small figures (page 68). In the same field and during the same years (520–510 B.C.) the Nikosthenes Painter also made very skilful use of the recently invented technique, introducing a further element of innovation in the decorative content (page 70). From around 520 B.C., the "pioneers," artists who were also exceptionally well versed in literature, decorated many large vases, especially calyx-craters and straight-sided craters (it has been estimated that roughly one per cent of the original output has survived). Their works reveal the fulfilment of the new technique's potential. Colour is reduced to a minimum and there is a clear interest in more accurate anatomical portrayal and in poses that are less stiff than their traditional equivalent. It was not until later, however, that examples of true foreshortening appeared, thus making it possible to portray the body as a real mass rather than making it look like a "cut-out" on the flat surface of the vase.

The most outstanding of these pioneers, many of whom are known to us, are Euphronios and Euthymides. The scenes painted by the famous Euphronios, which betray a thoughtful, balanced quality in both their composition and their draughtsmanship, portray figures of gods, heroes, athletes and characters from the Homeric epics (page 71). Euthymides, on the other hand, depicted a group of carefree figures, drinking and dancing, in one scene painted on a wine jar. His interest in human anatomy is clear, as is the fact that, in his portrayal of the figures, he had begun to sense the need to abandon the conventions of profile or frontal views (page 72).

The generation following that of the pioneers achieved complete mastery of the technique, with the Berlin Painter and the Kleophrades Painter being regarded as the finest artists. Neither of them, however, appears to have concentrated his interest on decorative effects or narrative content: the former is more concerned with refined and elegant figures standing out against a black ground, almost as though they were on stage (page 74), while the latter devoted himself to monumental compositions of austere and solemn figures (page 76), reminiscent of the characters being introduced at the time to Athenians by the genius of Aeschylus.

A separate development is represented by the Attic "white-ground" style (page 73), which on first sight recalls the ancient Orientalizing techniques and which can also help us to understand what panel or wall paintings must have looked like in around 500 B.C. The white-ground style was a technique which, in terms of realism, offered certain advantages as far as pictorial representation was concerned. In around 490–480 B.C., even a specialist in the red-figure technique like the Brygos Painter could exploit the pale roundel in a cup to include one of his tumultuous pictures (page 75).

Many of the subjects favoured by red-figure pain-

Two-handled cup in the shape of a female breast (mastos) with black-figure decoration depicting a battle between soldiers on horseback; c. 530 B.C. London, British Museum.

Cup (kotyle or skyphos). Red-figure decoration by the Brygos Painter. On the interior, it shows a maenad holding a panther in the left hand and a thyrsus in the right. Attic. From Greece; c. 480 B.C. Boston, Museum of Fine Art.

ters had already been introduced by black-figure painters, but as a whole their repertoire was very much more extensive. It included mythological subjects that had never before been depicted, as well as displaying a new interest in the Homeric epics and paying greater attention to the Olympic deities, with particular emphasis on the figure of a new hero, Theseus. In addition, it reflected such great contemporary events as the struggle against the Persians, while humorous scenes and parodies attest to the popularity and success of the comic theater. More than ever before, pottery confirmed its role as a magic eye that sees and records historical events and figments of the imagination, religious myths and vignettes of everyday life. The opening decades of the fifth century B.C., which saw the activities of artists such as the Kleophrades Painter, the Berlin Painter and the Brygos Painter, represent the most inventive period of Athenian vase painting: they correspond to the highest point of the arc. Later on, important and even outstanding works were made, but often they were inspired by other fields of artistic endeavour, becoming less and less the product of independent research.

During the Early Classical period, vases by artists such as the Niobid Painter show clear signs of the influence of wall painting, which, having previously been regarded as being roughly on a par with vase painting, at a certain stage began to be much more highly prized. Prior to the middle of the fifth century B.C. important buildings in Athens had been decorated with paintings by Polygnotos and other artists. We know that these took the form of large compositions containing many figures, which were arranged in long friezes and, rather than being tied to a single ground line, were distributed on different levels. An example of this practice can be seen in a famous calyx-crater by the Niobid Painter (page 77), which shows the influence of this new style of composition whereby, rather than trying to represent depth, the artist sought to find a way of arranging complex groups within the space. Other, large-sized vases, such as the amazing volute crater, again by the Niobid Painter, which portrays the legendary war against the Amazons (page 36), reveal a similar method, which involved only slight variations in the ground line but, when compared to the earlier style of composition, provided a greater opportunity for suggesting the third dimension, and allowed for particularly monumental friezes. This, too, was a method clearly derived from wall painting.

Wall paintings were executed on a white ground, a technique which, as we have already seen, is echoed in the works of certain Athenian vase painters. The use of a white ground now became increasingly common, particularly in certain tall *lekythoi*, oil flasks used for funerary offerings, examples of which were created around 450–440 B.C. by the Bosanquet Painter (page 79) and by the last of the great Greek vase painters, the Achilles Painter (page 78). If the statue-like figures and compositions of the Niobid Painter reflected the spirit and "Severe Style" of contemporary sculpture, the serene and idealized images of the Achilles Painter can be equally persuasively compared to the great contemporary works created by Pheidias for the Parthenon.

Similarly, when towards the end of the fifth century B.C. the Meidias Painter emphasized the contours of his figures by exploiting the tight folds of their garments, depicting them clinging so tightly to the body as to be almost transparent (page 82), he was not echoing some distant precedent in vase painting, but adopting a technique that had been

Attic red-figure crater by the Berlin Painter depicting the figure of Ganymede. From an Etruscan Tomb; c. 480–470 B.C. Paris, Musée du Louvre.

White-ground lekythos by the Achilles Painter depicting the figure of a woman; c. 440 B.C. Boston, Museum of Fine Arts.

introduced by contemporary plastic art. It was not only the major arts of wall painting and sculpture that provided a fertile source of decorative inspiration, however: some moulded vases and cups from around the middle of the fifth century B.C. represent ceramic versions of metal vessels that had first been introduced as part of the booty from the Persian armies (pages 80–81).

Potters of the Classical period created shapes that differed very little from the traditional ones. They invented no really new shapes, restricting themselves to following the dictates of popular taste, when, for example, the latter favoured bell craters.

The scenes depicted on vases of the fifth and fourth centuries B.C. showed a marked change from the past. There was a conscious effort to avoid bloody scenes of battle and a greater preference for more emotionally restrained subjects, such as the warrior leaving home for the wars and so on. The images increasingly celebrated festivals in the Athenian calendar, religious rituals and scenes of domestic life in which women appear, for example attending to their toilet. There was a new vogue for the personification of such abstract concepts as Fortune, Peace and Concord, whose likelinesses appear both in isolation and also in more complex groupings, in which case they always wear female dress. Certain mythological scenes also reveal the presence of strange, elegantly mannered figures, an element that contains no parallels in archaic iconography.

The progressive decline that can be detected in Greek ceramics, both in the inventiveness and in the quality of the moulding and painting of figured vases, culminated in the abandonment of the red-figure technique in Athens in the second half of the fourth century B.C. During the new Hellenistic era vessels became covered in a fine, shiny black glaze, sometimes, but not always, decorated with small, impressed decorations. In fact, this was a type of ware whose production had already begun in Athens in the second half of the sixth century B.C.

It was not long before Greek ceramics in Italy ceased to be made in conscious imitation of mainland wares and began to display their own specific characteristics. This was to some extent the case in Lucania (page 83), where as early as 440–430 B.C. Attic artists had established the first new workshops, but it was even more marked in other cities, beginning with Taranto, where highly ambitious items were produced, starting in around 420 B.C. and lasting throughout the fourth century B.C. These took the form of large funerary vases, whose most outstanding feature is their complex and florid decoration. The many figures are arranged on several levels, in some cases with the gods placed at the top, looking down on the scene below. Sometimes, not content with just red figures, the potters added touches of white, elements of gilding and raised decoration on the edges and the handles. At Paestum there were Greek workshops producing pottery during the fourth century B.C. that is remarkable more for the subjects it portrays rather than for the quality of its modelling or painting: it reflects the passion of the inhabitants of southern Italy for the comic theater, with scenes apparently inspired by the performances of strolling players.

There is a completely different quality to the so-called "Gnathian wares" (page 85) of the fourth century B.C. and early third century, which come mainly from Apulia and represent the transposition to southern Italy and Sicily of the polished black Athenian vases. Bearing a simple additional decoration of

Gnathian ware, black-glazed crater with geometric and vegetal decoration; c. fourth century B.C. Naples, Museo Nazionale.

Red-figure oinochoe *with scene from a phlyax play of the slave Xanthias standing by the statue of Heracles. Campanian pottery; c. fourth century B.C. London, British Museum.*

garlands or other floral motifs, they also display figurative decoration, often of some quality, although the figures are normally isolated, with no groups or narrative scenes. In Italy, the production of red-figure wares had ceased in around 300 B.C. This was much later than in Athens, but here too it was irrevocable. Totally black vases with modest decorative and chromatic additions continued to be made in Greece for some centuries, but in terms of shape and style they were definitely a lesser art form (page 86).

Both on the mainland and in the colonies, Greek vase painting was now at an end, proof of which is provided, paradoxically, by the beautiful, third-century B.C. polychrome vases discovered at Centuripae and other sites in Sicily. Their decoration of large figures (page 87), painted in tempera on the clay after firing, reflects the language of panel or wall paintings and is completely alien to ceramics.

During the Hellenistic period, leaving aside its Roman counterpart, which constitutes our main source of information on Greek art, painted vases were little known and not highly prized. We do not therefore owe our considerable knowledge of the work of Greek potters and vase painters to this period: we owe it to the almost indestructible nature of terra cotta and to the work of rescue, analysis and attribution carried out by modern scholars. In earlier times, however, particularly in Greek pre-Classical society, the intrinsic value of ceramic wares was acknowledged. The "pioneers," for example, would appear to have enjoyed the same respect and admiration that a century later would be accorded to sculptors and painters.

A hymn has survived in honour of Greek potters, which was probably composed during the sixth century B.C. It includes the following lines: "If you give me a reward, I will sing your praises, potters. Come, Athena, and extend your hand over the kiln, and may the cups darken well, and may the vases be well baked, may they obtain a fair price, since many are sold at the market, many others on the streets, and may the profit be great ..." The very existence of the hymn is indicative of an interest in the ceramics industry at a time when people were able to appreciate both technical skills and commercial values.

As regards prices, there is information that a vase of unexceptional size, with figured decoration, did not cost much more than a working day's wage. This, combined with the fact that the cost of transport by sea was relatively low, helps us to understand the vast extent of the market for Greek wares, which were, naturally enough, prized above all for their quality. Following the gradual decline in Etruscan interest in Attic wares, starting in the fifth century B.C., the Athenians had no difficulty in finding new markets in the northern Adriatic, in cities such as Spina (a rich source of Attic ceramics for the modern archaeologist), or in increasing their trade with the Black Sea area. Vases from Laconia were also exported to Egypt and North Africa, and we have already recorded the entrepreneurial success of the Corinthians, but there are other examples as well. Individual initiative was also of crucial importance and in this context mention should be made of a famous figure, the Athenian Nikosthenes. Nikosthenes took a typically Etruscan shape of amphora, with a ribbed body and broad, stirrup-shaped handles, which had previously been known only in a local bucchero-ware version, and re-invented it, creating an extraordinarily successful variant with a lively figured decoration that he produced in large numbers in his workshop for export to customers in Cerveteri.

Apulian crater with coiled handles by the Karneia Painter; c. fourth century B.C. Taranto, Museo Nazionale.

Calyx-crater for pouring, with red-figure decoration of Bacchus, Ariadne, satyrs and maenads by the Athens Painter 12592. Attic. From Greece; c. 350 B.C. Athens, National Museum.

The shape of this jug shows the proto-Geometric feeling for definition and balance; the decoration is an admirable example of the dark ground style with here only a narrow band of ornament round the belly, acting optically as a belt to hold it in. The ornament itself is a simple zigzag in a dilute solution of the dark "paint" and fired into a golden brown, the only contrast of painted colour admitted in the proto-Geometric.

The neck-handled amphora is a favourite Geometric shape. The meander, the characteristic Geometric ornament, is still tentative on the example opposite: on the belly the simple "battlement" form is filled with parallel lines; on the neck the standard form has its hatching all in one direction. This amphora served as a cinerary urn.

Opposite: Grave jar ("amphora"). Attic, Late Geometric IA, by the Dipylon Painter; c. 760 B.C. Height: 60¾ in (155 cm). Found at Athens. Athens, National Museum (no. 804, "the Dipylon amphora").

———

Below: Box with lid ("pyxis"). Attic, Late Geometric IB; c. 740 B.C. Height with lid: 7½ in (19.5 cm). Found at Athens. Athens, Agora Museum (no. P. 4784).

The enormous amphora opposite was made to stand as a marker on a grave, apparently a woman's (men's graves had craters). Its painter, in his way classical, established the human figure as a, or rather, the subject of Greek art. The main field shows the mourning of a dead woman. The human anatomy is reduced to a geometrical abstraction, clothing and sexual organs being irrelevant; the mourners are women, except for two men – with sword and dagger – at the far left. The chequering above the bier is the pall, raised for artistic clarity.

As often on the *pyxis* of this type and time, the knop of the lid is replaced by a team of horses (presumably for a racing chariot). The decoration of the box itself follows a new system of panels of about equal size and emphasis, and the effect is restless and even – because of the chequers – strident. The name "*pyxis*" refers in origin to box wood, and the shape looks as if it too was derived from wood.

Ahead as aperture was an occasional conceit of Greek potters. In the jug opposite it is a griffin's, of a type fashionably attached to the shoulder of bronze cauldrons. The body of the pot too is Orientalizing in most of its decoration, though the meander and lozenges remain Geometric. In the central panel a lion kills a deer and in each side panel a horse grazes. The decorative treatment of animals' shoulders is frequent in Cycladic work.

The Bird Cup group seems to be an original product of Boeotian taste. Its character, which suggests the cruder forms of folk art, is exceptional in Greek painted pottery. Other common shapes of the group are a dish with low foot and the *kantharos*. The birds on dishes are regularly upside-down, as if these pots were to be seen standing on their rims (as in this plate). The late date is surprising, but assured by associated pottery in graves.

The details and the use of purple in this cup are lavish and coarse and the filling ornaments are so crowded that it is easy to notice only the general effect. This new "Corinthian" style though busy, does not require delicacy and was well suited to manufacture in quantity.

The shape of the jug opposite is a Corinthian development of the mid seventh century B.C. The handsome effect depends partly on general design – notably the black polychrome decoration of the upper part of the body and the now solid bands which separate the fields below – and partly on the neat though uninspired execution. The dogs reveal signs of negligence, which warn of the coming mass production of the animal style at Corinth.

*Below: Water jar ("hydria"). Orange-red slip over yellowish clay. Black-figure. Corinthian; c.
560 B.C. Height: 17½ in (45 cm). Found at Cerveteri, Etruria. Paris, Musée du Louvre
(no. E 642).*

*Opposite: Grave jar ("amphora"). Black-figure. Attic, by the Nessos Painter; c. 615 B.C. Height:
32 in (82 cm). Found at Athens. Athens, National Museum (no. 1002, "the Nessos amphora").*

The subject opposite is a soldier's departure from home. According to Greek legend the heroes went to war and travelled in chariots, but after the Mycenaean period chariots were used only for racing. So it is evident that the scene on this pot is set in the heroic past, though – as is regular in Greek art – dress and armour are contemporary, so much so that the charioteer is defenseless in the standard costume of the racing driver.

This grave jar is one of the last Attic amphoras made to stand on graves. Its style, now disciplined, reaches the grandeur which earlier proto-Attic had missed. The neck shows Heracles, the most popular Greek hero, killing the centaur Nessos, and on the body there is another legendary subject – Perseus, who unusually is not shown, pursued by the monstrous Gorgons after he had beheaded their sister Medusa (on the left). White and purple details have mostly perished. The back of the pot is smeared roughly with dark "paint."

The broader, flat-shouldered version of the amphora seen on this page with offset neck was developed in the 540s B.C. The main subject of the face illustrated is Dionysus, the god of wine, welcoming two maenads (female votaries) who have been hunting; above is written "Dionysus" and "Amasis made me." On the shoulder there is an infantry battle, for artistic convenience broken up into duels.

The shape of the wine jar opposite is also the new version of the amphora with offset neck. Each face shows Ajax carrying from the battlefield the body of Achilles, the great Greek hero of the legendary Trojan War. Characteristically, this painter gives a deeper pathos to the incident through Ajax's patient stoop and the limpness of the corpse.

The size of the pot opposite is unusual. The subject of the face illustrated, which had a short-lived popularity, is Achilles and Ajax playing backgammon while on guard at the siege of Troy; other versions have the goddess Athena rousing them to their duty, but Exekias does not need her to show their unsoldierly absorption in their game, nor does he let the minute detail of the cloaks diminish the grandeur of the figures. On the mouth Exekias signs as both painter and "maker," whether "making" means owning the workshop or shaping the pot.

So-called "lip cups" were popular from the 560s to the 530s B.C. The shape has an elegant precision, being finished carefully underneath the foot and in the hollow of the stem. The decoration, if any, of the lip is restricted to the middle; the handle field has at most a decorative inscription–signature (as here), toast or even a nonsensical row of letters.

The shape of this cup is much like that of the "lip cup" (p. 61) but the outside is covered with bands of ornament. The inside has the most ambitious of surviving Laconian paintings – Arkesilas, presumably the nearly contemporary king of Cyrene, sits under an awning and supervises the packing of wool. The style, which owes much to Corinth, lacks fineness but has a lively assurance.

The composition on the wine jar opposite is unusual for painted pottery in that the human figures are scaled down to match their surroundings. The Antimenes Painter, so-called because he wrote on one of his pots "Antimenes is beautiful" (such tributes to fashionable Athenian youths were common around this time), was one of the less progressive but competent painters who remained faithful to the black-figure technique and style after the introduction of red-figure. The subject is olive picking.

By the late seventh century Chios had its own variant of the East Greek Wild Goat style, which among other peculiarities had a fondness for plastic ornamentation – in this bowl the female heads flanking the handles and perched incongruously on the rim. The inscription inside was not part of the original design, but scratched on after the pot was fired; it reads "Sostratos dedicated me to Aphrodite" – an offering in that goddess' sanctuary in the Greek settlement at Naucratis.

The wine jar opposite is in the Fikellura style, current from Samos to Rhodes in the 560s B.C. It is derived from the Wild Goat style but revises and adds to its inheritance, and often aims at black-figure effects though in a reserving technique. The style varies from careful to negligent, the composition from banding – at first narrow – to free field.

Below: Cup ("kantharos") Grey clay. Etruscan bucchero ware; late seventh– early sixth century B.C. Height: 4¾ in (12.1 cm). Finding place unknown. London, British Museum (no. 1953.4–26.1)

What is called "bucchero" ware is pottery of a clay fairly rich in iron oxide, which was fired with a final reducing stage so that the oxide turned throughout black and not red. Bucchero was traditional in the north of the East Greek region and emerged, probably independently, in Etruria around 650 B.C. Often, as here, there is no decoration and the effect depends on colour and shape. This type of *kantharos* seems to have been developed in Etruria, but was admired enough by Greeks for them to import it.

The painter – it may have been two painters – of the Caeretan hydrias (example illustrated opposite), so-called since most of them have been found at the Etruscan city of Caere (Cerveteri), wrote Greek and painted in a Greek style, though presumably at Caere. His connections are generally considered East Greek, though close parallels are wanting. The Caeretan master is a moderate draughtsman, but in his better work has a bolder appreciation of colour and more of a comic element than is usual in Greek vase painting.

Water jar ("hydria.") Black-figure. Etruscan Greek, by the painter of the Caeretan hydrias;
520–510 B.C. Height: 15¾ in (40.5 cm). Found in Etruria. Paris, Musée du Louvre (no. E 697).

Below: Cup. Red-figure. Attic, by Epiktetos (signed); 520–510 B.C. Diameter: 12½ in (32.5 cm). Found at Vulci in Etruria. London, British Museum (no. E 38).

—

Opposite: Wine jar ("amphora"). Red-figure with some details in purple. Attic, by the Andokides Painter; c. 520 B.C. Height: 20¾ in (53.5 cm). Found at Vulci in Etruria. Munich, Staatliche Antikensammlungen (no. 2301).

The red-figure technique was introduced by the Andokides Painter about 530 B.C. Epiktetos, who specialized in painting cups, was a half-generation younger than the Andokides Painter and his red-figure style has an easy assurance: he excels in accuracy of line. Usually until about 500 B.C. the inside field of the cup had a single figure; but here there is a girl dancing with castanets and a youth playing the double flute, held in place by a band round the head.

The wine jar opposite is an early example of the red-figure technique. Here the considerable use of purple and the elaborate patterning of Athena's dress still belong to the black-figure tradition, but comparison with the black-figure version on the back of the pot shows that the new technique is leading to a new style. The subject is the goddess Athena visiting her protegé Heracles as he reclines, in the proper Greek way, at dinner.

The typical decorative elements found on "eye cups" gave way to full-length figure decoration, particularly around the handles; in this example, there are pegasuses or winged horses in place of the previous palmettes. The scene depicts armed warriors, with the one on the far left apparently blowing on a conch shell.

The so-called "calyx-crater" appears first at Athens about 540 B.C.; the shape gradually became taller and narrower. Euphronios, who painted the specimen opposite, was one of the two dominant red-figure painters of the end of the sixth century B.C. By now the red-figure technique was being extended to floral ornament too. The subject here is from the legendary Trojan War – Sleep and Death carry away the corpse of Sarpedon, supervised by the messenger god Hermes (with herald's staff).

Mixing bowl ("calyx-crater"). Red-figure. Attic, by Euphronios (signed); c. 510 B.C. Height: 18¾ in (45.8 cm). Finding place unknown. New York, Metropolitan Museum of Art (no. 1972.11.10).

Opposite: Wine jar ("amphora"). Red-figure. Attic, by Euthymides (signed); 510–500 B.C. Height: 23½ in (60 cm). Found at Vulci in Etruria. Munich, Staatliche Antikensammlungen (no. 2307).

Below: Oil or perfume flask ("alabastron"). White slip over brownish clay, yellow on dresses of women. Attic, by the Pasiades Painter; 510–500 B.C. Height: 5½ in (14.6 cm). Found at Marion in Cyprus. London, British Museum (no. B 668).

Euthymides is the best exponent of the new anatomical interest of the years just before 500 B.C.; until then only strictly profile or frontal views of figures and parts of figures had been considered, but, in the example opposite, poses are oblique or twisting. The novelty is emphasized by an inscription – "as never Euphronios." The subject is an upper-class drinking party.

What is called the Attic white-ground style is that in which figures done in outline (like those of red-figure) are set on a white background; the white ground was, it seems, an imitation of picture painting and so was the use of flat washes of colour (as here on the dress). The white-ground style began around 500 B.C., but did not become common until the 460s.

In the wine jar opposite, the prevalence of the figurative over the decorative concentrates our attention on the figure and on the design, perhaps at the expense of the narrative element. Heracles is shown proffering a cup (*kantharos*) to be filled by Athena, who appears on the other side of the jar. Its author, a famous painter of Attic red-figure wares, owes his name to his greatest work, the amphora preserved in Berlin.

The technique of white-ground drawing is the same as that of red-figure drawing, apart from the fact that the ground is no longer black. The interior of this calyx shows a maenad, a follower of Dionysus, holding a leopard in her left hand and the thyrsus in her right. Over her shoulders she wears a leopardskin and in her hair she has a live snake.

Below: Water jar ("hydria"). Attic red-figure pottery. Kleophrades Painter; c. 480–475 B.C. Height: 16½ in (42 cm). From Nola, southern Italy. Naples, Museo Archeologico (no. 2422).

Opposite: Mixing bowl ("calyx-crater"). Attic red-figure pottery. Niobid Painter; c. 460 B.C. Height: 21 in (54 cm). From Orvieto in Etruria. Paris, Musée du Louvre (no. G 341)

The water jar opposite is a new type of hydria, known as a kalpis. On the shoulder the potter has painted a masterly scene depicting five episodes from the siege of Troy. At the center is King Priam, seated on an altar and holding in his lap the sprawled body of his beloved grandson Astyanax, killed by Neoptolemus, son of Ajax. To the left stands Ajax, son of Oïleus, forcibly removing Cassandra from the temple of Athena, while to the right Andromache, the legendary wife of Hector, is shown fighting the Greeks with a pestle.

Until about 400 B.C. picture painting – on panels and walls – differed from pot painting mainly in using a white background and flat washes of colour. Then, led by Polygnotus, picture painting began to represent depth, with figures tiered on uneven ground lines, no longer aligned with the plane of surface. A few vase painters tried to follow, as on this pot, but soon resigned themselves to their old spatial tradition.

Oil flask ("lekythos"). White-ground. Attic, by the Achilles Painter; 450–440 B.C. Height: 16.5 in (42.5 cm). From Eretria in Euboea. Athens, National Museum (no. 1818).

A larger version of the *lekythos* was fashionable at Athens from about 460 to 400 B.C. as a gift to be put on or in graves. Decoration was in the white-ground technique and, since it was only for show, could use fugitive pigments, put on after firing. These pigments have mostly vanished – here the man's dress and the woman's undergarment had a flat wash of yellow and her cloak of dark red. The scene – of leave taking – has a classical serenity. Its painter was the last of the great Greek painters of pottery.

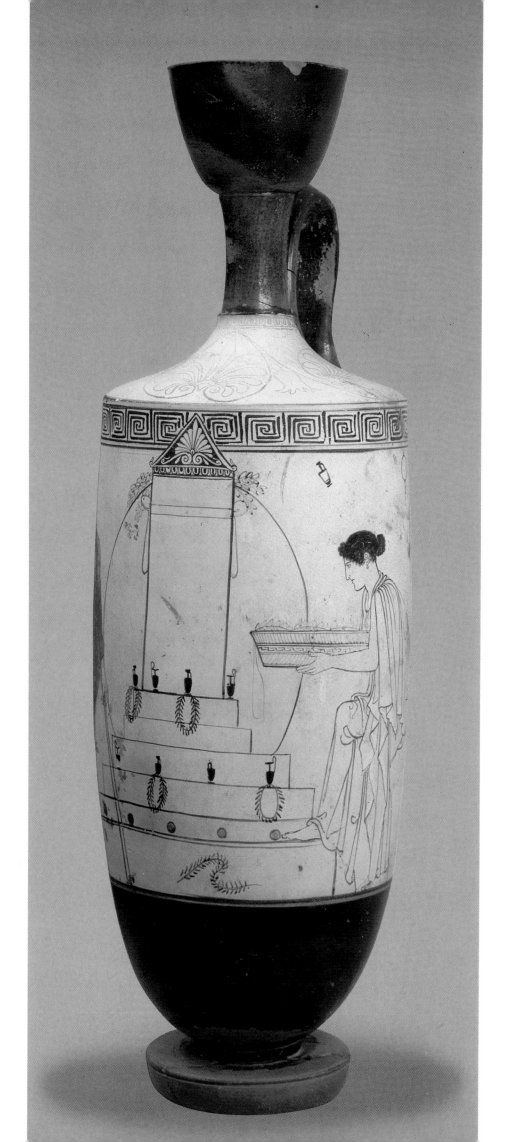

Oil flask ("lekythos"). White-ground, the normal "paint" supplemented by red, pink and white pigments. Attic, by the Bosanquet Painter; c. 440 B.C. Height: 18¼ in (47 cm). Found at Eretria in Euboea. Athens, National Museum (no. 1935).

The earlier white-ground *lekythoi* preferred quiet domestic subjects, but soon more specifically funerary subjects came in. Here a woman brings gifts to the grave, marked by a headstone (which has *lekythoi* and jugs on its base); the figure opposite, whom she does not notice, may be the spirit of a young man buried there. The ovoid object behind must be the grave mound, for artistic reasons drawn much too narrow. The style is still restrained: later scenes on *lekythoi* are often freely emotional.

Opposite: Drinking-vessel ("rhyton"). Attic red-figure pottery. Sotades Painter and Sotades Potter; c. 460 B.C. Height: 11½ in (29.2 cm). From Capua, southern Italy. London, British Museum (no. E.788).

Below: Drinking vessel ("rhyton"). Red-figure. Attic, Sotadean class, manner of the Sotade Painter; c. 450 B.C. Length: 8¾ in (22.7 cm). From Capua, southern Italy. London, British Museum (no. 73.8–20.271).

The Sotades workshop was renowned for its production of animal-shaped vases and tazzas, of which the piece opposite represents one of the most elaborate and detailed examples. It is a typical *rhyton* shape, painted in white with touches of red and gold, with a small hole between the paws of the sphinx through which to pour liquids. The red-figure painting depicts a satyr holding a staff.

Drinking vessels based on a mould-made head, human or animal, were produced in respectable quantity at Athens during the fifth century B.C. and in Apulia during the fourth. The rim section was made separately on the wheel and often decorated with figures; it was attached to the head before firing. The head itself may in the main be painted black or left in the natural colour of the clay.

Opposite: Water jar ("hydria" or "kalpis"). Red-figure with a little gilding. Attic, by the Meidias Painter; 420–410 B.C. Height: 20¼ in (52 cm). Presumably found in southern Italy. London, British Museum (no. E 224).

Below: Mixing bowl ("calyx-crater"). Red-figure. Southern Italian Greek (Lucanian) by the Dolon Painter; 390–380 B.C. Height: 18¾ in (48 cm). Found at Pisticci in southern Italy. Paris, Bibliothèque Nationale (no 422).

In the water jar opposite the subjects are legendary. Above, Castor and Pollux abduct the daughters of Leucippus from a sanctuary, indicated by an altar; below, Heracles, beardless and sitting idly with his club and lion skin, waits for the apples in the garden of the Hesperides.

The southern Italian schools of red-figure pottery, initiated around 440–430 B.C. by Attic immigrants, soon tended to deviate on their own. Much of the earlier work shows a dull, if competent, classicism; in this mixing bowl there is more originality and spirit. The subject – from Homer's *Odyssey* – shows the hero Odysseus summoning up the ghost of Tiresias by a blood offering.

The Apulian school, centered around Taranto, was the most successful of the southern Italian schools. During the fourth century its style burgeoned into floridity, especially on large pots, some of them fairly certainly made to be deposited in tombs. The subject opposite is the wind spirit Boreas abducting Orithyia. The style is ornate and in its presentation of spatial depth and foreshortening negligently assured.

Some Apulian red-figure painters had for a time been using applied pigments for part of their subsidiary decoration and in Gnathian production, which began towards 360 B.C., this technique was employed alone. At first human figures occur, but soon the Gnathian painters settled down to vegetable and other unambitious motifs, as above, done of course with decreasing care. Manufacture spread over much of Italy and lasted until around 270 B.C.

Below: Wine jar ("amphora"). Black "paint" over brownish clay, decoration in white pigment and thinned clay. Attic. West Slope ware; c. 200–150 B.C. Height: 9¼ in (23.6 cm). Found at Athens. Athens, Agora Museum (no. P 599).

Opposite: Bowl ("lebes gamikos"). Brownish clay covered, after firing, with white coat over which painting in tempera. Sicilian Greek, Centuripae ware; mid third century B.C. Height of field: 7½ in (19 cm). Finding place unknown. New York, Metropolitan Museum of Art (no. 53.11.5).

West Slope ware developed at Athens from, at least in part, the decorated Black ware. As seen in the example opposite, compared with Gnathian, its western counterpart, it tends to be heavier in both shapes and style and has more taste for abstract ornament. West Slope ware came to be made in many parts of Greece, but remained of minor importance. Its duration seems to be from the late fourth to the late first century B.C.

Centuripae ware is the name given to a group of big ornate pots, painted after firing in a fully pictorial style and often of unpractical shape – lids, as in the example above, may be in one piece with the pot – and found at or near Centuripae, well inland in Sicily. The subjects are concerned with weddings. This kind of painting is quite exceptional on pottery and presumably the product of an isolated but competent workshop, active perhaps throughout the third century B.C.

The Kilns of Ancient Rome

Any comparison between the characteristics of Roman ceramics and those of Archaic and Classical Greece will almost inevitably degenerate into a lengthy catalogue of differences. In the production of vases, for example, Greece displayed very marked differences from area to area and from city to city, whereas Roman civilization revealed its capacity for unification and amalgamation and its ability to impose homogenous styles and tastes on countries separated both by geography and by local traditions. In other words, it was a question of highly productive individualism versus a no less surprising universalism. Confirmation of this is provided by the fact that an Athenian red-figure crater is unmistakable, whereas it can prove very difficult to establish whether some first-century B.C. cups were made in Italy or Egypt. Another important fact to remember, when considering ceramics of the Imperial Roman era, is that although during certain parts of the sixth and fifth centuries they could display great quality and imagination, they were mainly the product of an industry that created wares for use in the home and on the whole they never ventured far beyond the limits imposed by this market. It could also be added that on Roman pottery the painted decoration, which was a hallmark of Greek wares, plays a role that is so secondary as to be barely perceptible.

In pursuing this course, however, one runs the risk of being forced into a position that is not only biased, but actually misleading, given that Roman wares were actually derived from Hellenistic models in many important aspects. The result is yet further confirmation of the belief that, from a cultural point of view, Rome was by and large subservient to Greece. Such elements of continuity as there are between these two phases in the history of ceramics,

Jug. Lead-glazed earthenware. Lezoux or Rhineland; second half of second or early third century A.D. Height: 11½ in (29.5 cm). Trier, Rheinisches Landesmuseum (no. PM3746D). This jug was found in a grave at Trier with a coin of the Emperor Hadrian (117–138 A.D.). It is possible that it was made at Cologne or at Bonn.

Ceramic styles of Ancient Rome

Terra-cotta pitcher with lead glaze. Asia Minor (?); first century A.D. Oxford, Ashmolean Museum.

and they are very strong ones, are echoed in the terminology of scholars who use the term "sigillata" to denote vases, from both the Hellenistic and Imperial Roman eras, characterized by a clay rich in red iron oxide and the presence in many cases of a *sigillum* (seal) bearing the name of the maker or the owner of the workshop. Another Hellenistic legacy was the Roman preference for relief decoration, a common feature of Imperial ceramics.

This type of decoration could be achieved in a number of ways. Sometimes the decorative reliefs were stamped out separately and then applied as required to the body of the vase, using a thin veil of slip (page 92, right). Sometimes the decoration was created *à la barbotine*, a technique that consisted of tracing ornamental motifs on the vessel's surface by means of a brush dipped in slip (page 92, left). Sometimes, instead of turning the piece on the wheel and then decorating it, the potter used a mould on which he had already stamped the required decorative motifs. Applied decoration of separately made reliefs, freehand decoration *à la barbotine* and moulded decoration are all techniques found in pre-Roman ceramics. The third technique could be used to decorate not only "open" vessels (the crater type), but also "closed" ones (the pitcher type).

It is widely believed that Roman ceramics were mostly of rather poor quality, but this means ignoring the exceptions that prove the rule, for example the extraordinarily beautiful sigillated wares known as "Arretine pottery." These "red-gloss" vessels were made in and around the Tuscan city of Arezzo (ancient Arretium) between approximately 30 and 20 B.C. or slightly later. Of elegant shape and bearing impressed decoration, they were made mainly for domestic use: shallow dishes, pitchers, craters,

straight-sided tazzas and the characteristic deep cups. The decoration is mainly floral, but there are also examples of more complex, figurative compositions, in certain cases of quite high quality, while its arrangement in horizontal bands respects the canons of the Augustan age. The decoration is derived directly from the relief ornament found on contemporary metal vessels. In other words, potters were seeking inspiration from metal workers, which is hardly surprising, given the fact that pottery had for a long time been trying to imitate metal, a clearly more valuable material. Vases also sometimes displayed reeding and isolated decorative elements that could be impressed using a roulette, a technique that had already been used in much earlier times. Apart from such manually applied patterns, however, the decoration consisted mainly of moulded reliefs (page 93, right), the most suitable technique for the creation of a cheap, yet attractive style of mass-produced pottery.

The production of Arretine pottery was a real industry, and a remarkably well-organized one at that. Thanks to the impressed stamps on the vases and information revealed by archaeologists, we know the different workshops in which the wares were made and also the names of their owners and many of the workmen. Vases were exported from Arezzo, which was situated on the Via Cassia, to more distant provinces and examples of Arretine pottery have even been found beyond the boundaries of the Empire. It was also a type of pottery that inspired many other craftsmen.

Very similar red-gloss wares were produced in Gaul from the beginning of the first century A.D. and well into the third century. These are not merely provincial imitations, however: sometimes the glaze

Red terra-cotta bowl with raised decoration. Sigillated ware; c. first century A.D. Naples, Museo Archeologico Nazionale.

Pink terra-cotta pitcher, with yellow glaze and painted in red and purple. From Nubia; first or second century A.D. Oxford, Ashmolean Museum.

is better than on Arretine pottery and the clay more solid. The figurative compositions may be a little crude and occasionally slightly clumsy, but this is compensated for by some of the shapes, which reveal astonishing originality (page 93, left). A type of pottery resembling that produced in Gaul was also made in Germany, Britain and Spain, while in North Africa there was a similar tradition until the collapse of the Empire. In fact, it was the kilns of North Africa which took over the exporting role that in the early days of the Roman Empire had been filled by the workshops of Italy and later, at least as far as the Eastern provinces were concerned, by those of Asia Minor. During the latter days of the Empire and up until the advent of the Arabs, North Africa appears to have been the source of those typical, flared tazzas that have been discovered from Cornwall to Russia and from Persia to the Sudan. As time went by, the quality declined: the wares became more fragile and the colour changed to dark red, a pale reflection of the beautiful Greek black and glossy Arretine red.

It was in Egypt that a major innovation was introduced during the first century B.C., in the form of lead glazes exploiting the range of colours obtainable by the admixture of metal oxides (copper, for example, produces a brilliant green). The glaze, used even on the most familiar forms of clay vessel, was overlaid on the decoration, which was normally in the form of floral motifs but sometimes comprised a more ambitious decoration of high-relief figures, either applied or modelled directly on the surface of the vase. The technique spread rapidly eastwards, then to Italy and thence to Gaul. In Asia Minor, vases covered in a lead glaze have been discovered in places such as Tarsus, an ancient city in Cilicia where fragments of the old moulds have also been found. The shapes show a clear intention to imitate silverware, particularly in the reintroduction of ring handles, an element commonly found on metalwork of the Late Hellenistic and Roman eras. A very characteristic feature of certain first-century A.D. cups were their colours, leaf green on the exterior and yellow on the inside, but there are exceptions to the rule (page 94). By contrast, there are other vessels, from the same period and also attributable to the kilns of Asia Minor, on which the glaze covers areas of white, red or buff slip and whose highly unusual decoration makes use of very skilfully executed relief mouldings (page 95). During the second century A.D. lead glazes were also used in workshops in central Gaul and the Rhineland (page 88).

Also in Egypt, there was another, very ancient method of glazing, based on the use of a quartz frit and characterized by a very broad range of colours. The bodies of the vessels were probably modelled by hand or moulded, rather than being turned on the wheel. They are distinguished by their rich, brilliant colouring which, while completely unlike that found on contemporary pottery, is to be seen on certain items of glassware, which were clearly an influence. The decoration, which allowed for highly unusual motifs, was obtained partly by using a brush to spread the colours and partly by scraping them away to obtain the desired effect (page 96). Later, in other areas, we find confirmation of the gradual emergence of new tastes in the matter of decoration: in the Rhineland during the third century A.D., for example, one potter concentrated on creating colour contrasts by decorating items of black-surfaced pottery with white and brownish-red slips (page 97). The original Roman ceramic models were gradually becoming a thing of the past.

Gaulish pottery with shiny red glaze and incised "cut crystal" decoration. Produced at Lezoux (France); mid second century A.D. Oxford, Ashmolean Museum.

Beaker in shiny red-glazed pottery with scrolling decoration outlined à la barbotine. Probably made at Rheinzabern (Rhineland); third century A.D. London, British Museum.

Below left: Flagon. "Red-gloss" pottery (probably "Eastern Sigillata A"). Asia Minor (perhaps Antioch); first century A.D. Height: 6½ in (16.5 cm). Leiden, Rijksmuseum van Oudheden (no. I.1908/1.1.).

Below right: Vase. "Red-gloss" pottery with applied decoration. Near Eastern (possibly Pergamum); perhaps first century B.C. Height: 6¼ in (16 cm). London, British Museum (no. 1902.10–12.2).

The flagon was found at Olbia in South Russia, near the mouth of the Dniester, on the north coast of the Black Sea. Olbia was an old Greek colony, and maintained trading contacts with the Hellenized Near East. It was natural enough, therefore, that a flagon made in Asia Minor should find its way there. The jug is decorated with scrolling leafy stems executed by slip trailing, an exacting technique in which the slip was poured from a small spouted vessel. The skill of the potter is seen in the spontaneous freedom with which these scrolls are "drawn." This is a precocious example of the technique, which is found later in the "red-gloss" wares of Gaul.

By contrast with most of the early relief-decorated "red-gloss" wares, this elegantly turned vase has moulded applied reliefs fixed to the surface by means of a film of slip. The vase originally had a pair of horizontal handles at the shoulder, now broken away. It was found at Laodicea, in Syria.

*Below left: Flagon. "Red-gloss" pottery. Eastern Gaul; first half of third century A.D. Height:
6 in (15 cm). Oxford, Ashmolean Museum (no. 1885–591).*

---

*Below right: Ewer. "Red-gloss" pottery with relief-moulded decoration. Arretium (P. Cornelius
factory); early first century A.D. Height: 7 in (17.4 cm). London, British Museum (no. L 56).*

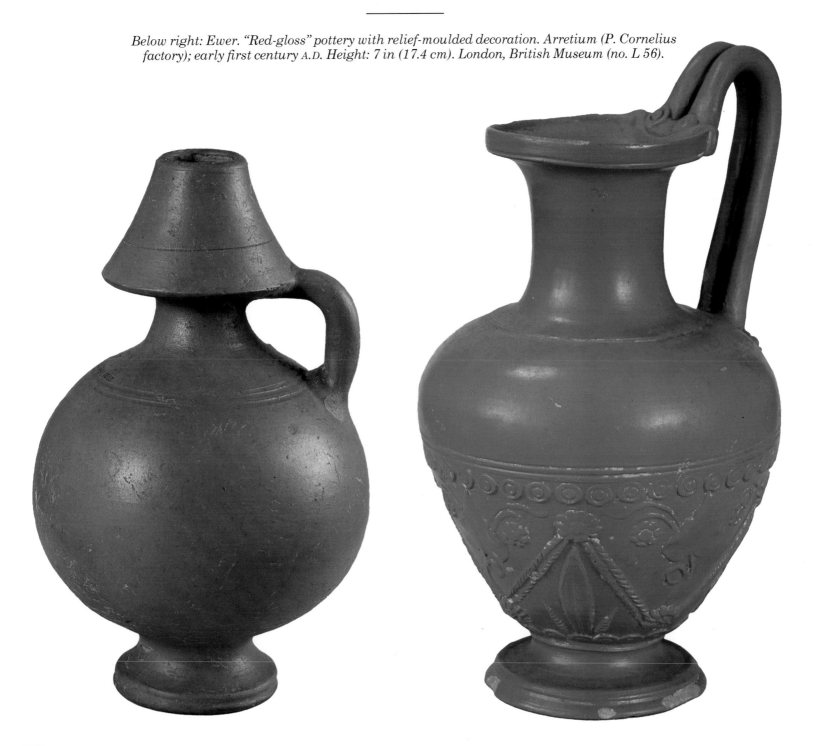

Flagons of the shape above have been found in graves at Krefeld-Gellup, in Germany, dating from the end of the third century, and were certainly made in the Eastern Gaulish factories. A similar, but more elongated, shape also occurs in Germany with white-slip decoration on the "red-gloss" surface. Here the native potter has taken the rim feature and exaggerated it beyond any practical purpose, thereby producing a shape of singular harmony which reiterates the same downward-spreading theme in rim, neck–shoulder, and foot, with telling effect. The originality of this shape, with its clean outline, is perhaps a greater source of aesthetic satisfaction than the confused compositions of the more pretentious traditional relief-decorated wares.

The principles of relief moulding already described could be applied also to closed forms such as the ewer shown here, the part above the decorative frieze being either worked by the potter in the normal way, or made separately, like the turned pedestal foot, and "luted" on with slip. The two-strand handle betrays by the two imitation rivets at its upper terminal its derivation from metalwork. The ewer bears the stamp of the factory owner P. Cornelius, who employed a number of craftsmen, at least seven of whom are known by name.

Footed bowl. Lead-glazed earthenware. Asia Minor; probably first century A.D. Height: 5½ in (14.2 cm). Diameter of mouth: 7 in (18.2 cm). Boston, Museum of Fine Arts (no. 50.2300).

The footed bowl was one of the less common shapes of green-glazed ware and was derived from metalwork. Here the vessel is, exceptionally, glazed green inside and out, its brilliance much affected by burial. The greater part of the bowl is decorated with vine sprays, but in the center of the side visible here a centaur (half horse and half man) moves to the right, holding possibly a club in his right hand and apparently a human head in his left. The remaining space is filled with figures of cupids holding vases in both hands, and with no less than fifteen dolphins. The vine motif and the cupids with raised vessels suggest wine drinking, a suitable theme to decorate a mixing bowl ("crater").

A few vessels of this handled beaker shape ("modiolus") are known, the present example from Komotini, in southern Thrace; a second from Olbia; and a third from Kenchreai, near Corinth. They are distinguished from the lead-glazed wares already described by having decoration partly trailed in slip and partly applied. The slips used are white and buff or red, the glaze overlying these colours thereby producing a variation of tone not found in the normal relief-moulded wares. The grotesque "comic" figure on the side is matched by the even more macabre skeleton on the front of the beaker. The divided handle and the general shape (also found in Arretine pottery and in glass) suggest an origin in metalwork.

Below: Dish. Glazed quartz fritware. Egypt (perhaps Memphis); first century A.D. Depth: 8¼ in (21.5 cm). London, Victoria and Albert Museum (no. C. 208–1926).

Opposite: Jug and beaker. Black-surfaced pottery with rouletted and slip-trailed decoration. Germany (Rhineland, perhaps Trier); third century A.D. Height of jug: 10¾ in (27 cm). Cologne, Kölnisches Stadtmuseum (nos. 29, 1723 and 175).

The dish opposite, which echoes in shape the contemporary dishes in "red-gloss" pottery, is decorated in turquoise and manganese brown, probably mainly by painting, partly by scraping away the design. Kiln wasters of this character have been found on a pottery site at Memphis, in Egypt. A number of them reveal decoration in delicate colours on the face combined with a brilliant turquoise on the back. This emphasis on brilliant colouring is perhaps inspired by the competition of the contemporary coloured glasswares.

The fashion for dark-surfaced pottery never died out in the northern provinces of the Roman Empire, and it was frequently decorated with slip trailing (à la barbotine), either in self-coloured clay in relief or in slips of contrasting colour or colours. The jug has the "thumb-indents" characteristic of this period, and is decorated with white and brownish-red slips in friezes delimited by horizontal rouletted lines. The design includes the inscription "SVME" ("Take!"). The barrel-shaped beaker is decorated similarly to the jug, but with the inscription "DA VITA[M]" ("Give life").

Ceramics of the Islamic World

The rapid expansion of the Muslim world marked the beginning of a particularly important chapter in the history of ceramics. An examination of this very particular episode in the evolution of the art brings to light two salient features. On the one hand the work of Muslim potters reveals clear links with the artistic traditions of those countries that were either gradually absorbed into the Islamic world or merely came into contact with it. On the other, it displays a constant ability to research and perfect new working techniques and an extraordinarily fertile inventiveness in the development of styles and subjects.

As far as decoration is concerned, various observations and hypotheses have been made. For example, it is interesting to note that likenesses of living creatures do appear with some frequency, which means that the widely held belief amongst non-Muslims that these were banned from Islamic art on religious grounds is also misplaced with regard to ceramics. The jewel-like colours that characterize the abstract decoration on so many wares have been interpreted as a form of compensation for a shortage of subject matter. Clearly, this is not the case. Rather, note should be made of the important role played by calligraphic motifs, for which a variety of characters were used, such as Kufic, one of the oldest and noblest, or Nashki, which has softer and more rounded shapes. Writing was used more for its formal values than for any verbal messages it might convey: the language that interested the decorators most was the visual one, as is illustrated by the numerous "pseudo-inscriptions."

Materials and working methods represent another extremely interesting facet of Islamic ceramics, which in this respect may be regarded as a sort of

Tile panel. Alkaline-glazed earthenware painted in luster. Iran (Kashan); c. 1260–1265. 46½ × 29½ in (119×76 cm). London, Victoria and Albert Museum (no. s 1487, etc.–1876).

Ceramic styles and decoration of the Islamic world

Bowl with opaque white glaze. It was the custom to paint only cobalt-blue decoration or merely the signature of the artist on this sort of pottery. Iraq; ninth–tenth century.

inexhaustible and highly talented laboratory. Among the most influential inventions was that of luster, which appeared towards the end of the ninth century. A rather complex process, its first stage involved painting the required pattern on the white-glazed surface of an already fired pot, using special metallic pigments, after which the pot was returned to the kiln at a relatively low temperature, using special devices that allowed for a reduction in oxygen when the glaze began to soften. The result is a glaze that incorporates a thin metallic layer which can be of a variety of colours and can also display touches of iridescence. This "invention," (even though Coptic artists had already adopted a similar form of decoration in another medium, that of glass), would appear to have originated in Mesopotamia, a region containing important centers of ceramic production.

Although certain characteristics of these luster wares clearly betray signs of their having been inspired by metalwork, other items reveal noticeable traces of the influence of Chinese porcelain. However, here, as in other instances, Islamic potters welcomed other challenges and stimuli, using them to enrich their own experience rather than confining themselves to stale imitation. They were working in an area teeming with different influences and inspirations, and this was not a one-way process. For a long while it was believed that at a certain stage Chinese blue-and-white Ming porcelain became a model for Middle Eastern potters. This supposition was in a way justified, and it was supported by the discovery of vast quantities of that particular type of Chinese ware in archaeological sites in the Islamic world. But there is a further detail, which is that the Chinese potters originally had a model of their own, an even more ancient type of Islamic ware. Indeed, cobalt blue was known in China as "Mohammedan blue."

During the seventh century the Arabs, under the leadership of the first caliphs, took the world of Islam by force of arms well beyond the confines of their historical homelands, moving simultaneously against two great empires, the Byzantine, an essentially Roman institution, and the Sassanian, further to the east. They had soon subdued Syria, Palestine, Mesopotamia, Persia and other lands in the heart of Asia. Their campaigns in the west were equally successful and the invasion of Egypt, begun in 639, was followed by the rapid conquest of a large part of North Africa. In 661 the caliphate passed into the hands of the Ommayad dynasty and the capital was moved to Damascus, in Syria. By the end of the century other territories on the borders of China and beyond the river Indus were added, while in 717 occupation began of a large part of the Iberian peninsula. These grandiose achievements also altered the original premises on which the Arab world had been founded. A few years after the death of Mohammed, for example, Mecca and Medina, traditionally regarded as Holy Cities because of their links with the life of the Prophet, were joined by other Islamic centers located outside the Arabian peninsula. Basra and Kufa in Mesopotamia and Fustat in Egypt were all important bases for military expeditions, to name but three. In the mid eighth century the Ommayads were replaced by the Abbasids and the capital was moved to Baghdad, and for a while to Samarra, both Mesopotamian cities, a move completely in keeping with the importance now being assumed by the eastern territories. The latter included Persia, which for many centuries was to play a leading role throughout the Islamic world in both literature, art and culture. This primacy also extended to the realm of ceramics.

Dish with luster decoration. The camel, executed in monochrome on a white ground, was one of the favourite motifs on this type of ware. Iraq; twelfth century.

Mina'i wares (wares with over-glaze decoration) were often decorated with subjects from the Shahnama *or Book of Kings. Kashan, Iran; twelfth century.*

The Arab conquests had laid the conditions for the establishment of a new art with its roots in, on the one hand, the heritage of Hellenism and, on the other, the Sassanian and Central Asiatic conventions of the East. The latter left their most visible marks on the art of the Abbasid period, while signs of the former are more clearly seen in works of the Ommayad period.

The ceramics which concern us here are the most costly and refined wares, not those used by the common people: they were luxury products, sold on the local market and destined either for the court and members of the upper echelons of society or for export. It is therefore understandable that caliphs, emirs, sultans and similar potentates should have expressed an interest in ceramics, either as sponsors of its manufacture or as patrons, and that they should have tried to attract artists from other countries to their cities, giving them sanctuary when they sought asylum, or even, as was the policy of the Timurids, deporting them from occupied territories. It is partly for this reason that, when subdividing the history of Islamic ceramics into various periods, the matching of specific groups of wares with the names of contemporary dynasties can be slightly less extrinsic than might first appear.

When the Muslim Arabs made their entrance on to the Mediterranean scene they discovered a well-established ceramic industry, based on technical and artistic traditions that had developed over many centuries. In the Roman Empire there were two basic types of pottery, examples of which were produced over a large area; one consisted of unglazed pottery, "sigillated ware," mainly bearing impressed or applied decoration, while the other comprised pottery with a lead or alkaline glaze. Ommayad ceram-

ics, of which little was known until recently, repeated this duality, albeit without renouncing the quest for more unusual possibilities. An illustration of this phenomenon, although there are a number of precedents in other areas, is provided by certain simple earthenware vessels with incised decoration, mainly shallow bowls and plates, the walls of which were engraved to a considerable depth so as to leave only the pre-selected geometrical patterns in relief.

Signs of the enduring influence of Romano-Byzantine ceramics can also be detected in wares of the early Abbasid period, particularly in the lead-glazed relief pottery that represents one of its basic forms. In fact, their lead glaze and their typical relief decoration, obtainable by pressing a lump of clay against a stamp bearing an incised pattern, both hark back to that tradition, while the ornamental motifs adopted (one thinks of the frequent palmettes and rosettes) are also part of a very ancient heritage. The links between pottery of this sort and metalwork are further reminders of a distant past, and all that remains now is to point out that these links were further strengthened by the specific Islamic prohibition on the use of gold and silver vessels. Potters tried to get round this ban by producing items which, in both shape and decoration, replicated the forbidden articles. But it is not possible to maintain that we are dealing with wares that possess no qualities of originality: such arguments can be easily refuted by an examination of the luster decoration on certain plates (page 110).

Tin-glazed pottery represents another of the main groups found in early Abbasid ceramics. Chinese grès and porcelain were soon being imported and it was not long before they had inspired the Islamic world to produce something similar. The Muslim potters, however, lacked an essential ingredient of porcelain,

Pitcher. Luster-painted decoration. The decoration was often combined with epigraphs or lines of poetry within vertical panels. Iran; twelfth–thirteenth century.

Ewer. Animal-shaped vessels, in both metal and pottery, were very common in the Islamic world during the twelfth–thirteenth centuries. Iran; thirteenth century.

namely kaolin, so they tried to cover the red or buff earthenware available to them with an opaque white glaze. For this they resorted to tin oxide and succeeded in creating a surface that was not only white, but also satisfactorily smooth and shiny. Initially, they produced undecorated white pottery and then began experimenting with painted decoration on the glazed surface, particularly in cobalt blue (page 111), achieving results of notable freshness and elegance.

During the early Abbasid period, lead-glazed ceramics with splashed decoration form a group apart. Originally the colours, applied in spots or stripes, ran rather haphazardly during firing, but the potters later learned to control this. It seems that to begin with only green was used, with other colours being introduced in stages, starting with brown (page 112). There are also examples of white-glazed pottery on which the green or, more rarely, yellow splashes are combined with a figurative decoration painted in cobalt blue (page 113).

The advent of luster as a decorative element on white-glazed wares, which also dates from this period, is to be regarded as a revolutionary step in the long history of Islamic ceramics. The men responsible for this advance would appear to have been the potters of cities such as Samarra, Basra and Kufa, whose wares can be divided into two main groups: the polychrome type, possibly the least interesting, and the monochrome. The colours found on polychrome wares are ruby red and two shades of brown, mustard and golden yellow, whereas the monochrome wares are either golden yellow or yellow–green in colour. The subjects of the latter's decoration include human figures, generally in isolation, rabbits, birds, camels and half palmettes (page 114), the remaining area being covered with dashes and spots; in other cases

the decoration is abstract. It is fairly common to find a word or brief benedictory inscription in the Arabic characters that take their name from the city of Kufa. Luster enjoyed great popularity, and between the ninth and tenth century vases similar to those produced in the Abbasid workshops of Mesopotamia were already being made elsewhere in the Islamic world (page 115).

Whereas in the Iraq region the pottery was first glazed and then given its splashed or luster decoration, the potters of Persia and central Asia took the opposite course, favouring a type of ceramics normally described as earthenware painted with liquid slips. Between the ninth and tenth century they discovered that, by applying a thin clay slip to the body of a vessel before firing, the lead glaze retains greater stability, thus making it possible to create more finished and sophisticated decoration. They made use of colours such as manganese purple, tomato red, olive green, yellow and brown, mixed with very dilute clay, in order to decorate the surface of the vase, which they then covered with a transparent lead glaze. The most widespread, most interesting and probably the most ancient group of this type comprises wares with a white or cream-coloured slip and a decoration in black. The decoration is always spare and simple, based mainly on Arabic script. Rather than inscriptions, the most highly decorated examples display figures of birds (page 116) or other animals. Another group is composed of polychrome wares with a white ground: together with black, the commonest colour is tomato red and in many cases the decoration also contains writing, with the center of the piece sometimes containing motifs of varying intricacy. This group includes "Sari" pottery, named after a small city situated to the south of the Caspian Sea in which

Long-necked vase. There was always a frequent exchange of ideas between ceramics and metalware, which vied with each other for the elegance of their shapes and their decoration. Iran; thirteenth century.

Tray with seven compartments. Luster decoration. This type of object was very popular in the Islamic world, especially in Syria. Raqqa, Syria; thirteenth century.

a number of examples have been discovered. It is easily recognizable by the presence of stylized birds at the center and stemmed circular motifs on the sides (page 118).

A similarly important position is occupied by another type of polychrome pottery, called "animate buff ware," which appears to have been made exclusively at the city of Nishapur in eastern Persia. These wares include cups, plates, trays, small pitchers, jars and oil lamps. The decoration, normally in three colours, is fairly varied: floral and geometrical decorations are relatively common, but the most usual type depicts scenes of figures. Given the absence of any miniatures or paintings from the period, these images represent an invaluable source of information on Persian art of the day. They are charming and enjoyable scenes in their own right, however, and not just interesting historical documents. Some pieces display one or two human figures, sitting cross-legged and holding cups, while others depict a warrior or a huntsman on horseback (page 119). Ceramics painted with coloured slips are also sometimes called "Samanid" pottery, from the name of the dynasty which ruled Transoxiana, the north-eastern region of Persia now called Khorasan, and Kirman, situated to the south-east of the country. The chronological limits of this typology are, however, much broader than the duration of Samanid rule.

Towards the end of the tenth century the production of Islamic ceramics shifted not only from Iraq to Iran, but also to Egypt, a development which took place against a historical background that needs some explanation. Because of its vast geographical extent the Muslim empire ran the risk, if not of easy dissolution, then of becoming divided up into different zones, each enjoying a measure of autonomy. Af-

ter the conquest of the caliphate by the Abbasids in 750, there gradually began a process of fragmentation whose main protagonists were the countries located farthest from the center of the Empire: first Spain, where a deposed member of the Ommayad dynasty established a stronghold (756), then Morocco and Tunisia. Finally, in 868, Egypt saw the establishment of emirates that broke the early solidarity of the Islamic world. During the tenth century two new caliphates were established in competition with the one in Baghdad: in Egypt there were the Fatimids, who extended their rule over Palestine, Syria, the Holy Cities and the whole of Muslim Africa, and in Spain the Ommayads. This process of political dismemberment should not, however, be interpreted as an indication of general decline: on the contrary, it was a sign of maturity in a civilization that had now become polycentric and was set fair for its golden age.

It is possible that Mesopotamian potters from Basra and Kufa had arrived in Egypt by the second half of the ninth century, after these cities were destroyed in slave revolts, but there can be no doubt that the golden age of ceramics began after the Fatimid conquest, and in particular following the establishment in 969 of the new capital, Cairo. Luster ware appears to be the most common type of Fatimid pottery, whose decoration comprises vegetal motifs, calligraphic patterns and figured subjects. One of its most remarkable characteristics is the way in which the human figures are presented, with great attention paid to the details of their faces, their poses and their dress, a feature which seems to bear out the theory that these artists were familiar with the painting of illuminated manuscripts. Sometimes there are also interesting variations on the usual decorative technique. In the work of one artist, for example, called

Albarello. This type of container was very widespread in Syria and Mongol Iran during the thirteenth and fourteenth centuries. Syria; thirteenth century.

Mina'i dish. The rich decoration depicts the Sun, with a human face, surrounded by the planets, represented as figures. Iran; thirteenth century.

Sa'ad, who was active between the end of the eleventh century and beginning of the twelfth, details of the pattern, painted in luster on an opaque white ground, were scratched out with a point in order to reveal the underlying colour (page 120). In Egypt, during the Fatimid period and beyond, there was also a considerable output of lead-glazed polychrome pottery, a development of the Abbasid-Iraqi splashed ware, although the most interesting type is represented by items whose decoration recalls certain papyrus paintings discovered in the ruins of Fustat and Fayyum. Wares of the same type have also been unearthed in a number of archaeological sites in North Africa, although it is fairly unusual to find the sort of particularly interesting decoration that occurs on one famous bowl, produced either in Tunisia or Majorca during the eleventh century (page 121).

The "sgraffiato" technique, with which Sa'ad was familiar, brings us back to Persia, where, from the beginning of the tenth century, a type of pottery was produced which exploited it to the full. Once again there are clear signs of the influence of metalworking techniques, and here too there are precedents, ranging from Coptic wares, which take us back to Egypt several centuries earlier, to those linked to certain late developments in splashed ware that can be traced back to the Iraqi area. The Persian potters appear to have taken a completely independent course, however. They incised their decorative motifs on the thin layer of slip with which they covered their pottery, only to re-cover it with a transparent coloured glaze, and also, as can be seen in many pieces made between the twelfth and thirteenth century excavated in the Garrus district of north-west Persia, they carved away large areas of the very thick slip with a knife or some other sharp instrument so as to leave only the decoration in relief. This decoration sometimes takes the form of palmette-shaped volutes (page 122), while elsewhere (page 123) it depicts animal or human subjects. The background appears darker than the subject which is in a transparent, greenish-coloured lead glaze.

During the first half of the eleventh century a new dynasty emerged in the Islamic world, that of the Seljuk Turks. Natives of Central Asia, the Seljuks had embraced Islam towards the end of the tenth century. In 1038 they invaded Persia and less than 20 years later they had also occupied Baghdad, where they became the self-appointed protectors of the Abbasid caliphs, who were deprived of all authority. By force of arms they established dominion over Anatolia, until then (1077) a Byzantine possession, apart from the south-eastern strip, which had already fallen within the Muslim sphere of influence. The settlement of new peoples in the ancient Muslim lands modified their ethnic make-up and marked the start of a new chapter in the story that had been begun by the preachings of Mohammed.

At a certain undefined stage of Seljuk rule, but certainly during the eleventh century, a radical change occurred in ceramics. A new material was introduced, at least in the main Persian centers, to replace earthenware. Chinese porcelain of the Sung dynasty (960–1279), which had been extensively imported into the Middle East, was certainly the model that the Islamic potters had in mind when, centuries after it had been forgotten, they adopted a product that had been used since the second millennium in the Nile Valley, in Syria and in Mesopotamia. A manuscript from 1301 reveals the "recipe" for this new paste, which was almost translucent and white or greyish white in appearance and, although not

Bowl. Islamic pottery of the thirteenth–fourteenth century has strong affinities with metalware, whose shapes and decorative motifs it imitated. Iran; fourteenth century.

Bowl decorated with a band of inscriptions around the rim. From Sultanabad, Iran; fourteenth century.

very malleable, was ideally suited to moulding and to the creation of thin-walled vessels. This composite involved a tenth part of white clay and the rest was made up of powdered glass and quartz. The new material allowed for beautiful decorative effects, achieved either by engraving, carving or piercing.

The thin-walled ceramics of the Seljuk period, produced first in Persia and later elsewhere in the Islamic world, can be subdivided into a broad range of types.

There are white, almost translucent wares, with incised, moulded, engraved or pierced decoration, which were then covered in a colourless, transparent glaze. There are "silhouette" wares, whose ceramic body is covered in a thick layer of black slip, on which, before glazing, ornamental motifs were carved, with details obtained by scraping the dark shapes until the white ground was revealed. There are wares painted beneath a glaze that can sometimes be colourless and sometimes coloured, generally in green, blue or turquoise: a cup with decoration in reserve on a black painted ground and beneath a turquoise glaze (page 124) reveals the sort of effects that could be achieved using this technique. There are wares with a monochrome glaze, of a type that also occurs on a certain number of figurines (page 125). There are also slightly eccentric wares on which, not without a certain amount of skill and success, under-glaze painted decoration is used in conjunction with pierced decoration, as, for example, in a double-walled ewer with a zoomorphic head (page 126). There are wares with an under-glaze painted decoration in more than one colour, with simultaneous use of incised ornamentation (page 127). There are luster wares, a technique that in Persia reached its greatest heights during the twelfth and thirteenth centuries:

it was a type characterized in its early stages by the so-called "monumental style," with large human or animal figures in a central position and, later, by the "miniaturist style," with a certain crowding and entanglement of the figured patterns, which are often accompanied by inscriptions in *thuluth* characters. Both styles can be traced back to Kashan, undoubtedly the most important, if not the only center of luster-ware production in Persia. It is also possible that there was another center at Gurgan, where hundreds of items of this type have been discovered. For example, the small figure of a seated man with a cup in his right hand (page 129) comes from Gurgan. Luster-ware vessels such as pitchers, ewers and bottles figure prominently and are characterized by rather elaborate decoration: one bottle discovered near Teheran displays a series of horizontal bands that are separated by a ring of inscriptions and in which horsemen amongst cypresses and arabesques alternate with lions within circular cartouches (page 128). Large quantities of luster tiles were also produced at Kashan, in workshops that were often handed down from father to son (page 98). Produced in star and cross shapes, they were used in appropriate combinations to decorate large wall surfaces on both religious and secular buildings. Their manufacture continued beyond the Seljuk period.

No list of the different types of thin-walled pottery made in Persia during the Seljuk period would be complete, however, without mention of the important over-glaze painted pottery known as *mina'i* ware. Painting on ceramics has always posed considerable technical difficulties because, if the artist paints the decoration before firing, the colours can easily "burn" in the high temperatures needed to melt the glaze or, equally, the glaze, while melting, may run and so

Dish with luster decoration depicting a shoal of fish surrounded by ornamental bands. Iran; fourteenth century.

Tile with decoration of a youth painted beneath a colourless glaze. Tiles of this sort adorned palaces and private homes. Kubachi, Iran; sixteenth century.

distort the entire painting. The alternative is to paint on an already-fired glaze and then subject the piece to a second firing at a lower temperature, but hot enough to soften the colours and the glaze and make them bond. In Persian *mina'i* means "enamel," and the technique is also sometimes known as *haft-rangi* ("seven-colour") because of the seven colours used: red, blue, green, yellow, gold, black and white, which were fixed by a secondary firing, with the exception of the blue, which was always applied beneath the glaze. This polychrome decoration, which offered the artist almost unlimited possibilities, was used to portray an elegant dream world of music and feasting, young ladies and important personages, horsemen and falconers (page 130), gardens and pools, animals and fantastic creatures. Some *mina'i* scenes are framed by inscriptions and pseudo-inscriptions; at other times the decoration comprises solely a combination of script and abstract motifs (page 131), while, in later examples, it takes the form of arabesques, reliefs and gilding (page 132): although the result is no less beautiful, it does perhaps make one feel a twinge of regret for the passing of the magical, figured decoration. Around the middle of the thirteenth century, a period that saw the rise of the Ilkhanid dynasty, *lajvardina* ware, whose name derives from a Persian word meaning "lapis lazuli," came to replace the more elaborate and ambitious *mina'i* ware. A simplified version of the latter, *lajvardina* ware has a mainly abstract decoration, which was painted on the blue or dark blue surface in white, red and black, with the further addition of gold leaf. The relatively restricted decorative repertoire is compensated for by the wide variety of shapes found in *lajvardina* ware, although clearly, alongside the new shapes, other, more traditional ones survived. A sig-

nificant indication of this is provided by the widespread popularity of certain flared bowls with a low, ring foot (page 134). Tiles made using the *lajvardina* technique display figured decorations inspired by Chinese art (page 133).

During the twelfth and thirteenth centuries Persian influences can be clearly detected in the flourishing ceramic output of Syria, whose greatest centers were located to the north of the country, at Raqqa, on the left bank of the Euphrates, and at Rusafa. Although its decoration is rather austere, the underglaze painted, polychrome pottery often reveals an attempt at imitating Persian *mina'i* ware. This is particularly evident where figured patterns are concerned, but it is also to an extent true even when the decoration is more abstract, whether floral or pseudo-calligraphic (page 135). The use of Persian models, particularly *mina'i* wares, was also a feature of thirteenth-century Anatolia, where ceramics played a very important role in architectural decoration.

During the thirteenth century, the devastating Mongol invasions, which resulted in the destruction of cities such as Kashan and even Baghdad (1258), had a profound effect on Islamic ceramics. The Mongols overran Persia, Mesopotamia, Syria and Palestine, as well as destroying the power of the Seljuks in Anatolia. With the Ilkhanid dynasty (1256–1353), founded by Hulagu and his successors, a lasting power base was established, whose center lay in northwest Persia. The closing years of the fourteenth century saw another invasion from the east, that of the blood-thirsty hordes of Timur. And yet the vitality of Persian and Islamic culture was not extinguished: in the empire founded by the Timurid dynasty the production of ceramics soon resumed and new centers emerged, such as Kirman, chief city of the epony-

Large vase with polychrome under-glaze decoration of intricate, mainly floral motifs. Iran; sixteenth century.

Mosque lamp. This type of religious item was characteristic of Iznik, Turkey; sixteenth century.

mous south-western Persian province. One type of pottery attributable to the end of the thirteenth century or beginning of the fourteenth is the so-called "Sultanabad type," a description applied basically to certain wares painted in black and turquoise (page 136) beneath a heavy and colourless alkaline glaze, whose decoration reveals the influence of Far Eastern art. Close copies of Sultanabad pottery have been discovered in Central Asia and southern Russia, confirming its appeal to Mongol tastes.

Under the Timurids there was a marked increase in architectural decoration, the principles of which had been established in Anatolia, where during the thirteenth century a new technique had been developed, that of faïence mosaic, used to cover vaults, the inside of domes and *mihrabs* (prayer niches). The small glazed squares, of different colours, which were put together and attached using a liquid fixative, were capable of creating much more elaborate and detailed patterns than tiles or bricks. In Persian monuments such as the mosques at Yazd and Kirman (fourteenth century) this type of architectural decoration reached extraordinary heights, while in Transoxiana, or more accurately in the territory of Samarkand, the city chosen by Timur as his capital, a different type of decoration was introduced and developed. This took the form of polychrome panels, mostly rectangular in shape, which were used extensively in funerary monuments and displayed a variety of decorative motifs: floral ones, entwined geometrical bands and inscriptions (page 137).

The domination of Egypt by the Ayyubids (1171–1250), who had succeeded the Fatimids, ended when the Mamelukes seized power. A people of Turkish and Mongol origins, the Mamelukes, who had already been living in the country for some time,

first as slaves and then as soldiers, had soon extended their empire, destined to last until the Ottoman invasion of 1517, to include Syria as well. Mameluke ceramics, which contain some very beautiful wares, display certain uniquely interesting characteristics, as is shown by the fluid yet vigorous decoration on certain jars (page 139). They also provide further confirmation of how, within the Islamic world, there was a constant exchange of men, ideas, products and information on artistic technique, as well as illustrating how "fashions" from even very distant lands were able to penetrate and take root there. One thinks, for example, of blue-and-white ceramics, a type that became popular at some point during the fourteenth century. The main centers of production in Syria were probably Hama, where the earliest pieces have been excavated, and Damascus, and in Egypt, Cairo. The arrangement and portrayal of the floral motifs appear to have been taken mainly from the repertoire of blue-and-white Ming porcelain, as can be seen in one albarello (drug jar) of extraordinary quality, whose decoration is arranged in horizontal registers (page 138). Another example of this phenomenon is provided by Syrian and Egyptian under-glaze painted pottery of the Mameluke period, whose decoration is often very similar, and sometimes actually identical to Sultanabad wares, with the result that there have been instances of pieces being identified as Persian when in fact they are not. While on the subject of blue-and-white ceramics, mention should also be made of the considerable output, which in Syria appears to have ended after the invasion of Timur, but in Egypt continued throughout the fifteenth century, of hexagonal tiles bearing a decoration of plumed leaves, branches of blossom, peonies, flowering trees etc. Panels of this

Dish with polychrome decoration of large flowers. Iznik, Turkey; sixteenth century.

Bottle in imitation of a Chinese prototype. Blue-and-white wares made in Iran during the sixteenth and seventeenth centuries, which were widely exported to Europe, sometimes even copied Chinese porcelain marks. Iran; seventeenth century.

type of tile, with borders painted turquoise and the remainder cobalt blue, contain faint echoes of Chinese ornamental motifs (page 140).

Spain was governed by the Ommayad dynasty until 1301, then by a number of small independent dynasties until, in 1230, the Nasrids took power. The latter, who were great patrons of the arts, were responsible for the beautiful buildings of the Alhambra. The early years of the thirteenth century, however, saw the beginnings of the *Reconquista*, the long struggle by the Spaniards against the Muslim presence on the peninsula, which culminated in the fall of Granada in 1492. Lead-glazed polychrome pottery and luster ware are among the most important types of Islamic ceramics in Spain, where one of the main centers of production was Malaga. When the Spanish fleet blockaded the ports still in Arab hands around the end of the fourteenth century, the potters of Malaga had no alternative but to emigrate to the Christian territories of the north, in search of new patrons. They settled at Manises, which is where the finest luster-painted wares of the fifteenth and sixteenth centuries were made: "Popes, cardinals order them ... and they express wonderment at the fact that things of such excellence and quality should be made of clay," we read in a document of 1383. The majority of Manises ware consists of broad trays, plates, deep cups and albarellos (page 141).

During the last important stages in the history of Islamic ceramics the main focus of attention returns once again to Persia and Anatolia. It was a golden age for both areas, with the two ruling dynasties, the Safavid and the Ottoman, producing such great figures as Abbas I and Suleiman the Magnificent. In Persia, united and made independent at the end of the fifteenth century by Ismail, it was Abbas I who, several generations later, was to emerge as a particularly generous protector and patron of the arts, but, in fact, for most of the period that takes its name from the Safavid dynasty, architecture, painting, weaving, carpet making, metalwork and ceramics all flourished.

As well as Isfahan, with its wonderful mosques, Kirman continued to be a very active center of ceramic production, the most notable wares being of the so-called "Kubachi" type, whose name is derived from a small Caucasian city in which large quantities of it have been discovered. These wares, whose origins lie in the Timurid period, took different forms at different periods. On the original type the decoration was painted in black under a coloured glaze, either blue or turquoise or, more rarely, green, with floral and plant motifs: in one bowl, attributable to the final quarter of the fifteenth century, the decorative details are engraved with a burin, a technique that had been used in "silhouette" ware (page 142). Another particularly attractive type of Kubachi ware consists of under-glaze painted polychrome pottery, in which green, yellow, ocher and brownish red are used, in addition to blue and black. They frequently display very interesting portraits, but the landscape scenes are of equally high quality, as is demonstrated by, for example, a large flat plate from the end of the seventeenth century, on which a flowering tree is depicted with a small stream in the foreground and scattered flowers that cover the entire surface of the piece and give it a feeling of lively elegance (page 143). As well as the Kubachi ware, mention should also be made of blue-and-white pottery, whose production increased notably in Persia in around 1600, a period that coincides with a decline in the production of similar porcelain wares in China. A certain num-

Vase. Wares made at Kirman included monochrome vases covered in a blue, green or brown glaze. Kirman, Iran; seventeenth century.

Bottle. The luster decoration found on Persian pottery of the Safavid period favours naturalistically-inspired motifs. Iran; seventeenth century.

ber of examples display a single figure standing out against a landscape (page 144) and it should also be noted that the decoration uses different shades of blue, with the darkest shades reserved for the outline of the design. There was another type of ceramics produced at Kirman whose decoration, painted under a colourless glaze, employed a relatively restricted range of colours: blue, green, ocher and brownish red. Its decorative motifs recall those used on blue-and-white wares, which may be explained by the fact that both types were produced in the same workshops and by the same craftsmen. In addition to floral and coiling motifs, the decoration often contains representations of figures. One seventeenth-century bottle displays arabesques enclosed within two medallions placed at either end of the piece, while the intervening space is occupied by a bird in flight surrounded by flowering branches and clouds (page 145).

Following the decline of the Seljuks, the Ottoman dynasty settled in the north-western part of Anatolia, where they embarked on an aggressively expansionist policy. Under the Ottomans Islam regained its early impetus: in 1453, after a struggle lasting eight centuries, Byzantium was conquered and in 1517 Syria and Egypt were overrun. There had been ceramic workshops at Iznik, the ancient Nicaea, since before the beginning of the sixteenth century. The decoration on Iznik tiles and vessels displays a certain variety in styles. The "Damascus" style used blue, green, sage, mauve or turquoise, with a decoration composed of flowers such as roses, tulips, hyacinths and carnations, with *saz* leaves and sometimes also inscriptions (page 147). The palette of the "Rhodos" style, however, made extensive use of a sealing-wax red colour. Introduced around the mid sixteenth century, the Rhodos style lasted for more than a century and enjoyed great success in the production of both pottery and tiles. The latter were used on important buildings in Istanbul, where the famous architect Sinan worked during Suleiman's reign, and also in other cities. In the fully mature style, the elegant range of colours was joined by a beautiful copper green and by "Armenian bole," a slip with a high percentage of iron (page 146). However, when it comes to the Rhodos style, there can be little more pleasing than the exuberant and carefully balanced floral designs decorating certain polychrome plates from the middle and end of the sixteenth century (pages 148, 149).

Tile with vegetal decoration surrounding an epigraphic motif. Iznik, Turkey; seventeenth century.

Dish. The decoration on Çanakkale wares classifies them as a type of peasant pottery because of the characteristic simple motifs. Çanakkale (Dardanelles), Turkey; eighteenth–nineteenth century.

Below: Moulded and luster-painted plate. Iraq, Abbasid period; ninth century. Height: 1 in (2.8 cm). Diameter: 11 in (28 cm). Washington D.C., Freer Gallery of Art (no. 57.23).

Opposite: Large dish. Tin-glazed earthenware with cobalt-painted decoration. Iraq; ninth century. Height: 1¾ in (4.5 cm). Diameter: 12 in (30.2 cm). Oxford, Ashmolean Museum (no. 1956.127, Barlow Gift).

This piece, which is moulded and entirely covered with golden luster, is one of the earliest examples of Islamic luster wares. The decoration, executed in low relief, consists of interlacing bands and palmettes centered around a four-petalled rosette. The combination of geometric motifs and palmettes is characteristic of early Islamic art and can also be found on contemporary architectural decoration and manuscript illumination. Both the shape and technique of the plate resemble gold repoussé work. Similar examples have been excavated in Samarra and Susa. The Freer piece is the largest and finest of its type and is said to have been discovered at the latter site.

This unusually large dish has a flat base and vertical rim, a shape not infrequently seen in this type of ware. It is, however, exceptional in its decoration. Normally the pottery of this class is decorated with formal or floral motifs or inscriptions only. This piece, however, represents a fish (a natural enough subject for a riverine area such as Mesopotamia) with two sprays of water weed issuing from its mouth. The narrow rim, however, permits no border pattern more ambitious than a row of dashes.

The writer Muhammad ibn al-Hussain Baihaki, writing in the middle of the eleventh century, stated that in the reign of Harun al-Rashid (786–809), Ali ibn-Isa, Governor of the easterly province of Khorasan, sent to the Caliph over two thousand pieces of "porcelain." Amongst these was a "mottled" ware, and it has been surmised that this was the lead-glazed pottery with splashed decoration, in mainly green and brown, made during the T'ang dynasty in China (618–906). This may have given the impetus for the production of comparable splashed wares in the Near East, from the ninth century at latest onwards. It is far from certain, however, that all the impulses went from East to West, for the making of lead-glazed earthenware was at home in the Mediterranean area, whereas there is no clear line of continuity in its manufacture in China from Han (206 B.C.–220 A.D.) to T'ang times.

The jar opposite was probably used for the storage of water or oil. The lid, now missing, was provided with a tongue, which was inserted inside the middle of the three handles, and on the opposite side with a pierced projection. The latter was secured to the pair of lugs, probably by a piece of wood or cord. The stonewares and porcelain of China were much sought after in the Near East from the eighth century onwards. The potters of the Islamic world never achieved the technique of true porcelain. In Mesopotamia, they tried to simulate its appearance by covering their vessels with an opaque white tin glaze. Sometimes, as here, they painted in cobalt on the white glaze and added splashes of green.

Dish. Tin-glazed earthenware painted in yellowish-brown luster. Iraq; ninth–tenth century.
Diameter: 12¼ in (30.6 cm). Height: 1½ in (3.5 cm). Copenhagen, C.L. David Collection
(no. 14-1962).

The dish illustrated here may perhaps be seen as a refinement of a design found on other ninth-century plates. Its rendering in yellow-luster pigment alone indicates a slightly later date. Here the half-palmette motifs have been composed into an angular symmetrical design within a "contour panel" reserved in a ground of dashes. Round the rim runs a repeated benedictory inscription of Kufic script similarly reserved on a ground of dashes: "blessing to the owner." The flat dish with broad rim echoes the form of dish used for decoration in cobalt blue, and since on some of the earliest luster-decorated pieces part of the design is in the high-fired blue, it seems probable that both types were made in the same workshops. The back of this dish repeats the motifs of "peacock's eyes" and circles enclosing filling patterns found on the earlier polychrome luster wares.

Deep plate with wide, horizontal rim. Buff earthenware, luster painted on opaque white glaze. From Estaxr; ninth–tenth century. Diameter: 13 in (32.5 cm). Height: 2 in (5 cm). Teheran, Iran Bastan Museum (no. 3050).

Much has been written on the question of the place of origin of luster painting. While this is not the proper place to take this question up, it should be said, however, that Estaxr must have been one of the main centers of luster painting in the early Islamic period. The decoration of this plate consists of a symmetrical arrangement of abstract motifs on both sides of a central axis. This may be a stylization of animal or vegetal motifs. The border of four rows of pearls resembling peacock's eyes is clearly reminiscent of the engraved and incised decoration of the famous unglazed Estaxr pottery of late Sassanian and early Islamic times.

Below: Bowl. Lead-glazed earthenware painted with coloured slips. East Iran (Nishapur); tenth century. Diameter: 14¼ in (35.5 cm). Height: 4¾ in (11.5 cm). From Nishapur. Teheran, Iran Bastan Museum (no. 8378).

Opposite: Dish. Lead-glazed earthenware painted with coloured slips. East Iran (perhaps Nishapur) or Transoxiana; tenth century. Diameter: 8¼ in (21 cm). Height: 1½ in (3.6 cm). Washington D.C., Freer Gallery of Art (no. 65.27).

Pottery painted in black or other coloured slips under a colourless lead glaze has been found over a wide expanse of Eastern Iran, Turkestan and Afghanistan, and is known to have been made in Nishapur and Afrasiyab (near Samarkand). It is not always easy to distinguish between the wares made in these centers, but the bowls of the type shown opposite, with a formalized bird in the center, seem to have been a Nishapur speciality. On one bowl found there two calligraphic renderings of the word "Allah" ("God") take the place of the two

birds shown on the piece illustrated here; in both, the artist has finished off his design in long tapering lines. The purplish-black pigment, the predominant colour in this whole class of pottery, is here supplemented by a touch of red.

The flat rim of this dish is ideally suited to the straightforward rendering of the Kufic inscription and here the text is simply and beautifully written, with diacritical marks, the scribe painter

using great skill in making the text fit exactly the diameter of the dish. The center has been decorated with a more than usually elaborate design of a scrolled fylfot, the scrolls each terminating in a trefoil and a half palmette, while the spaces are filled with a sketchy but beautiful strapwork rendered in brownish red scratched through to the underlying white slip. The inscription reads:"Generosity is one of the qualities of the people of Paradise."

A variety of Eastern Iranian slip-decorated pottery was made at various centers in Mazandaran. It has usually been associated with the town of Sari, near the south-eastern corner of the Caspian Sea. The designs, nearly always of birds, are outlined in purplish black, probably to stabilize the painting under the lead glaze. Characteristically, the black and red slips are supplemented by green and yellow, and the outlines of the simple designs are enlivened by white dots. The circular motifs, also found on other types of East Persian painted slip wares, are on this class usually embellished with pendant "strings." The internal patterning on the bird's body in black and white dots on the red ground, is also characteristic of much East Persian slip ware.

"Animate buff ware" was little known until familiarized by the excavations of the Metropolitan Museum of Art, New York, starting in 1935, at Nishapur in Khorasan, lying to the east of the southern end of the Caspian Sea. The pottery is characterized by a buff body showing a bone-coloured smooth surface on which the decoration has been painted in a pigment firing black, often with a purplish cast. The supplementary colours used are a mustard yellow rendered opaque with tin oxide, a thin transparent copper green, and occasionally a brick-red slip sparsely applied. Some of this pottery is decorated with conventional designs ("inanimate"), some with figures of human beings and animals ("animate"), all displaying a strong "horror vacui," the background filled in with small animals and birds, Kufic inscriptions (as here) and filling patterns such as rosettes, crosses, groups of dots, etc.

Bowl. Tin-glazed earthenware painted in luster. Egypt; first half of twelfth century. Diameter: 8¾ in (22.4 cm). Height: 3¾ in (9.8 cm). London, Victoria and Albert Museum (no. C. 49-1952).

One of the commonest potters' signatures found on Fatimid luster ware is that of Sa'ad, who signed the famous bowl illustrated here. It shows a Coptic priest holding in his hand what may be a censer or a mosque lamp of the traditional form. To his left is a motif resembling a cypress tree, and from this diverge knobby branches terminating in leaves, drawn in a manner characteristic of this period. The internal details of all these motifs were scratched out with a point before the luster decoration was fired. The painting of this piece is formalized with a static quality which is partly compensated for by the lively scrolling internal designs.

Bowl, painted in polychrome colours under clear lead glaze. Tunisia or Majorca; early eleventh century. Diameter: 13¼ in (33..5 cm). Height: 5¼ in (12.5 cm). From the Church of St. Peter, Grado, Italy. Pisa, Museo Nazionale di San Matteo (no.59).

The decoration of this polychrome vessel is somewhat unusual, presenting a large sailing ship and a boat with rowing men inside. The inspiration for this design should be sought in contemporary Fatimid painting, since similar drawings can be seen on several papyri and paper fragments which were discovered at Fustat, Fayyum and at other archaeological sites in Egypt. This decoration is remarkable, because it faithfully presents an Arab sailing ship. Similar vessels are still to be seen in the Gulf region of Saudi Arabia.

Below: Ewer. Lead-glazed earthenware with design carved in slip ("champlevé") under a green glaze. Iran (Garrus district); twelfth–thirteenth century. Height: 6¼ in (16 cm). Width: 3¼ in (8.3 cm). Cambridge, Fitzwilliam Museum (no. C. 161-1946).

Opposite: Bowl. Lead-glazed earthenware with design carved in slip ("champlevé") under a green glaze. Iran (Garrus district); twelfth–thirteenth century. Diameter: 10¼ in (26 cm). Height: 5 in (12.3 cm). Cambridge, Fitzwilliam Museum (no. C.155-1946).

Most of the Garrus "sgraffiato" wares are bowls, but occasionally a jar or a ewer, as here, is made in the same technique. This is often referred to as "champlevé," since the background is scratched away. This ewer has round the shoulder a border of Kufic writing, whilst two bands of cable pattern display again the predilection for knotted designs in this type of incised pottery. The wares of this class have in the past been mistakenly referred to as "gabri," a name for the fire-worshipping Zoroastrians of pre-Islamic times.

A variant from the brown–purple and white colour scheme in Garrus slip-decorated pottery is provided by the wares with green glaze. In this bowl a winged sphinx is represented against a background of leaf scrolls and a palmette. The wing of the sphinx terminates in a leafy scroll, and the rear flank is enlivened by an incised rosette, a reminiscence of Sassanian art, in which the joint of an animals' back leg is frequently emphasized in this way. A further Sassanian feature is provided by the pearled bands round neck and ankles. The sphinx's tail is neatly knotted, such knots being a convenient motif to render in this scratched technique. Round the outside of the rim runs a Kufic inscription in which similar effects appear.

Bowl. Alkaline-glazed earthenware painted black under turquoise glaze. Iran (Kashan?); early thirteenth century. Diameter: 8¾ in (22.3 cm). Height: 4 in (10 cm). Oxford, Ashmolean Museum (no. 1956–29, Barlow Gift).

Figure of a lion. Alkaline-glazed earthenware. Iran (Gurgan?); thirteenth century. Height: 7 in (17.7 cm). Length: 7¼ in (18.6 cm). From Gurgan. Cambridge, Fitzwilliam Museum (R. Ades Loan, no. 20-1948).

The black-on-white or black-on-turquoise colour scheme of the Persian "silhouette" wares has been reversed in the bowl opposite, the black pigment serving to delineate the decoration in reserve, and to pick out the internal details of the forms represented. It is painted with magnificent freedom in an overall design of animals and palmette-derived plant motifs. The central antelope is unenviably placed between two spotted predators (possibly cheetahs), while round the rim smaller creatures – a hare, a quail – browse inconspicuously amid the formalized vegetation. The blue line round the rim places this piece unobtrusively among the polychrome wares of this class.

A considerable number of figures are known in Persian pottery of the Seljuk period. These take the form of birds, animals and human beings. Occasionally the animal figures were intended to hold liquid while some have pouring spouts at the mouth and were presumably intended as aquamaniles; others may have served as flower holders. The diversity of these forms suggests that the figures are primarily of symbolic significance. On its flank is a streak of cobalt blue, such "deliberate imperfections" being a frequent occurrence in Islamic pottery.

Characteristic of the under-glaze painted Persian wares of the thirteenth century are those vessels which have a decorative pierced outer shell over the utilitarian inner form. In some ways the breaking up of the ground available to the painter may seem a negation of the aesthetic aim of this form of decoration, and it may perhaps be conceded that this type of painted pottery is more curious than beautiful. This ewer is in the form of a cock with a tail of recurved feathers which probably harks back to Sassanian metalwork prototypes. The existence of dated examples enables us to locate these pieces in the early years of the thirteenth century.

With regard to artistic composition, the piece opposite is a reminder of earlier traditions, but in pottery technique it is much finer in paste and firing. Two Persian quatrains are inscribed on the radial bands. Although it has not been possible to decipher them entirely, it is clear that they belong to the lyrico-mystical repertoire.

Opposite: Ewer. Alkaline-glazed earthenware with pierced decoration and black and blue painting under turquoise glaze. Iran (Kashan?); early thirteenth century. Height: 11½ in (29.1 cm). Width: 7 in (18.1 cm). Washington D.C., Freer Gallery of Art (no. 49.19).

Below: Bowl. Composite paste with decoration of black and blue over opaque white and under transparent glaze. From Kashan (?); thirteenth century A.D. Diameter: 9 in (22.8 cm). Height: 4 in (10 cm). Teheran, Iran Bastan Museum (no. 4761).

The chequered cypress trees alternating on the central register of the top bulb of this bottle with seated personages, and on two registers of the body with horsemen, were often used as funerary symbols in this period. The band of cartouches in the middle register may have been copied from metalwork where such cartouches often contain zodiacal signs. Here, however, they are only ten in number and the design is of a stereotyped, human-headed animal. Typical poems are inscribed in three registers and in the classical Nasx script.

Three-dimensional figures of birds, lions, deer and other creatures are not uncommon in Persian pottery of the Seljuk era, but human figures are rarer. Whole series of them, however, have been discovered at a place called Wasit, in Egypt, and it is possible that a figure like the one illustrated may have taken its place in an ensemble representing a courtly scene, in a way familiar in Chinese pottery of the T'ang dynasty. Many of the animal figures have orifices, presumably for receiving liquids, but not all have spouts for pouring, and their exact function is obscure. The figure here wears a Persian turban, and the lustered decoration on a blue glaze fits it into the category of "Rayy" wares. It was discovered at Gurgan, at the south-eastern corner of the Caspian Sea.

Bowl. Decoration of green, blue, brown, black, white and gilding over transparent turquoise glaze. From Rayy; early thirteenth century. Diameter of mouth: 8 in (20.3 cm). Height: 3½ in (9.2 cm). Teheran, Iran Bastan Museum (no. 3200).

*H*aft-rangi ("seven-colour") ware represents the highest level of achievement of Iranian pottery in a most complex technique. The secret was shared by the master ceramists of Rayy, Kashan, Sava and Gurgan. After the pottery was thrown and baked, the work of painting in various pigments was undertaken. The apogee of this school was between 1170 and 1200, but of course it continued well after the Mongol invasion and up to 1300. The name *mina'i* ("enamel") has been given to this category of over-glaze painted ceramics in auction rooms, and from there it has been adopted even in scientific publications. The present piece portrays a cavalier engaged in falconry, one of the most popular ancient Persian sports.

Tankard. Alkaline-glazed earthenware painted in enamel colours and gilt (mina'i ware). Iran (Kashan?); thirteenth century. Height: 5¾ in (14.7 cm). Width: 5¼ in (12.5 cm). London, Victoria and Albert Museum (no. C. 164-1928).

The finest figural designs of *mina'i* pottery are normally found on the insides of bowls and dishes which may be presumed to have had currency mainly in courtly or upper middle-class circles. Utilitarian vessels, however, seem also to have been made in the ware – notably long-necked bottles, beakers, spouted and handled posset pots, and, as here, cylindrical-necked tankards. These were also made in other types of pottery. The overall diaper design on the body of this tankard is not particularly well conceived or executed and the repeat pattern on the neck is positively naive. The colours, however, are bright and well preserved, and the shape is crisp and admirably balanced. Inside the rim runs a band of ornament suggesting a Kufic inscription.

Gilding became very popular during the second half of the thirteenth century, and it was applied to under-glaze, over-glaze or luster-painted pieces, both vessels and tiles for architectural revetment. During the Ilkhanid period entire walls of palaces were decorated with gilded tiles and faïence panels, and early in the fourteenth century the technique was at its most flamboyant. In Soltaniyych and Taxt-e Soleymān extremely elaborate and well preserved examples of this technique have been discovered *in situ* in the course of archaeological excavations in recent years. On the example opposite the main motif of the design is a half palmette in several sizes. Kashan masters also seem to have been in the forefront in gilding experience.

Some relief tiles with dark blue glaze have distinct affinity with the Kashan lustered relief tiles of the thirteenth century, and increase the likelihood that the *lajvardina* tiles were made in the same center. This tile of a rare shape, is painted in white and red enamels and further embellished with leaf gold. Its design of a dragon amid cloud scrolls illustrates yet again the Chinese influence which became so widely diffused and potent in the Mongol period.

Below: Bowl. Lajvardina *ware. Buff earthenware with decoration of red, white and leaf gilding over opaque cobalt-blue glaze. From Sultanabad; fourteenth century. Diameter of mouth: 8 in (19.7 cm). Height: 3½ in (8.7 cm). Teheran, Iran Bastan Museum (no. 3333).*

Opposite: Jar. Alkaline-glazed earthenware painted in under-glaze colours. Syria (Raqqa?); late twelfth–early thirteenth century. Height: 10 in (24.8 cm). New York, Metropolitan Museum of Art (no. 23.162.1).

This may be considered a late *lajvardina* piece. Although Sultanabad was a very important ceramic center during the fourteenth century, this piece is not typical of its workshops. The presence of these rich colours before the establishment of the typical grey Sultanabad ware may indicate the early examples still produced within the aesthetic canons of such centers as Rayy and Sava, from where they were imported. *Lajvardina* ware was produced in most of the ceramic centers of the fourteenth century.

The North Syrian/Mesopotamian potteries at Raqqa and Rusafa produced a distinctive type of painted ware which is characteristic of their area, although it was probably also made in Egypt, where many examples are found. This pottery is painted under the glaze in a distinctive palette of brownish red, black and blue which has an austere charm of its own, its qualities being unfortunately often obscured by the opalescent decay which has attacked the overlying glaze. The painting is often of a very high order, with a distinctive whiplash touch. Ceramic production probably ceased when Raqqa was sacked by the Mongols in 1259. The shape of the jar shown opposite is characteristic of the Syrian wares.

Bowl. Alkaline-glazed earthenware painted black under a colourless glaze picked out in blue and turquoise. Iran ("Sultanabad type"); first half of fourteenth century. Diameter: 8½ in (21.4 cm). Height: 4 in (9.7 cm). The Keir Collection, England (no. 203).

Tile panel. Alkaline-glazed earthenware with carved decoration and inscriptions picked out in opaque glazes. Transoxiana (Samarkand district); about 1360. Height: 17½ in (43.5 cm). London, Victoria and Albert Museum (no. 2031A-1899).

There is no evidence that pottery was made in Sultanabad, but many of the known pieces were first discovered in this general area. Sultaniye, not far away and an important city, is known to have made pottery, but only a rather coarse ware painted in black under a turquoise glaze. The bowl opposite shows characteristic painting in black outlines, with patches of turquoise and blue glaze colouring mainly filling in the ground and throwing into emphatic contrast the small areas left white. The hare and fleshy foliage filling the central medallion are common enough motifs of decoration in this class of ware, but the lobed quatrefoil panel, although not without parallels, makes a welcome change from the more stereotyped friezes and wedge-shaped divisions of the surface.

This tile panel comes from the tomb near Bukhara of Buyan Kuli Khan, who died about 1358. Its main feature is a Koranic inscription, in the *thuluth* form of Arabic calligraphy, placed against a background of sharply cut scrolls from which branch leaves and half palmettes. The letters and other decorative details are picked out in opaque white, purple or blue glazes on the turquoise ground colour. The ground is deeply carved away, the angle of the cutting being steeper on the underside, so that, seen from below, the design should stand out sharply against the shadow. Even architectural elements in the structure of the tomb, such as vertical columns, were covered with ornament in the same style.

Some of the earliest Near Eastern pottery showing the influence of Chinese porcelain painted in under-glaze blue has been discovered in Syria, notably at Hama, which, like Damascus, was laid waste by Timur in 1401. Here at least two copies of Chinese fourteenth-century porcelain were found. The albarello shown here is painted with scrollwork borders which are clearly derived from similar motifs on Chinese porcelain. Its coat of arms, which is partly painted in black and therefore forms a link with the black- and blue-painted origin, is not of Islamic origin, and almost certainly represents the device of Florence. In 1456 Piero di Cosimo de' Medici owned "3 alberegli domaschini" ("three Damascus albarelli"), and it is tempting to think that the vessel illustrated may have been one of this set.

Parallel with the luster-painted wares made in Damascus went a type of pottery with painting in black and blue pigments under a colourless, often green-tinged, glaze with a tendency to "craze." The shape of the jar opposite proclaims its affinity with the preceding item. Jars of this type were frequently exported to the West, probably in part for the sake of their contents. Thus the French Royal Accounts record a payment in 1416 "to Regnault Morel for a Damascus pot full of green ginger." On this jar a magnificently bold inscription in *thuluth* lettering with exaggerated ascenders contrasts markedly with the scrappy painting of the neck decoration.

Below: Tile panel. Alkaline-glazed earthenware painted in blue, black and green under a colourless glaze. Egypt or Syria; second half of fifteenth century. 19¾ in × 20¾ in (49.5 × 52 cm). London, Victoria and Albert Museum (no. 295-1900).

Opposite: Drug jar ("albarello"). Tin-glazed earthenware painted in blue and luster. Spain (Manises); first half of fifteenth century. Height: 14½ in (36.4 cm). Diameter of body: 5¾ in (14.6 cm). London, Victoria and Albert Museum (no. C 123-1931).

The tiles forming the panel opposite are part of a large series claiming to have come from the Umayyad mosque in Damascus. It has recently been shown, however, that these tiles may be of Egyptian origin. Their decoration, which is homogeneous in style although displaying many variants, is clearly influenced by Chinese porcelain of the fourteenth to fifteenth century, although there are no purely Chinese patterns among them. Thus, in the bottom row on the right-hand side, there is a form palpably derived from Islamic metalwork but shown on a leaf-scroll ground of distinctly Chinese character. The watery-green pigment used for the borders of these tiles adds a wholly un-Chinese touch to the ensemble.

Apart from Malaga, a number of centers in the south-east of Spain produced luster-painted pottery, notably Murcia, Almeria and possibly Granada itself. About the middle of the fourteenth century, however, Moorish potters from the Kingdom of Granada began to migrate in increasing numbers northwards to Christian Valencia, perhaps in part spurred by declining prosperity in the Nasrid dominions, in part by inducements offered by the de Buyl family, Lords of Manises, situated near the city of Valencia. There had long been a pottery industry in the province of Valencia, at Paterna, situated to the north-east of Manises. Here the potters had made a slipped ware painted in purple and green, and latterly in cobalt blue, a colour already used by the Andalusian potters in combination with their luster pigments. This combined colour scheme was taken up at Manises, and blue- and luster-painted wares were made there throughout the fifteenth century. The albarello illustrated differs in shape from that current at Malaga and is decorated in horizontal registers of purely Islamic designs, including inscriptions reserved in white on a luster ground, and mock "knotted Kufic" in blue on a ground of luster scrolls. The blue decoration had to be painted on or under the raw glaze, making allowance for the luster decoration which was to follow it on the fired glaze.

Below: Bowl. Alkaline-glazed earthenware painted in black and incised under a turquoise glaze. North Iran (Kubachi type); c. 1470–1490. Diameter: 12½ in (31.4 cm). New York, Metropolitan Museum of Art (no. 17.120.70).

Opposite: Large flat plate. Kubachi type, thin, white earthenware, decoration of blue, red, beige and green under transparent glaze. From Sava; seventeenth century. Diameter: 15 in (37.7 cm). Height: 2 in (5 cm). Teheran, Iran Bastan Museum (no. 3415).

In the fifteenth century there was a revival in more than one Near Eastern center of pottery painted in black under a turquoise glaze. Now, however, considerable play was made with areas of solid black through which tight scrollwork designs were incised with a joint to the underlying white body. The handsome bowl illustrated here shows this characteristic feature combined with sprays of leaves painted in lobed panels. The outside, however, is decorated with lotus panels clearly derived from Chinese porcelain. A closely similar dish is known bearing the date 1468, and others bear dates between 1473 and 1495. They belong to a group of wares with a soft, grainy white body and a thin glaze prone to crackling which then becomes stained.

This category of sixteenth- to seventeenth-century Persian pottery is known as Kubachi ware because important collections of it were first discovered in the village of that name in the mountains of Daghestan. The Tabriz region has been suggested as the place this ceramic was produced, and there are workshops and kilns active even today in Zonuz not far from Marand whose products are reminiscent of the Kubachi type. In most cases figures of the Safavid school of Reza Abbasi, such as those in Cehel Sotun wall paintings, are depicted on the ceramics of this category, and the present example with a blossoming tree in the foreground of a garden scene is rather unique.

Below: Under-glaze painted plate. Iran; Safavid period, late seventeenth–early eighteenth century. Diameter: 18 in (45.3 cm). Height: 3¼ in (8.2 cm). Washington D.C., Freer Gallery of Art (no. 70.23).

Opposite: Bottle. Alkaline-glazed earthenware painted in under-glaze blue and in white and ocher slips. Iran (Kirman?); seventeenth century. Height: 13¼ in (33 cm). New York, Metropolitan Museum of Art (no. 14.64.2).

The central medallion of the blue-and-white plate opposite represents a female figure in landscape. She holds an empty wine bottle by the neck in one hand and beckons with the other while tilting her head. The cavetto has an incised frieze consisting of a series of spade-shaped leaves filled with blossoms. The exterior reveals eight lotus panels, decorated with floral sprays. The Freer plate belongs to a group of blue-and-white wares which imitates the late Ming style. These wares are predominantly decorated with stylized landscape motifs executed in a sketchy manner and often include an incised and moulded cavetto.

The blue-and-white design of this slender bottle is derived from Chinese export porcelain of the Chia Ching period (1522–1566), but the design has been audaciously interrupted by the intrusion of lobed panels enclosing purely Islamic arabesque patterns rendered in a yellow ocher pigment, a colour occasionally found in the Kirman polychrome range, and a white-on-white border. Like many of the Kirman wares, this bottle is marked under the base with a blue "tassel mark," a series of strokes with a tail below, intended to imitate a Chinese character. The shape seems more Chinese than Persian, throwing into even greater prominence the curious hybrid character of this pottery.

The tile opposite is an example of the fully mature style of Iznik pottery in which the pale turquoise pigment gave place to a strong copper green. The combination of this colour with "Armenian bole," thickly applied to give a stronger tone, produced a palette of unrivalled power and brilliance.

The early sixteenth century at Iznik produced few tiles, and most of these were narrow rectangles designed to form borders to larger areas of hexagonal tiles with monochrome glazes. These tiles, from tombs at Bursa, are painted in blue only in a style akin to that of the "Abraham of Kutahya" group of vessels, a style which continued until about 1525.

Contemporaneously with the introduction of additional colours – first turquoise green and then sage green – the manufacture of tilework was stepped up, the tiles being now mostly hexagonal with radiating and star-shaped designs composed of arabesques and modifications of the lotus design.

Under-glaze painted plate. Turkey; Ottoman period, mid sixteenth century. Diameter: 12½ in (31.7 cm). Height: 2½ in (6.4 cm). Washington D.C., Freer Gallery of Art (no. 69.25).

This plate exemplifies the polychrome Turkish wares produced in Iznik. The clear white body forms the background for the bright blue, green, and red motifs, the latter of which appear in low relief due to the thickness of the pigment. The symmetrical composition consists of a large lotus blossom in the center, flanked by elegantly twisting leaves, roses, rosebuds, and hyacinths. The floral motifs grow from a source placed at the bottom of the plate. The foliate rim reveals a stylized wave pattern painted as a series of spirals and strokes, inspired by the theme utilized in Chinese porcelains.

Dish. Alkaline-glazed earthenware painted in polychrome. Turkey (Iznik); about 1560–1580. Diameter: 11 in (28 cm). Height: 1½ in (4.2 cm). Cambridge, Fitzwilliam Museum (no. C.15-1950).

About the middle of the sixteenth century a further colour was added to the Iznik palette – a strong sealing-wax red which was in reality an under-glaze slip, known as "Armenian bole" – first used in hesitant touches on the tilework commissioned by the Sultan Suleiman the Magnificent (reigned 1520–1566) for the decoration of the mosque in Istanbul which bears his name. The dish illustrated here shows an unusually sensitive and sparing use of painting on the beautiful white ground. Thin sprays of tulip, possibly hyacinth and a wheel-like flower, perhaps intended for a carnation, cover the dish in an open formation of symmetrical pairs which nevertheless give no impression of monotony. The three central stems are "clipped" together by a characteristic motif derived from a Chinese cloud scroll.

European Majolica

In the evolution of European majolica, the earliest sources drawn on must have been items of luster ware of Muslim Spain, dating back to as early as the end of the tenth century. The potters who imported this technique into the Iberian peninsula would have arrived from North Africa. The Andalusian city of Malaga became, during the golden age of Nasrid rule, one of the main centers of production: many thirteenth-century texts refer to items made there, and during the fifteenth century the famous Arab traveller Ibn Battuta was among those who mentioned its "gilded vases." However, throughout the country the *Reconquista* was then well under way, the Nasrid dynasty was in decline and large numbers of Arab potters, lured away from the kingdom of Granada to other, more inviting locations, moved to the Christian area of Valencia: Manises, a particularly favoured destination, assumed a very important position thanks to the patronage of the de Buyl family, Lords of Manises, with the result that from the fifteenth century onwards the finest examples of *obra dorada* came to be produced there.

Even before these developments, Paterna, another city in the province of Valencia, was already playing an important role in the production of what are known as "Hispano-Moresque" wares. The potters of Paterna produced a type of glazed earthenware painted in violet and green, and later cobalt blue, a colour that had already been used by Andalusian potters in association with metal lusters, a combination of colours later also adopted at Manises. As for decoration, the dominant elements at Paterna were originally geometric motifs, with coiling and calligraphic elements of clearly Islamic inspiration, but later, from the end of the fourteenth century, a new, more European iconography appeared, as is shown by one

Two-handled jar, from the Orsini-Colonna pharmacy group. Majolica, high-temperature polychrome. Faenza; c. 1520. Height: 18 in (45.3 cm). Width: 12 in (28 cm). London, British Museum (no. 52.11-29.2). The large number of containers of the Orsini-Colonna pharmacy that have survived were all apparently made at Faenza.

Marks of the Italian Renaissance

Mark of the painter and potter Virgilio Calamelli, called "Virgiliotto," owner of one of the most important workshops in Faenza during the mid sixteenth century.

dish depicting an elegant woman with two large fish (page 163). When compared to Arab models, the decoration to an extent evolved along similar thematic and stylistic lines, with adaptations to suit the preferences of a different ethos; what was preserved, however, was the fund of knowledge relating to techniques and methods, and during this transitional phase from Islamic to European ceramics this was of pivotal importance for the Spanish potters active in centers such as Malaga, Granada, Murcia, Almeria, Paterna and Manises.

Apart from luster ware, a tradition that lasted in Spain (albeit with a marked decline in quality) until the eighteenth century, there was another technique, that of *cuerda seca*, which originated in the East and was used mainly for decorative tiles. The potter traced his design on the surface to be decorated, using a mixture of sulphur and manganese to which grease was added (which volatilized during firing), then the outlined spaces were filled with coloured glazes: blue, green, honey, white and brown. This technique was also used to decorate large numbers of bowls, ewers and pitchers (page 162).

Hispano-Moresque luster ware, which was produced mainly in Valencia, generally took the form of decorative items and during the Late Middle Ages it was the first decoration of this kind to find a place in the aristocratic houses of Europe. Proof of this is provided by the large numbers of Valencia luster plates bearing European coats of arms at the center. There is also a reminder of the flourishing trade in ceramics, which were exported from Spain to Italy, in the word "majolica" itself. Even though it was later applied to all glazed earthenware, majolica was initially used for a long time to describe Spanish luster wares, with particular reference, it would seem, to the ones arriving in Italy from Valencia on board Majorcan ships. Another theory, according to which the word majolica is connected with Malaga rather than Majorca, still retains the link with Moorish Spain.

Majolica refers to a type of porous earthenware, covered in a tin-based glaze, on which ornamental patterns are painted. The item is dipped in order to obtain a white covering that completely covers the underlying clay; after a first drying comes the decoration and the firing, at a temperature of between 1560–1740°F (850–950°C) in kilns where the pieces are placed inside casings in order to protect them from direct contact with the flame. The rise of majolica should be seen within the context of a contemporary need for pottery with a white ground on which a clearly defined decoration could be painted. For a certain period of time the so-called *blanchetto* technique was used, which involved dipping the wares in a white clay slip, but this could not in itself provide an impervious covering, with the result that a further covering was needed. Tin enamel represented a better solution to the problem because it provided a covering that was both white and impervious.

It is hardly surprising that the first tin-glazed items produced in Italy should, at least in some respects, show a clear link with certain types of Spanish wares: for example, in the green and brown decoration on a white ground, reminiscent of that found typically on pottery made at Paterna. These Italian wares were made over a surprisingly wide area, even though it used to be the custom to group them all under the heading "Orvieto pottery" because that Umbrian town was the first place where these wares were discovered in any quantity. The shapes of Orvieto pottery display a certain originality,

Mark of the Casa Pirota, an important majolica factory active at Faenza during the first half of the sixteenth century and traditionally believed to have invented the berettino *decoration.*

Monogram used by Niccolò Pellipario to sign his wares. A sixteenth-century craftsman who worked at Casteldurante, he is regarded as the master of the Italian istoriato *style.*

although its early decorative repertoire differed little from the Spanish (page 164). The tin glaze on these early pieces covered only the decorated section, the remainder bearing the more common lead glaze. This early type occurred in Tuscany, at Florence and Siena, in Emilia and the Veneto.

From the fifteenth century onwards, Tuscany appears to have played an important role in determining the nature of majolica. In this context one thinks not so much of those famous works by Luca della Robbia and his workshop (page 165) which, precisely because of their highly individual treatment, are virtually in a class of their own and belong basically within the realm of Renaissance plastic art, but to a series of earlier works which relate specifically to the development of the art of ceramics.

Faenza, the city in Romagna destined to take a leading role in the history of Italian majolica, was, even at the beginning, quick to adopt the proposals formulated in the areas around Florence. The development of the ceramic industry at Faenza derived particular stimulus from the patronage and protection of the Manfredi family, who held power in the city from the opening decades of the fourteenth century and throughout the fifteenth. For example, when Florence saw the emergence of the decoration known as "relief blue" (*a zaffera in rilievo*), in which oak leaves stand out against a white ground with, in the middle, lions rampant, greyhounds, birds and fleurs-de-lys, all painted using a thick blue pigment ("zaffera"[zaffer] is derived from the Arabic word *'al safra*, meaning cobalt oxide), this original motif was also adopted simultaneously at Faenza. When, during the second half of the fifteenth century, the Florentines used a range of colours that included cobalt blue, a manganese brown verging sometimes on the violet, a copper green obtained from calcined copper oxide, an antimony yellow or a ferrous orangey yellow, the same was to be found at Faenza during this period. And yet Italian majolica, rather than relying on the richness of its colour to achieve the sort of magnificent effects found in the fifteenth-century floor of the Chapel of St. Sebastian in the Bolognese Church of San Petronio, a masterpiece of Faenza work (page 166), preferred to rely on a skilful and highly imaginative decoration that included, albeit with a new sense of balance, Classically derived designs, Orientally inspired motifs, Late Gothic patterns and other elements absorbed from contemporary iconography.

Another prominent feature of the ceramic decorative repertoire was the frequent inclusion of female figures and profile busts of men, but it cannot be said that in the early stages figures provided the main decorative impetus. In fact, the reverse is true, and the figurative elements normally formed part of a broader decorative rhythm, as is illustrated by the tiles in San Petronio. For a long time the luxuriant ornamental repertoire of Faenza displayed mainly Gothic foliage, acanthus leaves, pearls, scales, ovolos, Persian palmettes and rosettes, and peacock-feather patterns: other common motifs included pineapples, spirals and intertwined ribbons (page 167).

Only at the beginning of the sixteenth century, at a time when the Florentine area saw the rise of an important ceramic industry centered on a Medici villa at Cafaggiolo, did the *istoriato* style, in which the human figure was accorded a prominent role, reach its zenith at Faenza. In fact, Faenza's output had increased markedly during the final decades of the preceding century as a result of its search for new markets, and the style that had consolidated this

One of the marks of the Della Robbia family, a famous family of ceramic sculptors active in Florence during the fifteenth and sixteenth centuries. The workshop of Luca della Robbia, the founder of the dynasty, was later run by his nephew Andrea and by the latter's sons.

Mark of the famous ceramic center of Deruta, near Perugia. It started production during the fourteenth century, but its greatest period was from the end of the fifteenth to the end of the sixteenth century.

expansion was the *istoriato* style. The subjects portrayed were often taken from contemporary engravings, sometimes with considerable license and sometimes with great accuracy, as when pouncing was used, which involved using pierced paper designs placed over the piece to be decorated and then passing powdered charcoal through the perforations in order to create the outline of the image. But this does not mean to say that the products were in any way repetitive: a great deal of skill was still required of ceramic decorators, and their carefully structured and beautifully finished results can still be seen today (page 168). Further confirmation of this practice is provided by a new type of product, with no strictly functional use, namely painted tiles, which were directly influenced by engravings (page 169).

One particular technique used by the Faenza potters was *berettino* decoration. Generally attributed to the city's principal workshop, that of the Pirotti family, it consisted of applying the blue colours over a ground of grey blue or dark blue enamel. Another technique widely used in Faenza was *bianco sopra bianco*, a term that describes decoration thickly applied in an intense, opaque white over a whitish or greyish ground. Equally characteristic of sixteenth-century Faenza majolica is the presence of that typically Renaissance repertoire of swags, helmets, shields, cornucopias, putti, real and imaginary animals, masks and sphinxes, known as "grotesques." Elements such as weapons, busts and grotesques were the most frequent subjects of *berettino* decoration. Another means of exploiting the blue ground consisted of painting vine tendrils and grotesques in a thick, opaque white on a dark blue ground: this technique, known as *bianco sopra azzurro*, was frequently used for decorating the broad rims of those

pale ground plates known as *tondini* (page 170). *Berettino* decoration was not necessarily painted in white and could also be polychrome. Vessels such as the famous containers of the Orsini-Colonna pharmacy group provide further splendid examples of Faenza work: these include bottles, jars and albarellos, within whose precise decorative layout a privileged position is always accorded to a framed figure-subject, which is further emphasized by the rich decoration surrounding it (page 150).

A similar quality can be found in the sumptuous products of the Cafaggiolo factory. Its Medici patronage and its extensive contacts with patrician families explain why a considerable number of its wares bear an escutcheon (page 171) in a prominent position. In other examples the arabesques, grotesques or garlands surrounding the central element of the decoration set off figured scenes in the *istoriato* style.

Between the fifteenth and sixteenth century there was a widespread dispersal of Faenza majolica artists to other regions of Italy. One of the cities in which they were welcomed was certainly Siena, whose ceramics are characterized by a wealth of elaborate decoration (page 172) and by a palette whose most striking components are very intense orangey yellows and, for the background, sometimes particularly dark shades of blue, as well as the surprising appearance of a beautiful black, a colour normally used very rarely in majolica. Siena also appears to have been one of the first cities to introduce the blue decoration on a white ground known as the *porcellana* style, which was of Eastern inspiration (page 173). Another characteristic of Sienese majolica is the way in which the figures play second fiddle to a predominantly decorative taste, a notable aspect of which was the revival of the Faenza *candelieri*

Monogram of Orazio Fontana of the Fontana majolica factory at Urbino, founded at the beginning of the sixteenth century and active until the end of the seventeenth, which produced the famous Urbino istoriato *wares and later so-called* bianchi di Faenza.

Gubbio, whose workshops produced ceramics from the fourteenth century, became famous at the beginning of the sixteenth century for the use of the luster technique. Its wares are generally marked with the name or initials of the craftsman, as on this example.

layout, in which the grotesques are symmetrically arranged.

Deruta was another of the earliest centers of majolica production and, after a period during which its wares can be easily confused with those of Faenza, it became renowned for the lavishness and refinement, in both modelling and decoration, of its products. The great *piatti da pompa* or show dishes from the beginning of the sixteenth century are indicative of this trend (page 174), which also saw a resumption of the luster technique. Overall, Deruta wares are characterized by a decorativism that also absorbed figures into its motifs and which aimed to create an effect of great richness. Rather like Siena, Deruta largely ignored the *istoriato* style. At Urbino, during the same period, large numbers of very important majolica wares began to be produced by various named masters. Plaques, plates, ewers and albarellos reveal the widespread use, as sources of inspiration, of both literary and religious texts and also frescoes and paintings; the former were illustrated, while the latter were copied from the large numbers of engravings available at the time. Amongst the most outstanding figures working at Urbino were Niccolò Pellipario, who produced exceptional examples of *istoriato* wares, and Francesco Xanto Avelli, who signed a large number of very colourful pieces bearing solidly structured scenes (page 175).

Whereas in around the mid sixteenth century Faenza reacted against a certain misuse of colour by introducing the *compendiario* style, which greatly reduced the palette used in *istoriato* subjects, there was a different development at Urbino, where a new style of grotesque decoration emerged, inspired by the frescoes in the Vatican Loggias, painted after designs by Raphael and his pupils. This new style (page 176), known as "Raphaelesque," shows how majolica had expanded its horizons by dipping into the repertoire of Renaissance painting. Its characteristic elements are swags, volutes, mermaids, monsters and masks, all portrayed with a great sense of fantasy in a rich polychrome palette. Faenza took the opposite course, since attempts to emphasize the majolica and its luminous whiteness, to an extent implicit in the *compendiario* style, resulted in artists producing very sparsely decorated pieces, a trend that gave rise to the city's famous white-ground wares (page 177), in which the ornamentation was toned down and shape came into its own as the primary consideration.

Little study has been given to Venetian majolica, even though it is of great interest, partly for the way in which its variety betrays a multiplicity of contacts with other centers, as is the case, for example, with its *porcellana* decoration. One of its most noteworthy and interesting strands is perhaps represented by the beautiful monochrome wares with a *smaltino* ground (page 178). The piece illustrated has its rim decorated with trophies, a motif depicting arms and shields alternating with musical instruments that recurs on the majolica wares of several cities, not just Venice.

Italian majolica was also highly prized in other countries. The most popular examples were the famous white-ground wares (*bianchi*) of Faenza, as a result of which the city's name became used as a generic term for majolica in a number of European countries (*faïence, fayence*). There were families of potters from Florence, Faenza, Venice and Genoa working at Lyons, while at Nevers there were craftsmen from Albissola, and in around 1528 Girolamo della Robbia was invited to the court of François I.

One of the marks of the potters Piero and Stefano Fattori of Montelupo, who in around the mid fifteenth century were summoned by the Medici to found a majolica factory at Cafaggiolo near Florence.

A mark identifying some of the wares made in the workshops of Montelupo, a small town between Florence and Pisa, whose ceramic output, known since the fourteenth century, increased greatly during the sixteenth century.

The work of Masséot Abaquesne, who created the first examples of French faïence at Rouen, should not, however, be regarded as merely a re-working of Italian models: it has an originality that can be easily seen, for example, in the surviving faïence floor and wall tiles made for the château of the Constable de Montmorency at Ecouen (page 179).

The pharmacy jars produced at Antwerp, in the southern Low Countries, may be attributed to a factory established in around 1512 by an Italian ceramist from Casteldurante, a town that had contained a number of important workshops since the end of the fourteenth century thanks to the availability of an excellent local clay, in which very high-quality majolica wares were produced. There were other Italians working in the northern Low Countries and the output of countless workshops, from Haarlem to Amsterdam and from Rotterdam to Delft, for a long time showed signs of the influence of Faenza wares. It was an extremely profitable link, judging by such outstanding pieces as the famous stemmed cup in the Boymans Museum at Rotterdam, dated 1581, with its polychrome floral decoration on a white ground (page 180). At the beginning of the seventeenth century, under the influence of Urbino, grotesque decorative elements were adopted, whilst the influence of Faenza and Venice led to the appearance of blue-ground wares with polychrome birds, hares and other animals (page 181). The new factories also produced tiles which display echoes of Spanish influence (page 182); the name of Delft has become particularly strongly associated with this sector.

Germany was a law unto itself because, although it is true that faïence had first made its appearance during the course of the sixteenth century in towns such as Nuremberg, where there was an ancient tradition of manufacturing tiles for stoves, the commonest type of ceramic was not earthenware. The dominant type was, in fact, grès or "stoneware," which is very different from majolica, as can be seen in its hard, coloured, non-transparent, dense and impervious body, obtained by firing a special clay paste at temperatures of 2200–2400°F (1200–1300°C). It has often been noted that stoneware, which had been produced by the Chinese since the fourth century, appears more commonly in Northern Europe, and this fact has been explained by observing that the supplies of wood needed to stoke kilns capable of producing such extremely high temperatures were much more plentiful there than in the South. But it should also be said that in several regions of Germany, for example the Rhineland, potters had access to a clay suitable for producing very high-quality white stoneware. Because stoneware cannot be covered in a lead glaze due to the high firing temperatures, salt was used to obtain a vitreous coating: in the kiln the sodium combined with the silica and aluminium oxide in the clay. If the clay was refined it became possible to create very delicate relief figures on the surface of the piece, the favourite subjects being biblical and mythological characters. At Raeren, before the end of the sixteenth century, cobalt blue was also used in the decoration (page 183).

Rather than being just a stale continuation of the Renaissance tradition, the best examples of seventeenth-century Italian majolica experimented with a variety of new solutions, adopting elements that were less closely linked to the old decorative repertoire, generally using a more sober palette and creating shapes that on occasion possess a great feeling of movement and freedom. At Montelupo, for example, a center that had played an important role in early

Styles and decoration of majolica

Two-handled vase. Majolica with high-fired decoration in blue and manganese purple. Tuscany; late fifteenth century. Florence, Museo Nazionale del Bargello.

Tuscan majolica, there emerged, alongside the more elegant wares, another type that could be described as "popular" (even though it was, of course, destined for a wealthy clientele), which had figures depicted with a revolutionary sense of immediacy, with no apparent concern for formal considerations. It was the regions of northern Italy, however, which were most prominent in this process of renewal, most notably Liguria, the Veneto and Lombardy, a feature that applies equally to the eighteenth century. At the beginning of the seventeenth century, Genoa, Savona and Albissola favoured a pale ground, with lively decoration and rather full-bodied shapes (page 185) for their monochrome majolica, as well as revealing vague traces of Persian and Chinese influence.

In the Veneto, the factories of Bassano and nearby Angarano are known mainly for *latesini*, their peculiar wares characterized by a sky-blue ground, and by the elegant refinement of the decoration (page 184), whose composition reveals traces of a great painterly tradition. By contrast, the majolica produced at Lodi, which was of a very high technical standard, as seen in certain wares from the Ferretti factory (page 186), favoured Dutch, French and Chinese models. During the mid eighteenth century, the factory at Le Nove di Bassano almost always looked for inspiration to French porcelain of the day, as well as to imported Oriental wares. Its Chinese-inspired decoration should not, however, be regarded as pure imitation, but rather as a vague echo of Oriental motifs. Dragons, fantastic birds, small Chinese figures wearing exotic clothes, landscapes with pagodas and dwarf trees are all recurrent subjects. It reflected the fashion for chinoiserie. The shapes of the pieces also sometimes display remark-able originality (page 187, above).

Still in the eighteenth century, the Clerici factory in Milan, whose production lasted for more than 40 years, made use of decorative motifs from a variety of different sources, both European and Oriental. From Sèvres, for example, it took certain typical Chinese blue grounds, with spaces left white for brushwork decoration. Sometimes a character from the Italian Commedia dell'Arte, such as Harlequin, will appear, framed by trees (page 187, below). In the decoration of high-quality wares, as illustrated by one Venetian piece, eighteenth-century Italian majolica confirmed its keen interest in exotic settings and decorative motifs (page 188).

The seventeenth and eighteenth centuries saw the growth of a highly important faïence industry in various French towns. Nevers, which had already welcomed Italian potters and enamellers from Albissola during the sixteenth century, was initially in the forefront, both as regards tradition and invention. There was, for example, an extension of the Italian *compendiario* style in the form of *faïence blanche*, with large areas in which the underlying glaze was left exposed, and there was a whole range of wares that revived, albeit with a different iconography and a more markedly decorative taste, the layout of the *istoriato* style. The factories at Nevers became particularly famous for their beautiful blue-ground pottery, which in many respects surpassed the earlier wares made at Faenza and Venice and which, when it appeared in around 1630, with its very fine decorative motifs betraying a certain Oriental flavour, found a ready market. On the rarest examples the underlying colour is yellow, with blue being used in conjunction with white for the decoration (page 189). The entrepreneurial spirit of the *Compagnie*

Albarello. Majolica with high-fired decoration of grotesques. Siena; c. 1515. Sèvres, Musée National de Céramique.

Oval tray. Majolica with high-fired Raphaelesque decoration depicting, at the center, Joseph interpreting the Pharaoh's dreams. Urbino, workshop of Orazio Fontana; 1565–1571. The piece forms part of the service belonging to Guidobaldo, Duke of Urbino. Florence, Museo Nazionale del Bargello.

des Indes flooded Europe with Far Eastern porcelain during the second half of the seventeenth century and at Nevers, as elsewhere, Chinese landscapes and figures began to appear more frequently on blue-glazed and other faïence wares.

The decorators of Rouen, another great center of French faïence, also derived inspiration from Chinese genre scenes of the K'ang Hsi period (page 190). But in the patterns known as *broderies*, Rouen wares clearly display their originality: these patterns consist of a frieze of symmetrically-arranged lappets and garlands used to decorate, for example, the rim of a plate bearing a coat of arms or a chinoiserie decoration at the center. On other occasions the central motif comprised a wheel with spokes radiating outwards and touching the border, a pattern known as *décor rayonnant* (page 191). This justly famous decoration first appeared at the end of the seventeenth century, with the most sought-after colours during the first half of the eighteenth century being a combination of blue and red. There were numerous faïence factories scattered throughout southern France, but the most important ones, from the final decades of the seventeenth century, were located in the small village of Moustiers and at Marseilles.

At Moustiers we find the Clérissy family, masters of the *camaïeu* technique, which was based on the chiaroscuro effects obtainable from shaded gradations of the same colour. For several decades the Clérissy family produced pieces bearing coats of arms surrounded by decoration, others with hunting scenes taken from engravings by the Florentine Antonio Tempesta and, finally, pieces with compositions inspired by the ornamental style of contemporary decorators (page 192). The famous *décor Bérain* owes its name to a court designer who collaborated on the decoration of the Cabinet of Louis XIV. Other members of the Clérissy family worked in a suburb of Marseilles, at Saint-Jean-du-Désert, where they produced similar wares during the same period. Their output revived the decoration used at Moustiers, including hunting scenes enlivened by the addition of manganese-purple highlights (page 193). There are clearly many other wares that could be mentioned, from both Moustiers and Marseilles: Joseph Olérys, for example, who worked for a while at Moustiers, revealed a particular preference for polychrome decoration, as well as a great capacity for inventing popular decorative motifs.

There were countless faïence-producing centers in eighteenth-century France: the potters of La Rochelle created a very lively and imaginative "rustic" style, expressed in an airy, five-colour decoration; Samadet, in the south-west, produced wares whose decoration of butterflies displays an exemplary use of colour and extraordinarily elegant compositions (page 194); at Sinceny, in Picardy, a range of colours that included a unique and highly effective shade of yellow was used to evoke fabulous Oriental landscapes; at Saint-Amand-les-Eaux near Lille, the Fauquez factory produced pottery with a very subtle white decoration on a slate-blue ground (page 195); and there were many others. On a technical level, mention should also be made of low-temperature firing, a new process, introduced around the middle of the eighteenth century, which altered and extended the range of methods that could be used for decorating faïence, but also perhaps had the effect of somewhat diminishing its earlier qualities.

The course adopted until then had involved covering the clay with a glaze, allowing the glaze to dry, then painting the decoration and finally firing the

Chevrette *(drug jar). Majolica with high-fired polychrome decoration by Masséot Abaquesne. Rouen, France: c. 1545. Sèvres, Musée National de Céramique.*

Small, flattened flask of typically Italian shape. Majolica with high-fired polychrome decoration. Syjalon factory, Nîmes (France); 1581. New York, Metropolitan Museum.

piece, a process that called for fairly high temperatures. This method had its advantages and also its drawbacks: the advantages lay in the beauty of the results, since, by being fired together, the glaze and the colours combined very well; the drawbacks were that the potential range of colours was limited because some of them darkened or became volatile at the temperatures used, around 1560–1740°F (850–950°C), which is what happened with a colour as important as red. It should be added that great skill was needed to decorate the unfired glaze because the surface was absorbent and not very smooth; in addition, it was very difficult to correct any mistakes. Low-temperature firing involved considerable changes in procedure. The decoration was applied to a pre-fired glaze, which meant painting on a smooth and impervious, white surface. The colours, no longer subject to any restrictions, were then fixed and fused together by a further, relatively low-temperature firing. This technique, used for at least a century in the decoration of ceramics, was introduced via Strasbourg to Germany, where it supplemented the earlier process. In Italy, lower temperatures had already been used for firing gilding, while in China a similar process had emerged at the end of the twelfth century, during the Sung dynasty.

Over-glaze decoration expanded the potential of faïence in a variety of different ways. It allowed for very fine decoration and also for greater freedom of invention, as becomes immediately apparent in the wares produced at Strasbourg (page 196). It also allowed for a more naturalistic treatment, as exemplified by certain *trompe l'oeil* pieces, a speciality of the Strasbourg factory during the stewardship of Paul Hannong, a particularly skilful technician (page 197). Reds were no longer a problem and, apart from a limited output of monochrome purple wares, the extraordinary significance of this fact may be gauged from the polychrome decoration found on, for example, pieces made at Niderviller (page 198). Faïence was now able to compete with porcelain on a more equal level, as well as vying with its miniaturistic decoration. In the style practiced at Sceaux, a town near Paris, where in 1748 a factory was established that later became one of the main centers for the production of low-temperature wares, a rich range of colours was used to create a fantastic and very elegant decoration of Japanese inspiration (page 199). Marseilles also excelled in the decoration of low-temperature faïence, and the Bonnefoy factory, which began production relatively late on, reveals particularly clearly how manufacturers were able to call on the services of true artists rather than just craftsmen (page 200). Perfectly executed wares were now being created, but it is nevertheless hard not to feel that faïence had to become just a mirror in which the inventions of other forms of artistic expression were reflected, accurately, it is true, but also a trifle repetitively.

The evolutionary arc of majolica reveals a curious underlying paradox. Basically, the most satisfying wares (one thinks of the *décor rayonnant*) were produced in the face of the severe technical limitations imposed by the need for high-temperature firing. When, however, the low-temperature technique opened the door to previously unthinkable effects, capable of placing majolica on a par with other forms of artistic expression, such as porcelain, it rather lost its identity and in a sense began to suffer a decline.

In Spain, during the early sixteenth century, the tin-glazed earthenware of Moorish derivation was joined by a new type of Italian inspired majolica

Medicine jar from the Farmacia San Paolo, Savona. Majolica decorated in shades of blue. Savona, style of Giovanni Antonio Guidobono; c.1660. Faenza, Museo Internazionale delle Ceramiche.

Pitcher, the upper section modelled as the head of a rooster, the comb forming the cover. Faïence with high-fired red and blue decoration. Rouen (France); c.1700. Sèvres, Musée National de Céramique.

under the influence of artists such as Francisco Niculoso, who signed himself "the Italian" or "the Pisan." During the second half of the century the most characteristic examples of these wares were the pharmacy jars produced by the Talavera de la Reina factory in Castile, the decoration of whose wares was displaying marked Oriental and French influences by the seventeenth century. In the eighteenth century the Iberian peninsula's most important factory was that of Alcora, founded by a former ambassador to France, which employed a number of very talented French potters, including, for example, Joseph Olérys before he arrived at Moustiers. Alcora's output included pieces characterized by a richly decorative quality and others that are worthy heirs to the *istoriato* tradition (page 201).

There is good reason why, when faced with the word "faïence," to think particularly of the pottery made in Holland during the seventeenth and eighteenth centuries, above all that produced in Delft. The town of Delft achieved prominence during the mid seventeenth century, and in the following decades its factories further increased in number until, around 1700, there were 30 in all. Their output was sold well beyond the confines of Holland, finding particular favour in England, where the name of Delft became synonymous with faïence. It was only later, after several decades had elapsed, that a production which for many years had been at the forefront of the European ceramics industry began to decline, but even at the end of the century some dozen factories were still active. It would be too simplistic to say that Delftware owed its success to the fact that supplies of the Oriental porcelain which it imitated were not enough to meet the requirements of the market. For a long time there certainly were clear Far Eastern influences,

but the fact that Delftware, more than any other product, was able to bear comparison with Japanese and Chinese wares does it great credit. It should also be pointed out that not all Delftware was Orientally inspired: at a certain stage its main decorative motifs were European, either in style or derivation. Delftware is light, because of the quality of the clay, thin walled, remarkably thickly glazed and possessing a unique radiance due to the addition of a special, lead-based glaze called *kwaart* and special firing processes.

High-temperature, blue-decorated wares are one of the most popular and characteristic types of pottery produced at Delft during the second half of the seventeenth century: they depict landscapes, sometimes containing Chinese figures derived from scenes on Late Period Ming porcelain and sometimes taken from contemporary Dutch engravings or paintings (page 202). There is great sensitivity and refinement in the decoration of various dishes by, for example, Frederik van Frytom, who was responsible for the minute portrayal of a sweeping landscape, with trees, small figures and architectural elements (page 203). These wares thus owed their charm to the purity of the monochrome decoration, while the relationship between different colours, sometimes with very bright touches, lent itself particularly well to shapes with somewhat unusual elements, such as those found on a "puzzle jug" whose neck has an "openwork" decoration (page 204). There was a very broad range of decoration at Delft. There were wares with a blue ground, possibly derived from French faïence, with pale patterns painted in swift, very fluent and evocative brush strokes (page 205), and there was an altogether more traditional and formal decoration, epitomized by that found on one early eighteenth-

Rococo coffee pot. Faïence with low-fired polychrome decoration. Niderviller (Lorraine, France); c.1760. Sèvres, Musée National de Céramique.

Tulip vase, a unique piece probably used to adorn the dinner table. Lead-glazed earthenware with high-fired monochrome blue decoration. Delft; last quarter of the seventeenth century. Hamburg, Museum für Kunst und Gewerbe.

century dish, whose border is crowded with patterning and whose central medallion depicts a mythological scene with Juno and Mercury (page 206).

Polychrome was not perhaps very fashionable in Delft beyond the seventeenth century, but the highly important tile-painting sector, one of the glories of the city, is clearly an exception to this never very strictly enforced rule, and it cannot be denied that the fantastic compositions and evocations of exotic climes found on tiles profit greatly from its use (page 207). The prestige enjoyed by Delft, however, tends to make people forget that there were other factories in Holland. From the early part of the seventeenth century, for example, Rotterdam, as well as producing pottery, was home to a very flourishing tile-making industry, whose high-quality wares are decorated with scenes inspired by contemporary painting (page 208); in Friesland, tile panels and pottery were also produced in great quantities, with an attractive decoration betraying not a hint of heaviness (page 209); in Gelderland, the potters of Arnhem made a conscious choice to base certain details of their shapes on those found in metalware and then purposely emphasized them using colour (pages 210–211). During the late seventeenth century and throughout the eighteenth century, English pottery continued to draw inspiration from its Dutch counterpart. Such typically English pieces as a posset pot and stand (page 212) were decorated in perfect imitation of the Delft style. England, however, produced a major innovation in the form of creamware. Light, strong and ivory in colour, creamware provided earthenware and porcelain with very real competition during the nineteenth century, also because it was cheap and ideally suited to mass production. A leading figure in one of the many stages that lead up to the creation of this particular type of ware was Josiah Wedgwood, a native of Staffordshire. During the eighteenth century the Wedgwood factory produced vases made of a special, fine-paste stoneware with white relief decoration in the "antique style" on a blue ground (page 213). The name of the factory, Etruria, signals a new development in taste and brings us into the Neo-Classical period.

Hanau, Frankfurt, Berlin and Kassel are just some of the names linked to the flowering of German pottery during the second half of the seventeenth century. For much of the time, particularly during its early beginnings, this output harked back to Dutch wares. Some of the men who founded these new factories were Dutch, as were several of the craftsmen working in them, which meant that the subjects taken from Chinese and Japanese porcelain that had played such an important decorative role in towns like Delft, now became common in Germany as well. As well as Oriental-style scenes (page 214), however, other different decorative traditions asserted themselves, such as the use of hunting scenes, mythological scenes, *broderie* patterns and so on, which are amongst the elements found typically on wares produced at the two new factories founded during the eighteenth century at Nuremberg and Bayreuth. There is another feature of German pottery that springs more readily to mind, however: the appearance of a famous blue decoration of motifs taken from the local flora (page 215). As well as wares with a delightful decoration of exotic birds and slightly familiar Chinese figures (page 216), the Germans also produced large tankards with popular depictions of saints and anonymous figures from everyday life (page 217).

Tankard in the shape of a cask. Tin-glazed earthenware (Delftware) with cobalt-blue decoration. London, Southwark (?); dated 1632. London, Victoria and Albert Museum.

Tankard. Faïence. Made at Frankfurt and later decorated with flowers and peacocks at Augsburg in the workshop of Bartholomäus Seuter. Frankfurt-am-Main, Museum für Kunsthandwerk.

Below: Jug. Tin-glazed earthenware with cuerda seca *decoration in high-temperature colours. Seville; fifteenth century. Height: 11½ in (29 cm). Diameter: 6 in (15 cm). Sèvres, Musée National de Céramique (no. 8.440).*

Opposite: Dish. Green-glazed earthenware, high-temperature green and brown decoration. Paterna; fourteenth century. Diameter: 8 in (20 cm). Barcelona, Museo de Ceramica.

The form of the anthropomorphic jug opposite, one of the best-known examples of *cuerda seca* glazing, is doubtless derived from metalware, the cup-like neck affording space for the modelling of a human face. Decorative elements on the jug itself are traditional: leaves and flowers in a garland, an inscribed frieze, a simple ring pattern below. The Gothic lettering still shows traces of Arab influence.

After a period when Islamic influence was paramount (as it was also in the graphic arts), Hispano-Moresque potters turned to more definitely European forms, which were, without exception, somewhat stylized. This is a fine example of the "Archaic" style common in the Mediterranean countries, and which in Spain was adopted in Aragon and at Teruel, as well as at Paterna. The crowned female with a fish in either hand is described by some scholars as a lady of the court.

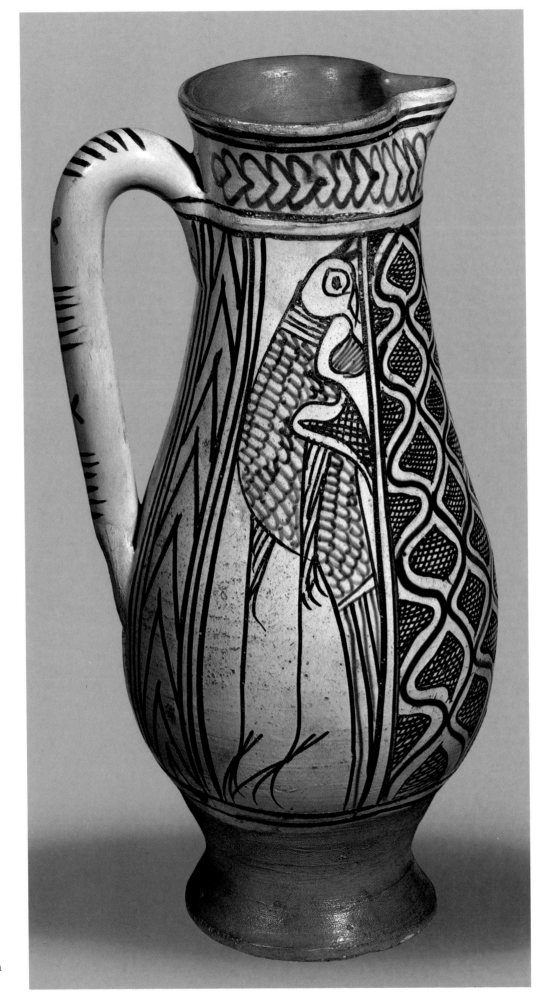

Right: Jug. Tin-glazed earthenware (majolica), high-temperature green and manganese purple. Italy; late fourteenth century. Height: 11¼ in (28 cm). Paris, Musée du Louvre (no. OA 7394, Brauer Bequest).

Opposite: Medallion in high relief. Majolica, high-temperature polychrome. Florence, Della Robbia workshop; sixteenth century. Diameter: 58 in (145 cm). Florence, Museo Nazionale del Bargello.

Orvieto pottery, as it used to be called, includes many jugs, frequently with trilobate spouts, in several styles of decoration. Geometrical motifs are common at first, then birds are often depicted – wading birds, eagles and double eagles, hawks, single or in pairs, affronted or back to back. They are often quite imaginary, of unquestionable Eastern origin though in very rare examples a more realistic representation is given.

The fame of the Della Robbia workshop rested chiefly on pieces like this, in high relief, designed for use as architectural adjuncts. The Virgin and Child group is another favourite theme.

Opposite: Pavement tiles. Majolica, high-temperature colours. Faenza; 1487. Length of each side: 3¾ in (9.5 cm). Bologna, St. Petronius (Chapel of St. Sebastian).

———————

Below: Jar ("albarello"). Majolica, high-temperature colours, "pineapple" pattern. Faenza or Cafaggiolo; c.1500–1510. Height: 8 in (20 cm). Paris, Musée du Louvre (no. OA 8233).

The pavement of the tiles opposite was commissioned in 1487 by Canon Donato Vaselli, and as the tiles are signed by members of the Bettini family and by Petrus Andrea of Faenza we can be sure of their date and origin. They provide a comprehensive selection of the Faenza patterns used at the time. They include abstract ornamental themes – scales, spirals, pearls and ovolos, with occasional waves, acanthus leaves and other Classical elements. Oriental and Western motifs include the broad coiled "Gothic" foliage and the "Persian palmette" as well as the hearts, cherub heads and single profile busts.

The "albarello" form is not of Italian origin; confectionery and drugs were kept in jars or vases of this shape in fourteenth-century Syria and Egypt. The confectionery and drugs were exported, and so, doubtless, the receptacles reached Italy, where people put flowers in them, or used them to store ointments and other solid medical supplies. (Syrups, essences and liquid medicines went into other containers, called *chevrettes*). Albarellos were produced in great numbers in the sixteenth century, some with striking, most with quiet, repetitive patterns. The "pineapple" design shown here, though not uncommon, is found mainly in Faenza and Cafaggiolo. Small spiral elements separate the pineapples, and on the neck of the jar is a twined, ribbon-like motif.

Plate. Majolica, high-temperature polychrome istoriato *decoration. Faenza; c.1510. Diameter: 13½ in (33.5 cm). London, British Museum (no. BL 1877).*

Tile. Majolica, high-temperature istoriato *decoration. Faenza, Master C.I.; 1518. 16¾ × 21½ in (42 × 54 cm). Venice, Museo Correr.*

The *istoriato* style is found on Faenza wares from the end of the fifteenth century onwards, subjects being copied from, or inspired by, engravings. In the plate opposite, the picture is a reversed adaptation of Dürer's *Satyr Family*.

As stated in the square panel in the lower left-hand corner, the subject of this picture is the Rape of Helen: *La grecha*

p(er) qui troia estinta faze, 1518 adi 15° dagosto. (The Greek woman for whom Troy was overthrown. 15 August, 1518). The lively figures are well-arranged in the airy landscape with temple ruins, a town, a large tree and, of course, the ships that will take Helen of Troy. Rich colouring gives a very effective sense of space. This scene is typical of the style of Master C.I., whose painting is normally on a smaller scale.

In many pieces with *berettino* glazing the technical accomplishment is such that almost all the ground may be dark blue, with only the decorative elements reserved in the lighter tone. In this example the *berettino* is confined to the sides of the central well, ringed with white motifs by way of contrast. The rim (with much-stylized grotesques in a lighter blue heightened with touches of white) thus seems darker, and the whole forms a most effective "composite" scheme. The portrait-bust is identified by the inscription CHL AUDYO as the Emperor Claudius. Wells of this type, with glaze, central bust and border of simplified grotesques, are frequent in Faentine *tondini* from 1520–1530.

Many Cafaggiolo pieces, such as the one opposite, are decorated with escutcheons, for the Medici were patrons of Fattorini's workshop there, and he had orders from other nobles and notables. The arms shown are those of the Altoviti-Ridolfi.

This type of decoration is attributed to Sienese potters of the early sixteenth century as it is very similar to the decoration on the floor tiles of the library in Siena cathedral and on those of the Palazzo Petrucci. It is remarkable for its elaborate detail, and for the striking colours.

Dish. Majolica, decorated in tones of blue. Siena, Maestro Benedetto; c.1510. Diameter: 9¾ in (24.3 cm). London, Victoria and Albert Museum (no. 4487-1858).

The inscription on the underside of this dish is "Fata I Siena da MᵒBenedetto." Benedetto is known to be the son of Giorgio of Faenza. Siena was one of the towns which welcomed potters from Faenza when the fall of the Manfredi family in 1501 deprived them of patronage in their home town. We know that Benedetto had a workshop there in 1503, and may have helped to make the paving tiles for the Palazzo Petrucci and for the cathedral library.

The dish illustrated, though not in the black and ocher palette of Siena, has many decorative details typical of the Sienese school. The central subject is St. Jerome in meditation, with a border of arabesques around the rim.

Show dish with istoriato *design. Majolica, yellow luster and blue. Deruta; first third of sixteenth century. Diameter: 16¼ in (40.7 cm). Sèvres, Musée National de Céramique.*

Islamic lustered pottery was produced in Mesopotamia as early as the eighth or ninth centuries. The technique spread along the Mediterranean to Spain and thence to Italy, probably via Majorca; the word majolica may well be a corruption of this. All glazed earthenware is now called majolica, but in sixteenth-century Italy the term definitely implied luster decoration. (In French, incidentally, *majolique* means Italian tin-glazed earthenware of the Renaissance period). The biggest Italian centers producing lustered majolica were Deruta and Gubbio; that of Deruta was normally painted a characteristic shade of yellow. The example opposite is typical: a large "show dish" for banquets, with a design of flowers and overlapping scales in sections on the rim. The central motif is based on an engraving entitled *La Vergine che legge e il Bambino* (the Virgin reading with the Christ-Child) attributed to Marco Dente, a pupil of Raphael. A scroll in the background bears the words, PER DORMI RE NŌ SE AQUISTA, roughly, Sluggards Prosper Not.

These are the only two remaining plaques of a set of five which illustrate the story of Cyrus. That on the left depicts his rescue as a baby by the shepherd and that on the right him being elected "king" of the village children. The inscription on the first reads: *Mosso il pasto/re del Re Astia/ge a pieta racco/lse il gettato/parto e quello element (...) come padre. n° 3* (King Astyages' shepherd, moved by pity, takes the abandoned child and raises him as his own son. no.3; on the second *Fan(n)o e familli Re Ciro gioca(n)do ond' hebbe Il Reger suo pote(n) te augurio come Troge'l descrive e dove e qua(n)do* (The children in a game make Cyrus their king, and this clearly presages his reign, as Trogus says, who tells us where and when[?]). The reference here is to the *Universal History* of Trogus Pompeius. In the lower right hand corner there are the words: *1536 i(n) Urbino/n°5*, and a monogram of the initials F.X.R.

Opposite: Vase with Raphaelesque decoration. Majolica, high-temperature colours. Urbino, workshop of Antonio Patanazzi; 1580. Height: 19¾ in (49.5 cm). Width: 12½ in (31 cm). Faenza, Museo Internazionale delle Ceramiche (no. 16722).

———

Below: Dish with white ground. Majolica, high-temperature colours. Faenza; mid sixteenth century. Diameter: 12½ in (31 cm). Faenza, Museo Internazionale delle Ceramiche (no. 14479).

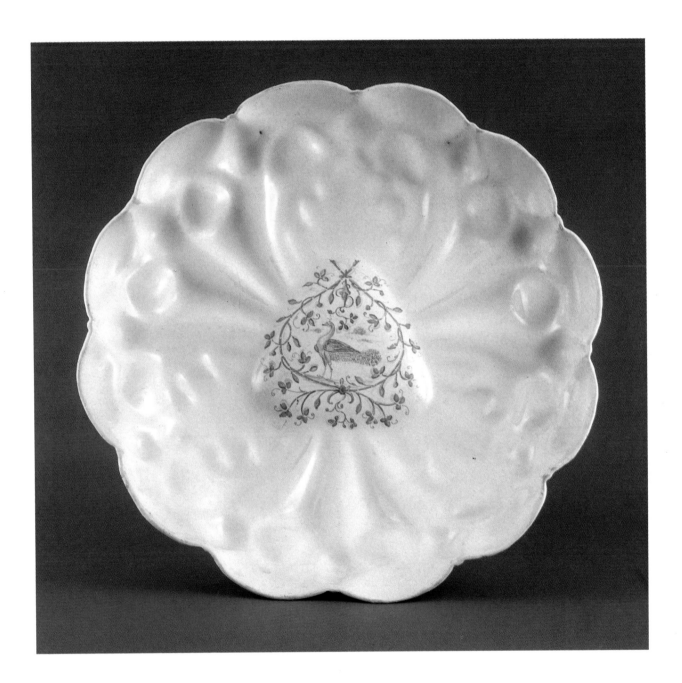

The main development in majolica painting during the latter part of the sixteenth century was the reinstatement of the white surface characteristic of tin-glazed earthenware. It was integrated into a strong sense of overall design; even when the white ground dominates, as in the case opposite, the decoration remains important. As we see from the bizarre handles, grotesque masks and raised ornament, it was a time when complicated shapes were popular and potters copied the work of goldsmiths.

In the second half of the sixteenth century, when the *compendiario* style was so popular in Italy, ceramic decoration became increasingly less ornate. Potters from Faenza consequently produced majolica with a milky-white surface of the highest quality. The plain majolica was fashioned in shapes often inspired by metal objects. Note the delicately-painted peacock motif on the piece above.

Between 1520 and 1530 Venice, like Faenza, produced majolica with a light blue ground by mixing the white tin glaze with cobalt. This technique was common to both centers, but in Venice the blue has its own peculiar slightly grey tone. In the example above the central design shows the straight streets, balconies, and doors with arches or architraves, of an Italian town. The flat rim of the dish is decorated with trophies, a common feature of Italian majolica (that of Casteldurante, for example); here the majority are military trophies with some representing the Liberal Arts, such as music and geography.

Masséot Abaquesne, the first man to make faïence in France, was in high favour with the Constable de Montmorency, for whose château at Ecouen he designed floor and wall tiles. One of two magnificent panels now at Chantilly is illustrated opposite: its subject, Marcus Curtius, sacrifices himself for Rome by leaping on horseback into the abyss. The predominant colours are yellow, blue and green, and a banner is inscribed "A ROUEN 1542."

A ROVEN
1547

This is a small dish, with short moulded stem and bosses round the rim. Inside, it has the date and three green-stalked marigolds in red and yellow: an elegant piece, one of the few dated sixteenth-century examples and, so far, unique in its kind. The shape is based on that of a goblet, probably in silver.

Dish, with painted bird. Tin- and lead-glazed earthenware. Majolica. High-temperature blue. Northern Netherlands; early seventeenth century. Diameter: 10¼ in (25.5 cm). Height: 2 in (4.7 cm). The Hague, Geementemuseum.

Faenza and Venice were by this date producing blue tin-glazed majolica, and the Dutch followed suit with plates and dishes whose backgrounds vary from sky to darkest blue. Here the central motif is a bird on a branch, with a border of berries in alternating yellow and manganese purple; it might equally well have been a hare, stag or other animal, for these were the most popular tile designs of the period. Borders are often spiral patterned.

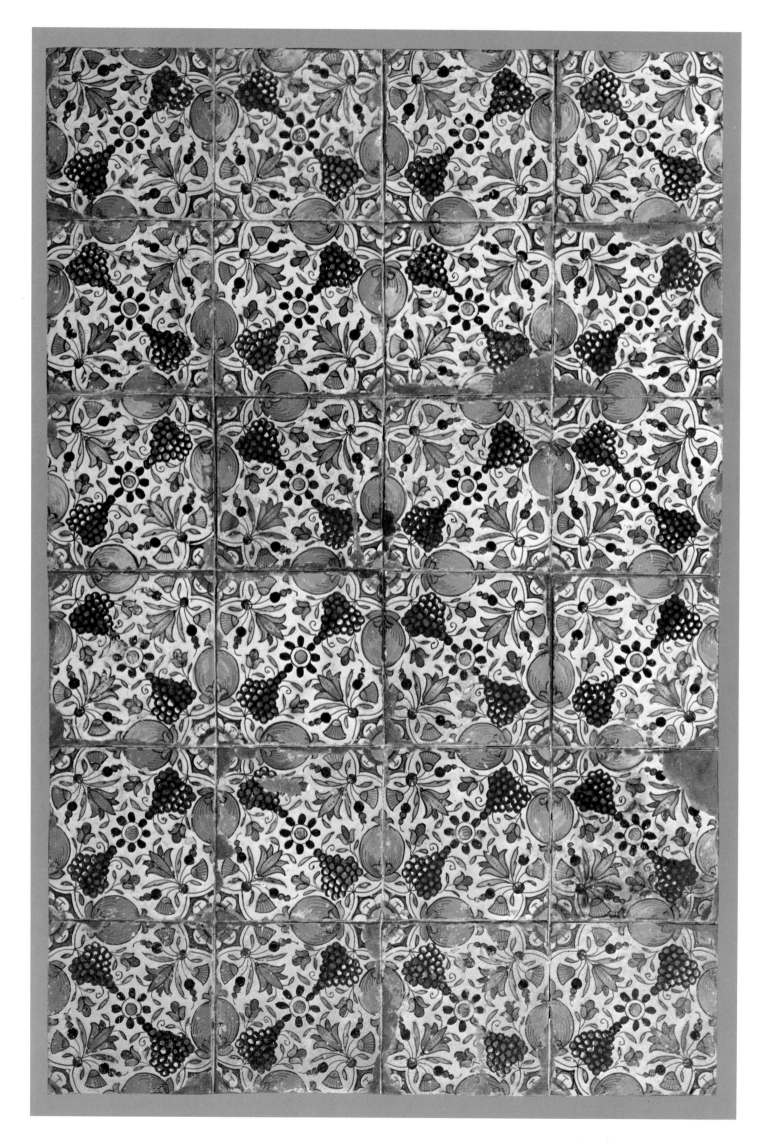

Opposite: Tiles, decorated with pomegranates and bunches of grapes. Majolica, high temperature polychrome. Delft or Rotterdam; early seventeenth century. Rotterdam, Museum Boymans-van Beuningen.

———

Right: Pitcher. Salt-glazed stoneware. Raeren, Jan Emens Mennicken; 1587. Height including lid: 22¾ in (57 cm). Diameter of body: 12½ in (31 cm). Diameter at base: 8 in (20 cm). Cologne, Kunstgewerbemuseum.

Though the fashion for tiling walls was probably more Spanish in origin than Dutch, and though geometrical patterns were due to foreign influences, the marvellous fruit designs of the tiles opposite were in fact invented by painters in the factories of Rotterdam or Delft. In units of four, they are decorated in blue, yellow and rust red, the most commonly-used colours in Holland in the first half of the seventeenth century.

This is the oldest stoneware jug known from Germany, with crisp decoration picked out in cobalt blue. The central frieze of nine moulded scenes from the life of Joseph is signed in full, on the band above the arcading, by Jan Emens Mennicken, the master of the Raeren potters. This inscription is exceptional, for his mark is usually limited to the monogram I.E.

The Manardi factory at Angarono, Veneto faced serious problems at the beginning of the eighteenth century but they kept going until the 1750s despite competition from the factories at Bassano and Venice itself. Pieces from these three centers are almost indistinguishable. The increasingly strong baroque influence meant pieces were no longer made in the usual spherical shape and had a varying degree of baroque relief decoration, often with garlands of foliage encircling the wells of dishes. The dish above, with a central painting of Neptune, was made by the moulding process.

Pictorial decoration of the early seventeenth century featured figures and animals among plants and flowers covering the entire surface. The liveliness of the designs is accentuated by stylization, and objects like the apothecary's vase in the illustration opposite show off the combination of a large number of motifs to the best advantage.

This truly remarkable dish is a fine example of the eighteenth-century enthusiasm for *trompe l'oeil*. But whereas *trompe l'oeil* is usually in relief, here we have a startlingly naturalistic painting on the flat surface of the dish. Moreover the painting is in *grand feu* colours, which means that the metal oxides have been exposed to extremely high temperatures in a single firing. Although the limited number of colours suitable for this technique tended to become very bright after firing, here they are soft and varied, and those of the border are equally delicate.

From the mid eighteenth century blue-ground colour became very popular. It had been used in the seventeenth century in Italy, France and Holland, but as an all-over, solid blue. Sèvres pottery, in imitation of Chinese designs, now left white spaces free for painted decoration, as in the plate opposite. The Clerici factory in Milan produced blue-ground majolica in large quantities and of excellent quality. The designs featured figures framed in trees. The figures, Harlequin and Columbine, on the plate opposite might be from the Italian Commedia dell'Arte.

The factory at Le Nove di Bassano, directed from 1738 to 1793 by Pasquale Antonibon, produced typically Italian baroque shapes, often derived quite clearly from the craft of the silversmith. The dish cover above is moulded to quite an unusual undulating, ribbed surface. The decoration draws on Chinese designs but is far removed from the parent style. Fantasy and imagination give the decoration of pieces such as this the bizarre, exotic flavour which often characterizes Italian pottery of the eighteenth century.

Opposite: Pharmacy vase with exotic decoration. Majolica, painted in polychrome. Venice (?); eighteenth century. Height including lid: 34 in (85 cm). Milan, Museo del Castello Sforzesco (no. 3541).

Below: Vase. Faïence, high-temperature blue and white on yellow ground. Nevers; c.1650. Height: 10½ in (26 cm). Diameter of body: 18 in (17.5 cm). Sèvres, Musée National de Céramique (no. 23.311).

Attribution of so exceptionally large and fine a piece as the vase opposite is difficult, for the other pieces of the factories which could have made it are much smaller and more modern. It is likely, however, that it was made in Venice in the eighteenth century. Whereas China is the usual source of inspiration for an exotic scene, this one is African, probably copied from some engraving or tapestry. Skilful construction of the design ensures that the rocky base of the picture occupies the lower surface and the swelling shoulder of the vase is filled with soaring palms; the artist, who is unknown, was among the master majolica painters of his time.

Yellow is the rarest of Nevers background colours, for the mixture of antimony and lead that gives the yellow tint also makes it extremely difficult to paint over it. The artist had to start by separating the blue parts of his design from the yellow with *blanc fixe* (opaque white), and decorative motifs had to be highly simplified. The Nevers vase illustrated here is of an Oriental shape widely reproduced in Europe.

Brument 1699

This celebrated piece shows how early polychrome painting was adopted at Rouen. The decoration, though contemporary with Delft chinoiserie, differs from it both in the motifs used and in the delicate execution of the border.

The pattern here is a supremely elegant example of the *décor rayonnant* of the golden age of Rouen. The central "rose" or wheel is made up of foliated scrollwork and trellised or diapered sections, with flower-tipped spokes leading the eye towards the intricate, lacy decoration of the rim, with its luminous interplay of white and coloured areas. The piece is marked on the back with the initials C.S.

Below: Oval dish. Faïence, high-temperature blue monochrome. Moustiers, Antoine Clérissy factory; c.1720. Length: 25¼ in (63 cm). Height: 2¼ in (5.7 cm). Sèvres, Musée National de Céramique (no. 8460, Davillier Bequest).

Opposite: Hunting dish. Faïence, high-temperature blue and manganese purple. St. Jean-du-Désert (Marseilles), Antoine Clérissy Factory; dated 1697. Diameter: 20 in (50 cm). Height: 2¼ in (5.5 cm). Limoges, Musée National de Céramique (no. 6906).

The style *décor Bérain*, named after Jean Bérain who, as *Dessinateur de la Chambre et du Cabinet du Roi*, designed furniture and stage scenery at the court of Louis XIV, was much favoured at the Clérissy factory. The small "grotesque" figures, the festoons, ribbons and garlands are assembled in beautifully balanced designs. On this piece the decorative elements frame a panel in which Orpheus is shown charming the animals, with a "lacy" pattern around the rim.

The large round or oval "hunting dishes" are so called because of their decoration: hunting scenes based on the engravings of the Florentine Antonio Tempesta. In this example a "petal" pattern surrounds the central picture and the design on the rim is a direct echo of Nevers designs. On the back of the dish we read, *A Clarissy à la bourgade du dezert 1697 à Marseille*. The use of manganese purple to bring out the blue is interesting and, it has been suggested, characteristic of Marseilles.

Below: Oval dish. Faïence, high-temperature polychrome. Samadet; c.1760. Length: 12¾ in (32 cm). Height: 3 in (3.3 cm). Sèvres, Musée National de Céramique (no. 12.844, M. Sentex Gift).

Opposite: Wall fountain. Faïence in three high-temperature colours. Saint-Amand-les-Eaux; c.1760. Height: 23½ in (58.5 cm). Width: 9¼ in (23 cm). Sèvres, Musée National de Céramique (no. 4.748).

Samadet, one of the most interesting *faïenceries* in south-west France, belonged first to the Abbé de Roquépine, and then to his nephew. It specialized, as did so many others, in flower designs in high-temperature colours in an attempt to compete with factories using low-temperature kilns and colours. Thanks to a very fine glaze and the delicate design in which the tones of pink painted in manganese blend with the greens and yellows, the pieces were extremely elegant. Samadet also specialized in the painting of butterflies, which may almost be considered its hall mark.

Dolphin-shaped vessels with relief decoration such as the one opposite were quite common in eighteenth-century France; the fact that the dolphin was the Dauphin's emblem surely helps to explain their popularity. The design and colouring of this piece are typical of the Fauquez factory: slate blue, with *bianco-sopra bianco* painting on a grey–blue ground.

This tray is remarkable for the elegance of the design and its arrangement. There are very few faïence trays with these bevelled corners and decoration with fantastic Oriental motifs. The design in fact draws upon the same repertoire of motifs as is to be found in other pieces of the time, but its originality lies in its combination of some Oriental and other European elements – the fountain and mask, the cobweb, birds and butterflies.

Strasbourg under Paul Hannong was a great center for *trompe l'oeil* pieces like the terrine opposite which were made, mostly in the mid eighteenth century, by several factories. Intended as ornaments for the table or sideboard, the terrines were shaped like farmyard animals, boars' heads, or vegetables, and meticulously painted in enamel colours to look as natural as possible.

Terrine in the form of a turkey. Faïence, low-temperature polychrome. Strasbourg; c.1755. Inclusive height: 19¾ in (49.5 cm). Width: 17½ in (44 cm). Paris, Musée de Cluny (no. 7.416).

Below: Bowl, with lid and stand. Faïence, low-temperature polychrome. Niderviller; c.1775. Bowl height including lid: 5½ in (13.5 cm); width: 7¾ in (19.5 cm). Plate diameter: 9¼ in (23.3 cm); height: 2 in (5.2 cm). Paris, Musée de Cluny (no. 7.372).

Opposite: Plate. Faïence, low-temperature polychrome. Sceaux, Jacques Chapelle; c.1750. Diameter: 10 in (25 cm). Height: 1¼ in (3 cm). Sèvres, Musée National de Céramique (no. 9622, M. Maillart Gift).

The elegant ware of Niderviller specialized in a *trompe l'oeil* decoration in which engravings in graduated tones of grey or crimson are apparently attached to a rose-wood background. The initials on the "pictures" here presumably indicate the work of the factory's celebrated artist, François Michel Anstett. Elaborate handles and naturalistic flowers are characteristic of rococo taste which was the prevailing fashion.

About 1749 the Duchesse du Maine, whose husband was a son of Louis XIV, extended her patronage to Jacques Chapelle at Sceaux. This plate bears the letters C.S. indicating that it was made by him. It has a crimped border and remarkable decoration. The fantastic pattern, inspired by Japanese design, consists of a dancing figure and flowering branch painted in a wide range of colours – yellow with touches of purple, azure blue, two greens and a dark iron red. Pieces bearing the mark C.S. or a fleur-de-lys were long attributed erroneously to Marseilles.

Dish. Faïence, low-temperature polychrome and gilding. Marseilles, Antoine Bonnefoy factory; c.1770. Diameter: 13¼ in (33 cm). Height: 1½ in (3.5 cm). Sèvres, Musée National de Céramique (no. 20927, Sagnier Bequest).

Bonnefoy's smooth glaze has almost the appearance of soft-paste porcelain and his factory was famous for its artists who could imitate miniature-painting to perfection. The pastoral theme of the picture in the center of the dish is in the Louis XVI style: a shepherd and shepherdess sitting by a stream in a rural landscape painted within a golden rim.

Plate. Faïence, high-temperature polychrome. Alcora; c.1735. Diameter: 10¾ in (27 cm).
New York, Metropolitan Museum (Seligmann Gift).

This piece certainly belongs to the period 1726–1737, when Joseph Olérys of Moustiers worked at Alcora; his influence is evident in the treatment of its central *istoriato* subject (Alexander's entry into Babylon), surrounded by a border. The rim is decorated in a delicate *broderies* pattern in blue. The artist is Miguel Soliva, one of the best painters of Alcora, who worked there from 1727 to 1750.

Dish, with winter landscape. Tin-glazed earthenware, high-temperature blue decoration. Delft; dated 1650. Diameter: 14¾ in (37 cm). Amsterdam, Rijksmuseum.

In the dish opposite, both the border of stylized branches, leaves and flowers, and the central subject of trees and houses by a frozen river, are clearly painted by a skilled artist. The view of the winter village is copied from or based on an engraving from the first half of the seventeenth century by Simon Frisius (c.1580–1628) or Jan van de Velde (1593–1641). Given the importance of landscape painting in Holland since the beginning of the century, it is not surprising that it became a source of inspiration for ceramic artists too.

The beautiful landscape of the tile above is minutely painted, with tiny figures of men and women, trees, a river with a bridge, and a palace on the right. Frederick van Friytom was famed for his miniature landscapes and ranks high among his contemporaries by virtue of his unique style. On the basis of five painted plaques, two of them dated 1692 other plaques and plates with similar compositions and undecorated rims have also been attributed to him. Some small dishes, round, oval and heart-shaped which were used for the tea ceremony were discovered in Japan after the last war and are also thought to be his. They are now in the Museum Het Prinsenhof in Delft.

Puzzle jug. Tin-glazed earthenware, high-temperature polychrome. Delft; first or second quarter of eighteenth century. Height: 8½ in (21.5 cm). Width: 6¼ in (15.5 cm). Enschede, Rijksmuseum Twenthe (M.G. van Heel Collection).

The "open work" neck of a puzzle jug is a hollow rim with three spouts, two of which are blocked; by covering the holes at the top and bottom of the hollow handle one can drink from the middle spout. On the body of this example is a Chinese lady, flanked by two dancing harlequins. These harlequin figures appear on plates made in China for the Dutch East India Company: the financial chaos of 1720 ruined many Dutch speculators, giving rise to many caricatures. Although the origin of puzzle jugs is uncertain, similar shapes were made in the Rhineland in stoneware as early as the end of the sixteenth century.

Pear-shaped jug. Tin-glazed earthenware, high-temperature white decoration on blue. Delft, "Peacock" factory, marked "de Paeuw"; pewter lid, opened by means of shell-shaped thumb guard, marked FVB; early eighteenth century. Height to rim: 8½ in (21 cm). Diameter of body: 5½ in (14 cm). Enschede, Rijksmuseum Twenthe (van Heel Collection).

This piece is decorated with flowers, birds and leafy branches in white tinged with blue and yellow on a blue glaze. This same glaze was used for a variety of other objects such as bottles, dishes, tureens. The "Peacock," and possibly other factories, produced bowls and jugs decorated in white, red or green. The Delft potters are thought to have learned their blue ground from Nevers which, during the period 1660–1680, produced blue-glazed dishes painted with brown and yellow branches and flowers in yellow or white.

The painting of the goddess and her peacock accompanied by Mercury on the dish opposite is based on a picture by Egbert van Panderen (1581–1637) in turn derived from a work by Bartholomeus Spranger. Shells, half circles, strapwork and garlands of leaves are among the Louis XIV-style motifs decorating the border. The palette consists of red, green, yellow and purple, with gold and two shades of blue. Two other dishes, one in the Rijksmuseum, Amsterdam, depicting the Rape of Europa, and the other, with Athena and Heracles, in the Boymans-van Beuningen Museum in Rotterdam, have the same border and are thought to date from the period 1713–1720.

The composition on this tile panel depicts the Bodhisattva Kuan Yin in the upper right-hand corner, seated on a lotus leaf dispensing the dew of mercy upon the world. Other motifs include palaces and tea pavilions, Chinese men and women, and Chinese horsemen below. The Negroes in the center and at the foot of the panel strike an unexpected note: carrying arms and other objects, they recalled the Tapuya Indians of Brazil, painted there by Albert van der Eeckhout in 1637. The palette consists of blue, red–brown, yellow, purple, green, black and red.

Four tiles, each with male or female figure. Tin-glazed earthenware, high-temperature polychrome. Rotterdam; 1620–1630. Each tile: 5¼ in² (13.3 cm²). Rotterdam, Museum Boymans-van Beuningen.

These superb examples of tiles, skilfully painted with men and women in early seventeenth-century costume, came to light after the bombardment of Rotterdam in 1941. Before then tiles with blue monochrome figures were known but here we have a palette of yellow, purple, green and brown. The subjects are based on pictures by Willem Buytewech (1591–1624), who painted in Rotterdam. After 1650 the figures on tiles tended to become smaller, leaving the white ground as an essential element in the design.

Dish, with boy holding an owl. Lead- and tin-glazed earthenware, high-temperature polychrome. Friesland; eighteenth century. Diameter: 14½ in (35.7 cm). Height: 2½ in (6 cm). Leewarden, Fries Museum.

The boy with the owl is painted in the central medallion, with drapery to left and right and a border of conventionalized fruit and branches, in purple, yellow and green. The Frisian potteries also had a border pattern of curves and stylized flowers, and though most of their polychrome pieces are of inferior quality the decoration is nevertheless characteristic and pleasing.

Below: Tureen. Tin-glazed earthenware, high- and low-temperature polychrome. Arnhem, mark in manganese, a cockerel facing to the left; late eighteenth century. Height including lid: 11 in (17.5 cm). Width: 14½ in (36.5 cm). Arnhem, Gemeentemuseum.

Opposite: Coffee pot. Tin-glazed earthenware, low-temperature polychrome. Arnhem, mark in red–brown, a cockerel facing to the left; late eighteenth century. Height including lid: 13½ in (34 cm). Diameter of body: 10½ in (26 cm). Arnhem, Gemeentemuseum.

The shape of this tureen is based on silverware. On the lid there is a scene after an engraving by George Philipp Rugendas (1666–1742).

The shape of the coffee pot or urn opposite, is known in Dutch as a *kraantjeskan* and is derived from metalwork. In the mid eighteenth century this type of pot was also made in silver.

Posset, a drink made of hot milk and spices curdled with ale, wine or other alcohol was poured into cups from spouted pots. In England these were also made in glass and silver. Illustrated opposite is a very grand example, for special occasions.

One of the most original technical innovations of Wedgwood was the development of a fine-grained white stoneware that could be tinted either when the compound was mixed or by the dipping of completed pieces. Most of this "jasper ware," perfected in 1774–1775, was tinted blue. The jug illustrated was coloured by dipping, and bears the mark WEDGWOOD, and an H, impressed. The central relief, in the style of Lady Templewood, an amateur artist who designed for the factory, is inspired by Goethe's *Sorrows of Werther*: Charlotte kneeling at Werther's tomb.

Opposite: Jug. Faïence, Hanau; c. 1705. Height including lid: 12½ in (31.5 cm). Diameter of body: 6¼ in (15.5 cm). Diameter of base: 4½ in (11.5 cm). Frankfurt-am-Main, Museum für Kunsthandwerk.

Below: Wine cooler. Faïence. Nuremberg; c. 1723. Diameter: 24 in (60 cm). Nuremberg, Germanisches Nationalmuseum.

The foundation of the Hanau factory near Frankfurt in 1661 marks the beginning of the best and most productive period of German and Austrian faïence. As can be seen from the jug opposite, the decorative styles in Germany are usually very close to those of Holland, inspired in their turn by porcelain from China and Japan.

Objects very similar to this wine cooler were being made by a Nuremberg workshop as early as the sixteenth century, though none are heard of after the beginning of the seventeenth. In 1712, however, production of such ware revived when a partnership of three Nuremberg merchants set up a factory that was to last until 1840. Its earliest decoration imitated that of Delft, with the addition of plant motifs taken from local flora. Its predominant colour was at first the under-glaze blue of this example. Before long the palette was enriched with other colours, among them lemon yellow, green and purple, the latter in every tone from very dark to palest lilac.

The faïence factory at Durlach, founded in 1723 by the Margrave Karl Wilhelm of Baden, was first managed by Johann Heinrich Wachenfeld, who had worked at Ansbach and Strasbourg and in the porcelain factory at Meissen. Durlach produced a wide range of pieces, but made no statuettes. The influence of Strasbourg is obvious in the decoration of its vases, and in Wachenfeld's time a blue ribbon motif, derived from Rouen, was frequently used. From 1755 the designs were based chiefly on polychrome Oriental flowers, and small Chinese figures were introduced after 1765, inspiration for which was often found in European copper-plate engravings; on the example here the decoration is possibly based on a copper-plate engraving by Elias Baeck, who died in Augsburg in 1747.

The Kunersberg factory was opened in 1745 by Johann von Kuner, a successful businessman. Having built the town and named it after himself, he applied for and received a license from the Municipal Council of nearby Memmingen to manufacture faïence there; and a year later the emperor granted him the monopoly for Swabia. He took over practically the whole Schrattenhofen establishment, where Prince Albrecht Ernst of Oettingen's enterprise was temporarily shut down; the painters, potters and workmen came to Kunersberg, soon established the factory and produced some magnificent pieces, notably the narrow-necked jugs which are among the most elegant produced in Germany. The cylindrical tankard with a figure of St. Bartholomew illustrated here is attributed to Johann Martin Frantz, a leading artist in subjects of this kind.

European Porcelain

To be comprehensive, a history of porcelain should look both at porcelain itself and at the long search to discover the secrets of its manufacture, to successfully duplicate its qualities and to invent satisfactory substitutes for it. When the nature of its composition was finally discovered in Germany around 1710 porcelain, with its dense, hard, resistant and translucent body, its characteristically white appearance, its shiny, nacreous surface and its mysterious resonance, had for centuries been regarded as an unattainable ideal.

Porcelain, imported from the Far East, had previously been viewed in Europe as first a myth and then a rarity. It was perhaps its beauty alone that had led generations of Islamic potters and decorators during the Middle Ages to first adopt a special white slip that gave particular prominence to line and colour, then, to the same end, a tin-based glaze, and then another material that differed from the clay which had been used from earliest times. The lure of porcelain, however, remained undimmed.

Europe would have to wait until the eighteenth century before receiving anything more than the most sketchy information concerning the techniques of its manufacture. The first man to mention it had been Marco Polo, but during the Renaissance porcelain was still such a rare commodity that it became suitable material for gifts between princes: the Sultan of Egypt, for example, sent a chest of porcelain to Lorenzo de' Medici. At the beginning of the seventeenth century the famous Florentine dictionary compiled by the Accademia della Crusca could only define porcelain in purely generic, albeit highly admiring terms, as "precious clay," and during the seventeenth and eighteenth centuries majolica wares were judged on the basis of their capacity to

Group, The Music Lesson. *Soft-paste porcelain, enamel colours and gold. Chelsea; 1760–1765. Height; 15 in (37.8 cm). Boston, Museum of Fine Arts. The subject is drawn from an engraving by R. Gaillard, based on Boucher's* L'Agréable Leçon *of 1748.*

Marks of European porcelain

Some of the marks used by German porcelain factories. From left to right: the crossed swords of Meissen, the Bavarian shield of Nymphenburg, the scepter of Berlin and the monogram of the Elector of the Palatinate used by the Frankenthal factory.

bear comparison with porcelain and on the extent to which they emulated the latter's properties. On a specific level, it was these criteria that determined the success enjoyed by Delftware, even beyond the frontiers of Holland, as well as explaining why, for instance, it was given such a particularly lustrous glaze. However, porcelain did not result in the downgrading of other types of wares. In a way, the opposite is true, because in Europe it was porcelain that raised the status of ceramics.

The princes and kings of Europe were not always content just to act as collectors and connoisseurs; many of them sought, whether out of enthusiasm or for reasons of prestige, to promote the manufacture of porcelain, sometimes even becoming personally involved in the process. This porcelain "fever," which during the eighteenth century affected many of the rulers of the small states into which Germany was then divided, appears to have first manifested itself years earlier in Italy. It is recorded in Florence as early as the second half of the sixteenth century, during the time of the Medici, when it is mentioned by no less an authoritative source as Vasari. Even more importantly, some 70 pieces, made around 1575, have survived as proof of the serious attempts being made at the time to imitate Oriental porcelain. At the center of these efforts stands the fascinating figure of Francesco I, Grand Duke of Tuscany, a lover of beautiful things who was intrigued by the secrets of nature, as is demonstrated by his *studiolo* in the Palazzo Vecchio. He was assisted in this enterprise by the brilliant architect Bernardo Buontalenti, who was in charge of production, and by a number of potters from Urbino and Faenza, who researched and created the new wares. The paste included one part of very impure kaolin and other parts of vitreous mat-

ter; the shapes of the pieces, which consist of cruets, pilgrim flasks, ewers, pitchers, bottles and dishes, are very varied and elegant; the decoration is mainly in shades of blue (page 228), but often with the addition of touches of manganese purple; the motifs are partly inspired by those on Chinese porcelain or, more accurately, by a Middle Eastern interpretation of them, but they also include such purely Italian elements as grotesques; another interesting feature are their marks, which generally take the form of an "F" crowned by a stylized dome of the Cathedral Santa Maria del Fiore.

Leaving the Renaissance, we have to wait until the eighteenth century before another similar, and at least as famous factory emerges in Italy this time much further to the south, within the royal palace of Capodimonte, in Naples. The factory was founded in 1743 by Charles, the intelligent and cultured Bourbon King of Naples. The white, translucent paste used here was similar in appearance to that used in contemporary French soft porcelain and the quality of the ware is impressive, as is immediately apparent when one admires the grace and powerful expressiveness of the celebrated Capodimonte figurines, which often portray characters from the Italian Commedia dell'Arte (page 229), as well as the table services or single masterpieces such as the porcelain room created by the factory for the royal villa at Portici. When it came to formal and decorative prototypes, the painters and modellers working for Charles found their inspiration in Germany, where several decades earlier the first European factory making "real" porcelain had been founded at Meissen under the patronage of Augustus II of Saxony, uncle to the Queen of Naples. After exchanging the throne of Naples for that of Spain in 1759, Charles trans-

French marks. From left to right: the crowned double "L"s of Sèvres, the inscription and "CD" monogram of Limoges, the dolphin of the Manufacture royale de Monseigneur le Dauphin *at Lille and the sun of Saint-Cloud.*

Italian marks. From left to right: the Bourbon lily of Capodimonte, the crowned "N" of the Neal Manifattura di Porcellane *at Naples, the armorial star of the Ginori family, owners of the Doccia factory of the same name, and the star and inscription of the Antonibon workshop at the Nove di Bassano.*

ferred production to the palace of Buen Retiro in Madrid, taking with him the numerous chemists and artists already in his service and using the same type of materials, making the same type of wares and even retaining the same mark. Only in 1771, in the reign of Ferdinand IV, did the Naples factory resume production, when its wares reflected the Neo-Classical taste (page 230). The soft-paste porcelain made by the Buen Retiro factory, by contrast, often reflects the influence of the great French ceramic-producing center of Sèvres.

French porcelain owes its glorious and well deserved reputation mainly to the wares produced at the royal porcelain factory, founded by private individuals at Vincennes in 1738 and then transferred to Sèvres in 1756. It can, however, lay claim to seventeenth-century origins, since the first chapters of its history had been written several decades earlier by ceramists working at Rouen and Saint-Cloud. Another factory, founded at Chantilly in 1725 under the patronage of the Prince de Condé, produced wares whose decoration, like that found on the earlier Saint-Cloud products, betrays the influence of the Japanese Imari style. Indeed, it was craftsmen from Chantilly who, under the patronage of a highly-placed figure at the French court, began creating porcelain in the château of Vincennes, where they were soon protected by the granting of an exclusive privilege running for 20 years. This privilege banned other factories from producing porcelain wares "in the manner of Saxony and Japan" and prohibited them from taking on workers who had previously been employed at Vincennes.

Having developed under state patronage, in 1750 the factory could count on the services of more than 100 workers, employed in seven specialist work-

shops: preparing pastes, turning, shaping, decorating, painting, sculpting and creating flowers. The latter *atelier* was run by Madame Gravant and vied with Meissen in the production of flowers modelled from nature (page 232, above): a very sought-after genre, these were either displayed in vases or used to adorn the gilt-bronze parts of inkwells, lamps and other decorative objects. The output of Vincennes, which employed famous chemists, silversmiths, enamellers and decorators, was in direct competition with that of Meissen, which explains why its early decoration, for example of flowers and insects, reflects the style of the famous Saxon factory rather than Imari-inspired motifs. But the arrival at Vincennes of so many qualified artists soon gave rise to an original style and a new, incomparably elegant taste, with a decoration characterized by extraordinary delicacy and sometimes achieved by very simple means (page 232, below).

In 1753, at the request of Madame de Pompadour, the factory was moved to Sèvres, situated between Paris and Versailles, while in 1760 the enterprise was nationalized by Louis XV. By this time, however, the famous coloured grounds, most notably the Chinese-inspired "clouded" blue, had already begun to appear at Vincennes, and these were used to give prominence to reserved areas in which there appeared light and airy polychrome forms (page 234).

The shade of pink known as *rose Pompadour*, which had already been used on monochrome Vincennes wares, became very fashionable at Sèvres, where brilliant new combinations of colour were tested: blue and green, green and pink, and so on, while the grounds were enlivened with special effects of gilding and mosaic or "partridge-eye" patterns (page 235). Highly original shapes were introduced,

English marks. From left to right: the anchor and trident of the Bow factory, the triangle and the anchor (two marks used by Chelsea), a Derby mark and the Plymouth mark.

Above, one of the marks of the Vienna factory, founded in 1719 and chronologically the second European hard-paste porcelain factory. Below, the mark used by the St. Petersburg factory during the Catherine II period.

which achieved a magical balance between fantasy and composure (page 236), and a wide variety of pieces were made: as well as services, there were vases of every shape and size, lamps, opera glasses, containers and, later, table clocks, decorative objects and ornamental plaques for furniture. The year 1759 was an important one since it marked the start of the production of hard-paste porcelain at Sèvres. It is significant that soft porcelain, although a more fragile and less malleable material and thus harder to work, continued to be made until the end of the century and is still the type of porcelain which has given Sèvres its legendary reputation in the history of ceramics. A rather late and, some would say, rather cold product of the royal factory was biscuit porcelain, which was inspired by the idea of leaving the paste unglazed in order to reveal the minute detailing of certain statuettes in all its beauty.

As the most important French workshop, Sèvres was soon showing the way, in matters of both taste and technique, for all the very many other French factories: one of these, Mennecy, was famous for its snuffboxes, its decorative boxes, its small cosmetic jars and other similar objects, but also for its figurines of peasant girls and the rustic themes that appear on the beautifully balanced decoration of its wares (page 233).

In Belgium, a factory like Tournai proved that, even when adopting from Sèvres and Meissen a whole series of elements relating to decorative themes and styles, there was still room for "personal" touches. Tournai produced splendid dinner services, whose strength sometimes lies in the extremely skilful use of the *camaïeu* technique, sometimes in their characteristic shapes, such as the swirling, ribbed edges of certain large and small plates (page 237),

and sometimes in the elegant simplicity of their highly restrained decoration.

Even in a very rapid and broadly-based resumé of European soft-paste porcelain, special mention should be made of England. The English produced large numbers of very fine wares that display a considerable degree of independence, even on the technical level. During the mid eighteenth century, for example, the Bow factory began to use a paste containing a high percentage of bone ash, an innovation that was adopted by other factories because it was more stable and also held its shape better during firing than its vitreous equivalent. In addition to this "phosphatic" porcelain, which was fired at a lower temperature than hard-paste porcelain, there was another type, a member of the "hybrid porcelain" group, which was produced at Bristol and used a new component, steatite or soapstone. Research was clearly developing along a number of different lines and experimentation was flourishing.

However, bearing in mind the results, the most successful wares were undoubtedly produced by Chelsea, the oldest English porcelain factory, with a paste whose composition was very similar to that used by the French. Meissen, Sèvres and Saint-Cloud, but also Chinese and Japanese ceramics, provided important sources of inspiration for the work carried out at Chelsea, while the shapes were in many cases inspired by those found in silverware, an art well known to Nicholas Sprimont, a French silversmith who was the factory's first director. But the new wares cannot be classified as imitations or mere derivatives since they distinguish themselves in a number of different ways, especially in their decoration, which at one stage in particular displayed a highly imaginative quality, both in its subject matter

Above, the three waves used to mark the wares of the Copenhagen porcelain factory. Below, the mark of the founder of the Swedish Marieberg factory.

Above, the tower, one of the marks used by the Belgian Tournai factory. Below, the stylized Bourbon lily of the Spanish Buen Retiro factory.

and in its elegant choice of colours. Landscape motifs were matched by portrayals of plants and insects inspired by plates from natural history books (page 238), while relief decoration of flowering sprays, derived from Chinese porcelain, alternated with scenes that echo paintings by artists such as Boucher and Watteau. Later on, figures painted in gold on a blue or pink ground, in a decidedly more ambitious but perhaps less spontaneous style, began to appear, while the decoration tended as a rule to become more and more crowded as the shapes became more elaborate and more complicated. But perhaps the most attractive feature of Chelsea's output, as revealed in its figurines and groups, is, independent of the greater or lesser profusion of its colours and gilding or the degree of crispness of its modelling, a certain magical blend of ingeniousness and sophistication (page 238).

Around 1756, Bow, whose porcelain is decorated with motifs that were often inspired by those found on Meissen vases and figurines, but sometimes also echo Oriental prototypes (page 239, below right), was probably the first factory to make use of transfer-print decoration, which gives a hint of the way in which mass-production techniques were gradually emerging in the manufacture of ceramics. At Lowestoft in Suffolk, phosphatic porcelain gave a new impetus and offered new possibilities for the imitation of Chinese blue-and-white wares, although a more original style later emerged in the lively decoration of pieces attributed to the so-called "Tulip Painter" (page 240). The magnificent flowers, painted from life (page 241), that decorate the soft-paste porcelain from the Derby factory in the Midlands, are in themselves enough to earn this English town a place amongst the most famous names in porcelain manufacturing, but experts also acknowledge that it owes

a very important part of its reputation to certain characteristic decorations of birds and butterflies, as well as to its biscuit figures. Another major center, both for the quality of its wares and for the continuity of its production, is Worcester. Soapstone porcelain, of which large quantities were produced at Worcester, was extensively used for tea services, given the fact that it withstood rapid changes in temperature much better than soft-paste porcelain; its quality, however, was not of the best, partly because of its slightly off-white colour.

Germany plays a dominant role in the history of European hard-paste porcelain. The discovery of the secret of the composition and thence the manufacture of "true porcelain" was, in fact, made at Dresden. The men responsible for this were the alchemist Johann Friedrich Böttger, who worked as a jeweller for Augustus the Strong, and a mathematician who helped him in his research. The factory founded by Augustus in the fortress of Albrechtsburg at Meissen began production in 1710, under Böttger's direction. The first pieces took the form of brown stoneware, and in their shapes and their decoration they betray clear, if not exclusively Oriental influences (page 242). By using the kaolin discovered at Aue, however, Böttger soon succeeded in producing an excellent white porcelain, similar to Chinese prototypes, covered with a felspathic glaze. This marked the early beginnings of an enterprise destined to enjoy extraordinary success: the workforce at Meissen in 1719, the year of Böttger's death, numbered a few more than 20, but at the end of the century this had increased to more than 500. The early decades were the most important, partly thanks to two excellent directors, the painter Johann Gregorius Höroldt and the modeller Johann Joachim Kändler, who

Styles and decoration of European porcelain

Small snuffbox in the form of a shell. Soft-paste porcelain painted in enamel colours. Capodimonte; c. 1750. London, Victoria and Albert Museum.

supervised a workforce of highly talented artists and craftsmen. The preference at Meissen for the models provided by Chinese and Japanese porcelain was to last for a long time, but Höroldt's genius, imagination and skill led to a rapid diversification of shapes and decorative motifs, just as they ensured an improvement in the pastes and a constant flow of discoveries and experiments in the field of colour. The chinoiserie decoration, invented during Höroldt's time and often enclosed in gilt-edged medallions, is particularly memorable (page 243). Meissen never slavishly copied Oriental examples, and there was always some development, some free reinterpretation, some personal touch (page 244) in their pieces. There was a decisively new quality to the scenes of landscapes, seascapes, harbours and tiny figures created during the 1740s by certain artists carrying on the work begun by Hörodolt (page 246, left).

By far the greatest of these figures was Kändler, who, starting in 1731, worked for more than 30 years in the service of Europe's first and greatest hard-paste porcelain factory. It was a period during which the most frequent form of painted decoration were Arcadian scenes (page 245) in the manner of Boucher or Watteau, with Oriental flower motifs replaced by "German flowers" (*deutsche Blumen*), whose warmth and naturalness also marked a departure from the earlier style of flower, copied from botanical books. Kändler, who for a while also held the post of artistic director, devoted himself to modelling with an almost boundless energy. When Augustus the Strong decided to decorate an entire palace with porcelain, Kändler contributed vases, statues and large figures of animals in white paste. In less than two years he created several hundred models for the animal series alone. No less important were the dinner services,

for which Kändler was assisted by other master craftsmen: the "Swan service," created for one of the Elector of Saxony's ministers, is probably the most famous one in the history of ceramics. However, Kändler achieved his greatest success with his brilliant statuettes, which were admired and imitated throughout Europe: their subjects were legion, but special mention should be made, on the one hand, of his figures of characters from the Commedia dell'Arte, such as Harlequin, a highly popular "mask" in Germany (page 246, right), and, on the other, his enchanting "crinoline" figures, which capture the very essence of woman in all her eighteenth-century elegance. The groups in which Kändler's ladies appear in their multi-coloured floral dresses accompanied by other figures are a delightful portrayal of the scenes, ceremonies and festivities of the fashionable world (page 247).

This was the moment of porcelain's greatest triumph, when it became one of the main passions of society and a symbol of such prestige that the encouragement of its production was considered to be almost a bounden duty for every ruler. The various kings and princes of Europe vied with each other in a competition that also involved trying to lure the best workers away from other factories. Particularly welcome were those in possession of some manufacturing secret, who had every sort of favour showered on them. One symbol of the public's insatiable appetite for porcelain was the appearance, most particularly in Germany, of a new artistic figure, that of the *Hausmaler* ("home painter"), artists who bought porcelain "blanks," decorated them in their own studio and then sold the result on the open market. Despite the authorities' attempts to curb this practice, which damaged official production, they never succeeded in

Pitcher with cover and fluted body. Soft-paste porcelain. Gerault d'Areaubert factory, Orléans (France). Sèvres, Musée National de Céramique.

Jardinière (plant container) with picture of children inspired by Boucher. Soft-paste porcelain. Vincennes; 1754. Sèvres, Musée National de Céramique.

stamping it out and *Hausmalerei* flourished, even though some people condemned the painters as amateur daub artists. Drinks such as tea, coffee and chocolate, which were now widely consumed by the nobility and the wealthy middle classes, as indeed was ice cream, helped to increase the market for cups, small bowls and so on.

During the second half of the eighteenth century Meissen's star gradually began to wane, partly as a result of the rise of Sèvres, and in around 1770 the most important German factory began to be Berlin, which for some years had been under the direct control of Frederick the Great of Prussia. The Berlin factory was particularly famous for its table ware, and the service made for Frederick's Neues Palais at Potsdam is a masterpiece of the rococo; the one made for his palace at Breslau (modern Wroclaw) is distinguished by its brightly coloured and sharply drawn decoration (page 248). Despite changes in the historical, social and artistic climate, Berlin retained its prestige well into the nineteenth century, but by then porcelain was no longer so fashionable and its decoration became influenced by the public's preference for illustrated scenes over purely ornamental motifs (page 249).

Whereas, during the second half of the eighteenth century, the Frankenthal factory had been able to enjoy the patronage of the Elector of the Palatinate and so capture a wide market, partly thanks to the hundreds of highly imaginative models created by Johann Wilhelm Lanz (page 250), the role of patron and financial backer at the Nymphenburg Palace was assumed by the Elector of Bavaria. The Nymphenburg enjoyed the services of an exceptional modeller, Swiss-born Franz Anton Bustelli, who, for a while, ensured that his factory became the arbiter of European taste as far as ceramics were concerned, mainly through his series of brilliantly executed rococo figurines (page 251).

The Vienna factory was, chronologically speaking, the second European manufacturer of hard-paste porcelain. It dated back to 1718, when it was founded by an official of the Imperial court, Claudius du Paquier, who was obliged to hand it over to the state in 1744 due to the costs of the enterprise. He was initially assisted by a kiln master and an enameller from Meissen, who had previously worked with Böttger. As at Meissen, the first Vienna wares were strongly influenced by the Japanese and Chinese porcelain that had been extensively imported into Europe by the different East India companies, but the factory soon adopted a style that exercised greater control over these exotic references, finally absorbing them completely. Some Vienna pieces appear to reflect the formal examples set by centers such as Rouen or Sèvres, while others repeat elements, like the use of a decoration of monochrome black glaze (*Schwarzlot*), that had been features of seventeenth-century German faïence. But Vienna porcelain displays a different taste: a liking for gilding, for example, and for a certain formal richness in the relief elements. During the course of the eighteenth century Vienna produced works that combined elegance with an extraordinarily life-like quality (page 252), after first passing through a phase of very controlled and sober decorativism (page 253).

The influence of Vienna and Meissen shines clearly through the style adopted by the Doccia factory, near Florence, founded by the Marchese Carlo Ginori in 1735. To begin with, Ginori did not just make a close study of the wares produced by Du Paquier, but also imported experts from Vienna to teach his Italian

Sauce boat. Soft-paste porcelain painted with enamel colours. Worcester (England); c. 1755. Northampton, Central Museum.

Lantern modelled in imitation of the Chinese. Hard-paste porcelain with over-glaze decoration by Johann Ehrenfried Stadler; end of the seventeenth century–beginning of eighteenth. Dresden, Staatliche Kunstsammlungen, Porzellansammlungen.

workers and assist him in the technical and artistic running of his enterprise. The main difficulty facing Doccia lay in obtaining sufficient supplies of kaolin, since Vincenza was unable to provide enough white clay for a rapidly developing factory and it was too expensive to try and obtain it from even more remote foreign sources. It was therefore decided to take what could be regarded as a backward step and use a type of clay found in the area round Lucca and then cover the paste with a thick tin glaze of the sort that had long been used for majolica. This hybrid porcelain, known in Italian as *masso bastardo*, was used to produce large numbers of wares and also allowed for very delicate results (page 254). Doccia also made hard-paste porcelain of a very high quality, both in its decoration and in other respects (page 255). The factory produced a wide range of shapes: figurines and monumental compositions, decorative items and crockery, plaques and friezes, capitals and altars, centerpieces for tables and vases. But all these different forms share the same quality: a sense of balance and clarity that is typically Tuscan.

The Le Nove factory, already mentioned in the chapter on majolica, was under the direction of Pasquale Antonibon when, during the mid eighteenth century, it also began to make porcelain. It was a hybrid porcelain, made with a slightly greyish paste, which nevertheless produced excellent results, even in pieces as potentially difficult as a figure group (page 256). Le Nove was not a small ceramic manufacturer: in fact, at one stage it employed more than 100 workers, while at the end of the century it also began making pottery. Its porcelain wares are remarkable for their very brilliant colours, particularly a bright red, a beautiful transparent pink and a very fresh green.

A porcelain factory had been established in Venice in around 1720, the third in Europe after Meissen and Vienna, but it was soon forced to close because of the ban imposed on kaolin exports from Aue by the Saxon authorities. The enterprise set up some fifty years later by Geminiano Cozzi, however, enjoyed much greater success. The porcelain, classified as hybrid because its paste is made up of a blend of different clays, was used to produce wares with rococo shapes (page 257), while the decoration clearly betrays the influence of first Meissen and then Sèvres. But the new wave of interest in subjects derived from Oriental art, which in around 1775 manifested itself throughout Europe, also had its effect on the decoration of Cozzi porcelain.

In France, the development of hard-paste porcelain production was hampered by a number of factors. Above all, the French lacked kaolin, and only after the discovery of deposits at Saint-Yrieix in 1768 could this problem be considered solved. In addition, the exclusive warrant enjoyed by Sèvres blocked any other initiative: in 1754, for example, an attempt to keep the Strasbourg factory open failed, and Paul Hannong, who had founded it a couple of years before, transferred his activities to Frankenthal in Germany. Finally, the success of soft-paste porcelain discouraged any diversification. However, once the problem of kaolin had been resolved, Sèvres, the greatest of the French factories, was the first one to become involved with the new medium in 1770. The advent of hard-paste porcelain did not in any way alter the preference of many customers for soft-paste wares, although it is true that the new material, with its greater resistance to high temperatures, offered new technical possibilities and to an extent encouraged Sèvres to adopt a style of decoration that

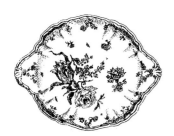

Tray from the service made for Frederick the Great's residence at Breslau (Wroclaw). Hard-paste porcelain with over-glaze painted decoration. Berlin; 1767–68. Berlin-Köpenick, Kunstgewerbemuseum.

Vase. Hard-paste porcelain with over-glaze painted decoration by Joseph Nigg. Vienna; 1835. Vienna, Oesterreichisches Museum für angewandte Kunst.

covered the entire available surface, leaving the way clear for previously impossible *tours de force*. The overall consequence is that hard-paste porcelain wares convey a feeling of particular richness, but are also a little cold. This period saw the introduction of gilded decoration on a black ground (page 258), gilded grounds, the use of platinum and such difficult feats as the imitation of other materials, such as wood and tortoiseshell. There was a revival of the fashion for naturalistic motifs portraying leaves, plants, birds etc. (page 259), with pieces sometimes bearing captions from some scientific treatise on the reverse, giving the name of the species represented. Hard-paste porcelain triumphed in the manufacture of biscuit wares, which were now produced in even greater numbers. All in all, decoration was either overabundant or absent: the old feeling of balance has been lost.

The relaxation of the Sèvres monopoly made it possible for other enterprises to be set up, although their founders took the wise precaution of placing them under the protection of some important personage. Various factories sprang up in Paris, where the Petit Carrousel specialized, with remarkable success, in the decoration of white porcelain blanks acquired from other factories (page 260). But there were other points of sale and production, such as the factory on the Rue Thiroux, under the protection of Queen Marie Antoinette, and the one on the Rue Clignancourt in Montmartre, where hard-paste wares with a highly inventive and very elegant style of decoration were produced (page 261, above).

The development of a factory at Limoges was clearly helped by the close proximity of Saint-Yrieix, but it used these favourable conditions to start production of a type of porcelain that has great merits in its own right. During the age of Louis XVI its wares were often decorated with a recurrent motif of roses, the famous Limoges roses, which became a sort of factory emblem (page 261, below).

In England it was the apothecary William Cookworthy who succeeded, after years of research and following the discovery of kaolin in Cornwall, in producing an Oriental type of porcelain. His factory moved from Plymouth to Bristol, and financial difficulties forced its closure in 1781. Many pieces have survived, including certain biscuit plaques with relief decoration, but the most famous pieces are figurines characterized by nervous modelling and the use of bright yet appropriate polychrome colours (page 262).

As can be seen in a chestnut vase from the Oude Amstel factory (page 263), Dutch hard-paste porcelain provides further confirmation that the two great reference points of eighteenth-century European ceramics were Meissen and Sèvres. In fact, there were painters and craftsmen from both France and Germany working in Holland. The main collaborators of the Dutchman who, in 1757, had founded the first porcelain factory in Holland, at Weesp, were German. This same factory reappears at Oude Amstel in 1782, having changed ownership and moved cities on several occasions. One gets the impression that making porcelain in Holland meant embarking on a rather difficult task, which may perhaps be explained by the extensive importation of Far Eastern wares by the Dutch East India Company.

As the century drew to a close, it became abundantly clear throughout Europe that the end of the eighteenth century had also marked the end of the halcyon days of porcelain.

Teapot of "bamboo" shape inspired by Chinese imports. Hard-paste porcelain. Sèvres. Sèvres, Musée National de Céramique.

Milk jug with "antique" decoration in the early nineteenth century Neo-Classical taste. Hard-paste porcelain. Nast factory, Paris; c. 1810. Sèvres, Musée National de Céramique.

The Medici porcelain of Florence produced in the last quarter of the sixteenth century is so called because it was the Grand Duke Francesco Maria de' Medici, who financed the research and production. Only two dated pieces are known: the flask illustrated, and a medallion dated 1586 in the Bargello Museum, Florence. Most examples are marked. On the back of this plate there is the cathedral dome, with the letter "F" for Francesco.

Meissen, which introduced porcelain figures into Europe, did not itself produce the best examples. The masterpieces are unquestionably those by Bustelli who worked at Nymphenburg and by Gricci at Capodimonte. The statuette opposite of Captain Spacca, a character from the Italian Commedia dell'Arte, is one of the most famous. His face is more expressive than is usual for a porcelain statuette. The piece certainly belongs to the early period at Capodimonte and is of rare quality, despite fire-cracks and other technical faults. Figures of this kind are rare, and very valuable.

Below: Plate. Soft-paste porcelain, enamel colours and gold. Naples; c. 1785–1795. Diameter: 10½ in (26 cm). London, Victoria and Albert Museum (no. C.1734–1919).

———

Opposite: Vase. Soft-paste porcelain, polychrome decoration. Buen Retiro; c. 1770–1775. Height: 13½ in (33.5 cm). London, Victoria and Albert Museum.

Most Capodimonte pieces of this later period are in the Neo-Classical style of the piece opposite, with clean lines and restrained decorative motifs derived from the Antique.

The paste and glaze used at Buen Retiro resembled those of Capodimonte and the French soft pastes. Since the designs of the Spanish factory also tended to imitate those of Sèvres the attribution of several pieces is disputed.

Below: Spray of flowers. Soft-paste porcelain. Vincennes; 1750. Length: 9½ in (24 cm). Sèvres, Musée National de Céramique (no. 1.895).

Below right: Snuffbox. Soft-paste porcelain, Vincennes; c. 1745. Height including lid: 2½ in (6 cm). Length: 3¼ in (8 cm). Limoges, Musée National Adrien-Dubouché (no. 1051).

Opposite: Plate. Soft-paste porcelain. Mennecy, with incised mark D.V.; c. 1770. Diameter: 9½ in (24 cm). Height: 1 in (2.5 cm). Sèvres, Musée National de Céramique (no. 22.296).

One of the most important departments at Vincennes was that devoted to the modelling of flowers, under the direction of Madame Gravant. An enormous variety of flowers were made, with fabric-covered stems, and these were much in vogue from 1748 onwards to decorate trinkets and to ornament chandeliers and wall brackets, or as bouquets. There were also vast arrangements in vases, such as that sent by the Dauphine Marie-Josèphe of Saxony as a present to her father in Dresden.

Opposite is one of the rare Vincennes snuffboxes, which is unusually large for its purpose. It is silver-mounted and delicately painted in tones of pink; the two birds may be emblematic of love or friendship.

The plates from the Mennecy factory are rare and are all similar, with a scalloped rim and "basket-weave" border moulded to resemble plaited wickerwork. Here the rustic scene in the middle is framed by a garland of leaves, a common motif of the period, found on faïence (for example that of Sceaux and Marseilles) as well as porcelain.

Below: Bowl with lid and stand. Soft-paste porcelain. Vincennes; 1753. Bowl height including lid: 6 in (15 cm); width: 8½ in (21.5 cm). Stand diameter: 9½ in (23.5 cm); height: 1¾ in (4.2 cm). Total height: 6¾ in (16.5 cm). Sèvres, Musée National de Ceramique, (no. 18.712).

Opposite: "Myrtle vase." Soft-paste porcelain. Sèvres; 1777. Height: 12½ in (31 cm). Width: 8¾ in (22.8 cm). London, Wallace Collection (no. XVIII 7).

This bowl is a fine example of the blue backgrounds of Vincennes. The artists of the factory were familiar with the blue of Chinese porcelain and sought the same charmingly "clouded" effect. The polychrome birds on the reserved areas surrounded by elaborate gold frames, are by the painter Chapelle.

The term "myrtle vase," used to describe contemporary designs for pieces such as the vase opposite, refers to the leaves which climb the sides of the vase to form handles. This is a particularly splendid example of Sèvres coloured ground, with the "partridge-eye" pattern on light blue. In the reserved panel is a basket of fruit tied with a ribbon, by the artist Taillandier who specialized in flower designs.

The purely ornamental vase opposite is of considerable historic interest. It was commissioned by Gustavus III of Sweden as a gift to Catherine the Great: in the painting the book lying on the barrel is open at a page which reads *"neutralité armée 1780. Catherine II. Gustave III"*. The decoration is by the painter and gilder Legrand, and the baluster form,

"celery-leaf" handles and reserved white fluting are all typical of the style of the period, as is the marine subject in the medallion.

The plate above with its fine ribbed edge, is typical of the porcelain of Tournai, which produced magnificent

pieces such as the splendid dinner services decorated with landscapes in crimson monochrome. Mireille Jottrand curator of the Mariemont Museum has pointed out that this type of monochrome appears to have been more widely used after the artist Duvivier joined the factory and ceased with his death in 1771.

Below: Plate. Soft-paste porcelain, enamel colours. Chelsea; c. 1755. Diameter: 9½ in (23.8 cm). Height: 1½ in (4 cm). London, Victoria and Albert Museum.

———————

Opposite left: Coffee pot with lid. Soft-paste porcelain, enamel colours. Chelsea; c. 1745–1749. Height including lid: 9 in (22.7 cm). Width: 5¼ in (13.3 cm). Boston, Museum of Fine Arts.

———————

Opposite right: Bottle. Soft-paste (phosphate) porcelain, enamel colours. Bow; c.1755. Height: 7½ in (19 cm). Diameter of body: 4½ in (10.5 cm). London, Victoria and Albert Museum.

This plate bears the red anchor mark, and the design is freely adapted from the botanical illustrations of Georg Dionysius Ehret, of Augsburg. Butterflies and insects have been added in characteristic Chelsea colours.

Both Bow and Chelsea copied the porcelain of Arita in Japan, especially the Kakiemon ware. They did so more or less faithfully, the design being modified according to the taste of each painter. The artist who painted the bottle opposite had a brilliant sense of design and has harmonized the Kakiemon colours perfectly. The iron red, manganese purple, blue and turquoise are used with exceptional intensity, matched by the predominantly turquoise design, on the other side of the bottle, of bamboo plants and rocks. In its boldness and impact such decoration is comparable with some Arita porcelain in the Ko-Kutani style – that is the style which imitated the old (Ko) late seventeenth-century style of Kutani in Honshu.

This coffee pot has the incised under-
glaze triangle that is the earliest known
mark of Chelsea ware. The relief
decoration of flowering sprays may be
derived from the *blanc-de-chine* ware of
Tê-hua in Fukien.

The East Anglian factory of Lowestoft was one of the first to adopt the formula for a paste containing bone ash invented at Bow, and this coffee pot is in its most ambitious style. The artist, whose bouquets often include a tulip in iron red, is known as the "Tulip Painter." There is a rose on the other side of this piece.

Opposite: Coffee pot. Soft-paste (phosphatic) porcelain, enamel colours. Lowestoft; c. 1775. Height including lid: 9 in (22.7 cm). Diameter at mouth: 3½ in (8.7 cm). London, Victoria and Albert Museum.

Below: Tureen with stand. Soft-paste porcelain, enamel colours and gold. Derby; c. 1800. Height including lid: 12½ in (31.7 cm). Width: 18 in (45.2 cm) London, Victoria and Albert Museum.

At the end of the eighteenth century the Derby factory produced some of the richest and most remarkable porcelain ever made in England. This piece was decorated by William Pegg, who painted his flowers from nature rather than from botanical drawings. The tureen bears the Derby mark of a crowned "D" with crossed batons and six dots, in blue enamel.

This coffee pot, its tapered outline derived from Turkey or Persia, is one of the earliest products of the Meissen factory. There are also Oriental details, such as the dragon's head at the base of the spout. The angular shape and the moulding and some of the handle betray the influence of silverware. The relief decoration is so unusual as to be exceptional. The design, in enamel colours, is of a branch with leaves, flowers and fruit, together with insects and birds. Garnets are set among the petals, in the center of some of the flowers.

The magnificent vase opposite is decorated by Johann Gregor Höroldt who, as artistic director at Meissen, invented a whole range of graduated colours. Although he drew on Oriental motifs, he also created a new and unmistakably European style that survives in porcelain painting to this day. In the 1720s his scenes are peopled with Chinese figures set in imaginary landscapes crowded with fantastic plants and animals. A dense flower pattern almost covers the medallion on the other side of this piece.

Plate. Hard-paste porcelain with over-glaze painting. Meissen, painted by Johann Ehrenfried Stadler; c. 1725. Diameter: 9¼ in (23.3 cm). Height: 1½ in (3.6 cm). Dresden, Staatliche Kunstsammlungen, Porzellansammlungen.

This piece shows how an original design may be modified by the individual artist who "copies" it. Stadler, to whom it is attributed, had worked at the Dresden *faïencerie* (founded in 1708), and was engaged at Meissen in 1723 or 1724, by Johann Gregor Höroldt, the art director. Stadler became one of the leading artists using on-glaze enamel painting. Not only did he transform his Oriental models in terms of design but he also developed a highly personal style of brushwork, using very delicate coloured hatching which resembles fine silk embroidery. In the piece illustrated the elegant, stylized border sets off the naturalistic subject in the center.

Dish. Hard-paste porcelain, over-glaze painting. Meissen; c. 1765. Diameter: 11¼ in (28 cm). Height: 2 in (5 cm). Dresden, Staatliche Kunstsammlungen, Porzellansammlungen.

This is one of many pieces decorated in the "Watteau" style with motifs painted in copper green over black lines, and usually showing a pair of lovers based on eighteenth-century copper-plate engravings after the paintings of Jean Antoine Watteau (1684–1721) and Nicolas Lancret (1690–1743). Unfortunately, the imitations on porcelain were sometimes executed without the skill of the original artists and some of them betray a certain clumsiness.

The very first Meissen statuettes, made in stoneware by Böttger about 1715, had been of Commedia dell'Arte figures. Harlequin, the most famous of these, appears in many versions in German porcelain of the eighteenth century. Meissen alone produced twenty-six different Commedia dell'Arte characters, including Pantaloon, the Doctor, Scaramouche and Columbine. It may well be that the modellers were inspired by the actors' expressive gestures.

Fine decoration of almost the entire surface, as on this bowl with lid, is characteristic of the best Meissen porcelain, and of that of other European centers. Christian Friedrich Höroldt joined Meissen in 1724. He became a leading painter there and though mentioned in a list of 1731 as a painter of "Japanese figures and landscapes," he was to specialize in non-Oriental harbour scenes. Note here his masterly treatment of a complex composition.

Group. Hard-paste porcelain with over-glaze painting. Meissen, Johann Joachim Kändler; 1737. Height: 7¼ in (18 cm). Length: 11½ in (29 cm). Dresden, Staatliche Kunstsammlungen, Porzellansammlungen.

Kändler entered the modelling department at Meissen in 1731. As its head he made large animal figures for the Japanese Palace and succeeded in producing dinner services more co-ordinated in shape and decoration than those hitherto known. From 1736 onwards he concentrated on small ornamental figures.

Below: Tureen. Hard-paste porcelain with over-glaze painting. Berlin: 1767–1768. Height including lid: 10 in (25 cm). Diameter of body: 9¾ in (24.7 cm). Berlin-Köpenick, Kunstgewerbemuseum.

Opposite: Vase. Hard-paste porcelain with over-glaze painting. Berlin; 1830. Height: 25½ in (64 cm). Diameter across top: 4½ in (11.2 cm). Berlin-Köpenick, Kunstgewerbemuseum.

The tureen opposite is from a service made for Frederick II's palace in Breslau. The design was repeated on another service commissioned in 1768 with scale-pattern medallions in crimson instead of blue, and in 1770–1771 the King ordered a third version for Potsdam. All three services have polychrome flower designs of bouquets, scattered blossoms and miniature garlands. On this Breslau tureen they are noticeably larger than they were on the Neues Palais service, more sharply drawn and brightly coloured, while the Potsdam pieces are decorated with even greater botanical accuracy. The flower painting of Berlin was at every stage influential on porcelain decoration in Germany.

This vase is evidence of attempts by factories such as Meissen, Berlin, even Vienna, to come to terms with changing aesthetic standards throughout Europe – changes which began during the last three decades of the eighteenth century. In the wake of the struggles of the middle classes against the aristocracy, who were seen as impeding social progress, the arts they had patronized came to be castigated as being neither serious nor useful. Luxurious, beautiful porcelain was singled out for particular disapproval, so greatly had it influenced European art as a whole in the final years of the splendour and ascendancy of the nobility, and many factories were forced to close as a result. A few managed to survive by dint of endless experiment with new shapes, but despite the considerable technical skill deployed it was clear – we need only examine the piece illustrated on the right – that the unique aesthetic qualities of porcelain were diminished in the process.

Formed of pierced rococo scrolls and set on its own matching bracket, the clock on the left is a masterpiece of Johann Wilhelm Lanz. The figures represent the Triumph of Time over Envy.

Bustelli created the most beautiful porcelain figures ever produced by a German factory. As the example opposite shows, they not only express great life and character, but also exploit to the full the qualities and possibilities peculiar to the medium.

Opposite: Figure group. Hard-paste porcelain, over-glaze painting. Vienna. Anton Grassi; c. 1780. Height: 15¼ in (38.2 cm). Vienna, Öesterreichisches Museum für angewandte Kunst.

Below: Place setting. Hard-paste porcelain with over-glaze painting. Vienna; c. 1745. Plate diameter: 9¼ in (23 cm); height: 1¾ in (4.2 cm). Cup height: 2½ in (6.4 cm); diameter across top: 2½ in (6 cm). Vienna, Öesterreichisches Museum für angewandte Kunst.

Most eighteenth-century European statuettes represent prototypes of all classes rather than individuals, but some – particularly in the case of busts – are actual likenesses, and there are figures and groups to which definite, if unverifiable, names have been attached. This group, for instance, is said to show the betrothal of the Archduchess Christina and Albrecht of Sachsen-Teschen. Copied time and again, the original was by Anton Grassi who, born in Vienna in 1755, became the factory's chief modeller in 1784. In a world dominated by Neo-Classicism his statuettes retained their rococo gaiety and charm.

Except for the gold rims this place setting, probably pieces from a larger service, is decorated in monochrome, unlike other Vienna ware of the period. Stylistically the design lies somewhere between East and West: details, such as the sharply-angled twigs and the treatment of leaves and chrysanthemum flowers, derive from China and Japan, while their composition in a unified pattern is in the tradition of Western formal design.

On the basis of comparison with two signed pieces, the dish above is attributed to Anton, son of the painter Karl Anreiter engaged by the Marchese Carlo Ginori, Doccia's founder; it dates from shortly before Anton's final return to Vienna in 1747. The unusual subject – a woman in Eastern dress, with a monkey – may have some hidden significance and is delicately executed. The flowers painted on the rim resemble those of Meissen from a slightly earlier period.

Doccia, near Florence, was founded in 1735 by the Marchese Carlo Ginori. After initial setbacks, it was enlarged by the founder's son, Lorenzo, who increased the production and made bigger objects. Karl Anreiter, a chemist and painter from Vienna, taught the Italian workmen, and this must explain the marked influence of the Viennese Du Paquier factory on the early ware of Doccia. The coffee pot illustrated opposite, with its mixture of styles, is a typical early piece. The general lines, and particularly those of the lid, are Italian, while the spout in the shape of a swan and the thickness of the handle are features inherited from Vienna.

Except for brief periods in other hands, Giovanni Battista Antonibon's factory, founded at Le Nove in 1728, remained in the possession of his family until the end of the nineteenth century. Perhaps as early as 1752, certainly from 1762, it was producing porcelain, and at the end of the eighteenth century creamware as well. The porcelain was hybrid, lacking the characteristics of German and Oriental hard paste but, though not normally of first-class quality, was occasionally used for such intricate and sensitive pieces as that illustrated opposite. The scene, with figures in Turkish costume, shows that a taste for exoticism was by no means dead at this date.

Cozzi's factory was active from 1765 until 1812, and its products reflect the Meissen and Oriental styles then most fashionable. A style of rococo moulding derived from contemporary silverware was evolved before the 1750s, and was combined with naturalistic flower paintings. The tureen above faithfully reproduces these characteristics. Note the swirling lines of base and handles, and the large flowers on the body and lid. Flowers tied in a bunch to form the handle is an example of the *trompe l'oeil* decoration used in *faienceries* and porcelain factories alike.

Below: Ewer and basin. Hard-paste porcelain, gilded on black background. Sèvres; c. 1790. Ewer height: 9¾ in (24.5 cm); width 6¾ in (17 cm). Basin length: 14¾ in (37 cm); height: 2¾ in (7 cm). Sèvres, Musée National de Céramique (no. 5291).

Opposite: Plate. Hard-paste porcelain. Sèvres; c. 1792. Diameter: 9½ in (24 cm). Height: 1¾ in (3 cm). Sèvres, Musée National de Céramique (no. 12.829).

The substances imitated by the artists of Sèvres included lacquer, for gilding, the luminosity of which was enhanced by platinum. Oriental motifs of this period are modified entirely in accordance with European taste. The decoration on these pieces is by one of the best gilders at Sèvres, Le Guay.

Technical advances made at the end of the century encouraged the Sèvres painters to all sorts of experiments, especially in the imitation of different materials such as tortoiseshell as seen from the illustration. The bird in the gold-bordered central medallion is not merely ornamental as bird motifs had been before, but is taken from a natural-history engraving.

Below: Cup and saucer. Hard-paste porcelain. Paris. Rue du Petit Carrousel factory; c. 1790. Cup height: 6¼ in (15.8 cm); width: 6¼ in (15.8 cm). Saucer diameter: 9½ in (24 cm); height: 1¼ in (3.3 cm). Total height: 6½ in (16.5 cm). Sèvres, Musée National de Céramique (no. 479).

—————

Opposite above: Bowl with lid and stand. Hard-paste porcelain. Paris. Rue de Clignancourt factory; 1783. Bowl height including lid: 4½ in (11.5 cm); width: 7¼ in (18 cm). Stand diameter: 8 in (20 cm); height: 1¼ in (3 cm). Total height: 5 in (12.5 cm). Sèvres, Musée National de Céramique (no. 7.802).

—————

Opposite below: Sugar basin with lid. Hard-paste porcelain. Limoges; c. 1780. Height including lid: 3½ in (9 cm). Diameter: 3½ in (8.5 cm). Limoges, Musée National Adrien-Dubouché (no. 1.414).

The charming decoration of coloured butterflies on a ground of finely gilded leaves and flowers exactly suits the chalice shape of the cup illustrated above. The interior in solid gilding shows that this style was no longer a monopoly of Sèvres. The Rue du Petit Carrousel mark which appears on this and other pieces may refer to a firm of porcelain dealers and decorators in Paris rather than to a factory.

The important Clignancourt factory at Montmartre was under the patronage of the King's brother, the Comte de Provence, and used his initials, LSX (Louis Stanislas Xavier), as a mark. It attracted talented artists, and among the special types of decoration they pioneered is a sepia monochrome, *camaïeu grisaille*, invented by the Viennese Georg Lamprecht who signs the bowl shown above. *"Georges Lamprecht pinxit à Paris 1783"* may be read on the painted milestone. In the following year he was summoned to work at Sèvres.

When kaolin was found at St. Yrieix near Limoges, André Massié set up a porcelain factory as part of his *faïencerie*. In partnership with the Grellet brothers he obtained a royal license and worked from 1773 to 1777 under the protection of the Comte d'Artois (hence the mark CD). The factory was amalgamated with Sèvres in 1784. There are many pieces with armorial decoration, such as this sugar basin.

Pheasants, being birds of Oriental origin, added an exotic touch to the range of birds and animals modelled as porcelain statuettes. A tendency of Plymouth figurines to droop in the kiln is counteracted in the pair opposite by the birds being perched in a somewhat unnatural manner on tree stumps as supports.

Vases such as the example above, with inner containers, were made of both metal and porcelain for serving hot roast chestnuts in eighteenth-century Holland. The tall lid of this example has a moulding of little arched indentations around the rim and below the knop, while the remaining surface of lid and vase is painted with coloured birds against a landscape background. Rings on either side act as handles.

North American Ceramics

Ceramics in the New World began as a continuation of European traditions. Early settlers brought with them the ceramic forms and techniques of their homelands, particularly those of England and Germany. From these European sources, augmented periodically by those of the Far East (particularly Japan), arose the basis of what was to become an American ceramic style. Eventually these influences would be assimilated and melded with the energy and spirit of the American ethos to produce the original and distinctive character of American ceramics today.

Of necessity, the earliest American wares were utilitarian in nature – these crocks, bowls, jugs and bottles were produced in both red earthenware and buff stoneware from the late 1600s until the end of the nineteenth century. The redware plates, jugs, crocks, jam jars and other useful items produced by German potters in both the northern and southern colonies were often cleverly decorated by trailing slip (clay thinned to a creamy consistency) over the surface before firing. Some of these plates and jugs were commemorative objects, carefully and often naively inscribed with names, dates and traditional German decorative motifs.

Ceramics in Canada had similar beginnings, with the most prevalent early influence coming from France. By the nineteenth century, however, England was supplying all but the most common functional wares. Redware was the basis of Canadian production as stoneware clays were not available locally. It was not until the arrival of American immigrants in the middle of the nineteenth century that the expertise and the necessary materials were available for expanded production.

The production of fine ceramic wares in the United

Hydrangea vase. Rookwood Pottery. Albert Valentien, decorator; 1904. Earthenware. Height: 14¼ in (36.5 cm). Syracuse, N.Y., Everson Museum of Art (Museum Purchase with Funds from the Dorothy and Robert Riester Ceramic Fund). Early Rookwood artists tried to simulate French barbotine ware, in which decoration was applied with coloured slips under the glaze.

Styles of American ceramics

Jug. W. H. Farrar and Company; 1841–57. Stoneware. The cobalt decoration on this New York State jug is derived from German folk motifs. Syracuse, N.Y., Everson Museum of Art (gift of Mrs William J. Davison).

States was impeded by the relatively low cost of imported wares and the lack of technical knowledge among American potters. Though soft-paste porcelain was successfully produced in Philadelphia before the American Revolution, it was not until the second decade of the nineteenth century that porcelain production became a viable undertaking. Creamware closely akin to English Staffordshire ware was produced in various locations following the Revolution. Rockingham ware was also made at various American manufactories, most successfully at Jersey City, New Jersey, and later at Bennington, Vermont, and in Canada in Quebec and Ontario. In the late nineteenth century, the United States Pottery Company, a Bennington firm, also made Parian ware, having a porcelain body said to resemble Parian marble. This successful firm produced vases, pitchers and figurines, many derived from English and French prototypes.

The earliest potteries in America were usually family establishments, many of them handed down from father to son, like the Crolius and Remmey potteries in New York. But as more English potters emigrated to America, they brought with them the technical knowledge and production methods of industrialized England, and soon the making of ceramic wares became a matter of mass production rather than handcraft. Here began the divergence of art and industry that was to be addressed by the potters of the Arts and Crafts period.

The production of what was to become the prototype of American art pottery began at Rookwood Pottery in Cincinnati, Ohio in 1880. In keeping with the Arts and Crafts ideals of the time, one of the main objectives of Maria Longworth Nichols in establishing Rookwood was to "advance the manufacture of artistic work as well as to make cheap ware pretty." She, and other ceramists who followed her lead, wished to have the best of two worlds: the aesthetic sensibilities of handcrafted wares combined with the economic advantages of mass production. This she accomplished by a division of labour: forms were thrown or moulded by potters and then decorated by other artisans. Thus the pieces, though handmade, were not the work of a single artistic sensibility.

Rookwood was a success, both artistically and eventually financially. It spawned many imitators, some of whom were successful, others only marginally so. Among the imitators of Rookwood Standard wares were J. B. Owens, Roseville, A. Radford, Edwin Bennett, Denver China and Weller potteries.

While many of the art potteries subscribed to the ideals of the Arts and Crafts movement, their wares did not always reflect the Arts and Crafts style. Many of the objects, including the ubiquitous Rookwood Standard wares, spoke more of Victoriana, with their high-gloss glazes, sentimental floral and figural decoration, and adherence to naturalistic renderings. But as the Arts and Crafts movement gained momentum in the United States and more and more homes were reflecting that taste, potteries heeded the demand for ceramic wares to complement this sparer, more restrained style.

William Grueby's pottery produced heavy, sculptural vessels with deep matte glazes. Gates (Teco), Marblehead, Walrath, and Newcomb potteries adopted the subdued matte glazes and the reserved stylized motifs now recognized as characteristic of the Arts and Crafts style. Even Rookwood and Weller, the progenitors of the art pottery phenomenon, turned to matte glazes and simplified forms and

Vase. Grueby Pottery; c. 1900. Earthenware. The heavy potting and ubiquitous matte-green glaze place this piece squarely within the Arts and Crafts style. Syracuse, N.Y., Everson Museum of Art (Museum Purchase with Funds from the Dorothy and Robert Riester Ceramic Fund).

Cookie Jar. Arthur Baggs; 1938. Stoneware. This "ultimate cookie jar" is one of the masterpieces of American ceramics. Syracuse, N.Y., Everson Museum of Art.

decoration, mindful of the demands of their buying public. Adelaide Robineau crusaded relentlessly for the more conventionalized designs of the Arts and Crafts style.

Robineau was a studio ceramist – she worked alone and created unique objects in whose formation she was involved from start to finish. Unlike the art potteries, where teams of decorators worked on forms created by others, Robineau's studio was a one-person operation (although her husband often helped her with the firing of her pieces). She devised her own clay bodies, concocted her own glazes, threw the forms and decorated, glazed and fired them herself. Few women at that time were involved in the technical aspects of ceramic production. It was considered proper for women to be decorators only, rather than be part of more intellectual technical pursuits, or to throw on the wheel, a physically demanding job regarded as better left to men.

The ideals of the art world gave way to the realities of the market place as art potteries became more and more reliant on mass production methods and less attention was given to handcraftsmanship. Ceramics as an art form became the mandate of studio potters like Robineau as the ceramics industry turned to the production of functional wares.

The Great Depression that struck in 1929 delivered the final blow to what was already a fading art pottery movement. The infrastructure of American ceramics had also changed. Formal university study was replacing the on-the-job training that was prevalent in the art potteries and family establishments of earlier years. Ceramics was taught at Ohio State University and Alfred University in New York, and at many other schools across the nation (Robineau taught at Syracuse University). The Cleveland Insti-tute of Art became a center of ceramic activity when its students, in the midst of the Depression, proceeded to produce innovative and lively clay sculpture. Relatively small in size, this figural work was brightly coloured, often whimsical and entirely approachable. Viktor Schreckengost, one of the most successful and original of the "Cleveland school," as the group came to be known, said that one of their aims in producing this witty work was to "relieve depression blues." Animals were a favourite subject for these artists as were mythological figures and performers of all kinds. Black figures were also popular.

Finding no American tradition of clay sculpture upon which to build, these young ceramists turned to Europe, specifically Vienna, for examples. Many young Viennese artists were working in a more expressionist vein. They respected the inherent qualities of the material; their work looked as if it was made of clay, pliant and wheel-thrown, with glazes applied loosely and allowed to flow freely over the forms. The Austrian work was witty, sophisticated, even at times sexually suggestive, and it completely entranced the Americans who had seen it in European exhibitions that had toured the United States.

While the majority of the clay sculpture produced between 1925 and 1950 was relatively small in size, a few artists did work on a very large scale. Viktor Schreckengost created immense figures and relief sculptures for public buildings, mainly in the northern Ohio area. Waylande Gregory, influenced by Renaissance and later European sculpture, produced allegorical figures for fountains and other public areas. His *Fountain of the Atom*, created for the New York World's Fair of 1939, remains one of the largest clay sculptural groupings of modern times.

Other European ceramists came to America during

Factory/Farm Worker. Waylande Gregory; 1938. Stoneware. This Janus-like figure was the centerpiece for a sculptural group called American Imports and Exports, *commissioned by General Motors for the 1939 New York World's Fair. Private Collection.*

The Dictator. Viktor Schreckengost; 1939. Earthenware. Schreckengost was one of the few artists who dared to speak out against the rise of Nazism. Here, a sleeping British lion lies at the feet of a strumming Nero, about whose throne cherubs gambol with the likenesses of Hitler, Mussolini, Stalin and Hirohito. Syracuse, N.Y., Everson Museum of Art (gift of the Artist).

the 1920s and 1930s, the most notable being the Austrians Gertrud and Otto Natzler. The Natzlers worked together, Gertrud throwing remarkably thin classic forms and Otto glazing and firing them, creating unique and luscious surfaces. Marguerite Wildenhain settled in California and established Pond Farm pottery, where she worked and taught for many years. Maija Grotell came from Finland and headed the ceramics department at Cranbrook Academy in Bloomfield Hills, Michigan. Under her direction, Cranbrook became one of the major American centers for ceramic education. Sam Haile, an Englishman, taught briefly at Alfred University, but nonetheless wielded a great influence on American ceramics, bringing a freer, more expressionist style to the medium.

World War II brought the heightened creativity of the American clay sculpture movement to an end. Many of the ceramists went on to pursue other interests after the war. When the interest in clay sculpture would be revived a few decades later, the whimsy would turn to a sharper humour and the figure would reappear in a radically different guise.

Extreme changes were to come about in American ceramics in the decades immediately following the war and significant to these developments were the influences felt from the American art scene in general. Abstract expressionism was not confined to painting alone; American ceramics also felt its touch. Just as painters became involved with the self-referential qualities of paint, so ceramists were caught up in the expressive qualities of the clay. This, combined with the influence of Japanese pottery, led young American ceramists to break with the traditional European aesthetic that had dominated American ceramics since its beginning. The results

were revolutionary. A moving force in this clay revolution was Peter Voulkos, a young talented artist who attracted a group of creative ceramists, many of them students, at the Otis Art Institute in Los Angeles.

These West Coast artists liberated clay from the confines of the vessel. No longer considered solely as a functional container, the vessel became a vehicle for expression and at this point it often was an expression of the medium itself, particularly in the hands of Voulkos. This exploration of the material took these artists, and others influenced by them, in many different directions, each exploring aspects of the art form such as volume, form, surface, line, colour, iconography, minimalism, constructivism, expressionism and other "isms" prevalent at the time. Work was by turns large and small, glazed and unglazed, sculptural and planar, figural and abstract.

Influenced by Japanese aesthetics, Voulkos and other American ceramists rejected the traditional European requisites of symmetry, perfection of form and artistic control. The intuitive approach of the Japanese folk potters appealed to the Americans who soon learned to allow the clay and the fire to play a freer role in the formation of the work. The result was a looser, fresher approach to form and the acceptance of accident as a relevant part of the creative process.

The focus on Japan was initiated mainly by the philosophy of Bernard Leach, an Englishman who had spent much of his life in the East and who had studied with the traditional folk potters in Japan. He espoused a return to functionalism and believed that pottery should spring from the lives and work of simple people who are close to nature and the land.

In dramatic contrast to the subtle, subdued work produced by the followers of Leach, there developed

Whiplash! Richard Shaw; 1978. Porcelain. Shaw is one of the most important figures in the American "Super-object" school. In this work, photo-silkscreen images create exact reproductions in porcelain of the ubiquitous blue bicycle playing cards. The trompe l'oeil *book is stamped on the spine with "Whiplash!" and "Richard Shaw." Syracuse, N.Y., Everson Museum of Art (Museum Purchase with Matching Funds from the National Endowment for the Arts).*

Vase. John Mason; 1986. Stoneware. The baroque twist given to this work imparts the sense of contained energy found in the work of a number of American ceramists in recent years. Syracuse, N.Y., Everson Museum of Art (Museum Purchase with Funds from the Dorothy and Robert Riester Ceramic Fund).

in California a new school of sculptural ceramists whose work was radical, irreverent, humorous, often offensive. The initiator of this style, aptly dubbed funk art, was Robert Arneson, a professor at the University of California at Davis. Funk artists drew inspiration and images from many sources and the work they produced was just as varied. Wordplay and visual puns played an important part in this style, and artists often seemed to be more concerned with shock value than with aesthetic value. The work was intentionally sloppy, a pointed rejection of the European tradition of highly crafted and delicate porcelain sculpture of the eighteenth and nineteenth centuries.

This revolution in American ceramics had deep and lasting effects. It led to wide experimentation and a great diversity of approaches by American ceramists. The super-object is the opposite of funk, meticulously crafted, illusory to the point of *trompe l'oeil*, exemplified by the work of Marilyn Levine and Richard Shaw. Clay sculpture reached immense proportions with the giant, often menacing, figures of businessmen and housewives created by Viola Frey and the haunting, archaic revenants of Stephen DeStaebler. Arneson and Richard Notkin speak out on political and social subjects, but in totally different styles.

The vessel returned with greater strength and presence than ever before, and with just as much diversity as contemporary clay sculpture. Variously termed the "smart pot" and the "gallery pot," it now was viewed in terms of aesthetics rather than function. Traditional sources, only too recently taboo for the vessel maker, enticed artists like Adrian Saxe, Ron Nagle, Michael Frimkess, Beatrice Wood, and Canadian ceramist Leopold Foulem into creating not imitations but exceedingly original works whose roots were not always immediately apparent.

Many Canadian ceramists such as Roseline Delisle and Paul Mathieu work in the United States as well as in Canada, and the distinction between Canadian and American ceramics is difficult to make, since ceramic style has become so complex, blurring international boundaries. But Canada, too, has experienced a resurgence of interest in ceramics, with artists such as Ann Mortimer and Les Manning campaigning for support and acknowledgement of the medium.

American ceramics is as diverse as the culture from which it has sprung, and this is one of its most telling characteristics. Without the baggage of tradition, Americans have been free to peruse the works of other cultures and other times and to choose only those elements that would serve their purposes. Out of this amalgam has grown a new and original body of work tempered by the American spirit that now influences many of those cultures to which it once referred.

Hare Basket. Kenneth Ferguson; 1987–88. Stoneware. Ferguson has been one of the most influential teachers of ceramics in America. His own work is honest and forthright, and he encourages his students to achieve the same honesty of purpose and materials, while also directing them to peruse the ceramics of other times and cultures for inspiration and technical knowledge. Syracuse, N.Y., Everson Museum of Art (Museum Purchase with Funds given by friends in memory of Lenore Goldstein).

Bonnin and Morris of Philadelphia made the first soft-paste porcelain in America, predating the factory of William Tucker by more than fifty years. The venture, patterned on contemporary English wares, was short-lived, however, and few pieces produced by Bonnin and Morris have survived. Apparent in this small dish with its traditional shell form and blue-and-white decoration are European influences.

Muller utilized American motifs in the creation of this vase for the Centennial Exposition of 1876, indicating that Americans were beginning to assert a sense of national identity in their work. The form is of traditional European origin, and the decorative style is derived from Sèvres and Wedgwood, although Muller chose to include typical American animals, scenes, figures and inventions, such as the steamboat, sewing machine, and telegraph, in this homage to his adopted land. The Centennial Exposition was a watershed in American ceramics; here, American ceramists were exposed to the best of European and Oriental ceramics.

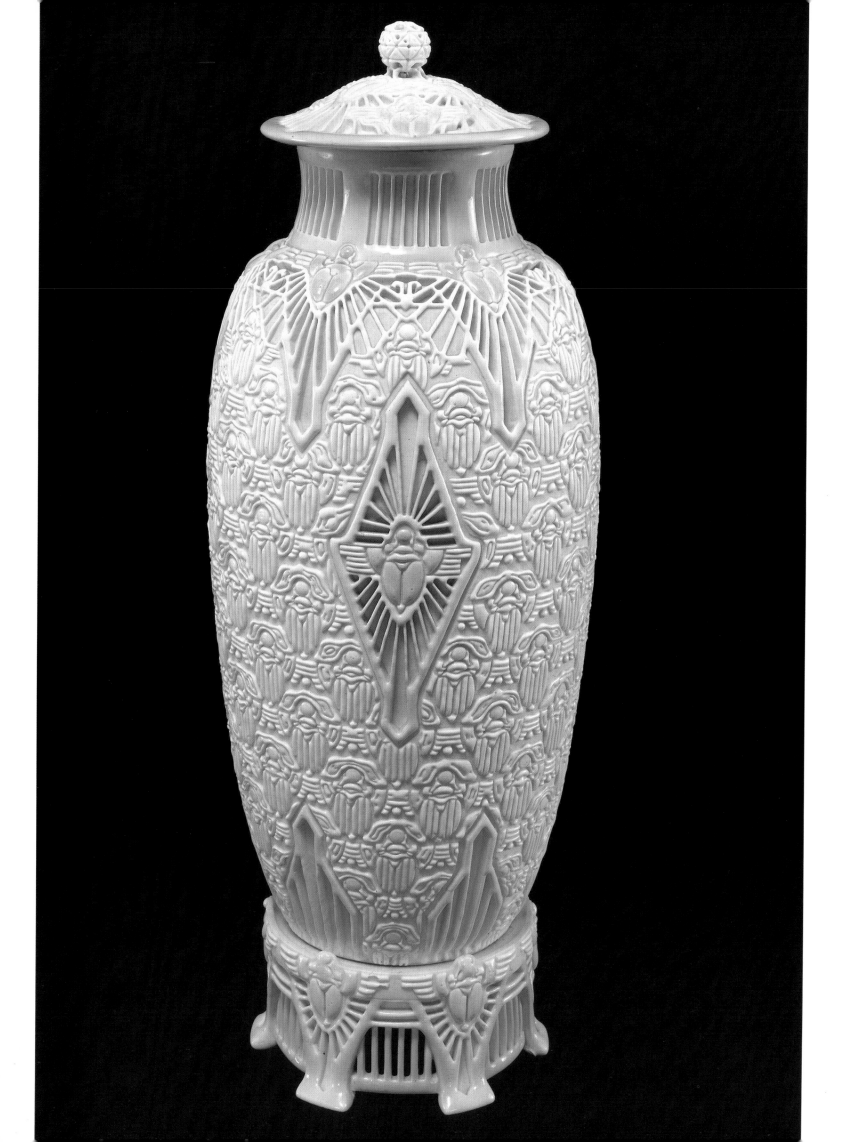

Rightly called *The Apotheosis of the Toiler*, the vase opposite reputedly took over one thousand hours to carve. The excised design of scarabs refers to the ancient Egyptian symbol for rebirth and creative powers. The piece is in three parts – lid, vase and base. Robineau, the doyenne of American studio ceramists, created exquisite porcelains that are among the most sought-after of American ceramics today. She experimented constantly, producing elegant pieces with carved, incised, and excised decoration. She created her own glazes, many of them unique crystallines used in combination with matte or gloss glazes, producing works as complex technically as they were aesthetically. Her work is refined, even precious at times, but always restrained and seemly. Robineau eschewed the naturalistic decoration of the art potteries and used stylized motifs in her own work; she continually encouraged American china painters and ceramists to adopt conventionalization. Her publication, *Keramic Studio*, provided examples and advice for fledgling American artists.

Sicard, a student of Clement Massier in France, came to Zanesville, Ohio, to work at Weller Pottery, where he used metallic lusters on iridescent grounds. The results were deeply rich backgrounds of reds, purples and blues with elegant linear decorations in metallic gold in the art-nouveau style. The simple forms further enhanced the elegance of the surface decoration. Weller Pottery in Zanesville was one of the most successful of the American art potteries. Over the years, hundreds of designs and shapes were added to the line of wares and less hand workmanship was used. Motifs ranged from flowers (the most common theme) to portraits, particularly those of American Indians.

While clay sculpture was a major focus during the pre-World War II years, the vessel was certainly not neglected. Glen Lukens explored materials indigenous to the West Coast to produce bowls, plates and other vessels; gritty unglazed areas reveal the nature of the clay and the hands that formed it, whereas thick, viscous glazes sensuously envelop the objects. This bowl, with its simple, almost primal form, has a luscious glaze whose brilliant colour and texture contrast markedly with the rough clay body. It speaks most clearly of the materials from which it was created, as well as of the processes that formed it. Arthur Baggs also worked during this period, creating classic vessels, the most famous being his "ultimate" cookie jar.

The piece opposite, made after Wieselthier's arrival in America, illustrates the Viennese style that she helped to promulgate here. The sections are hollow, with details applied and glazes used freely. The almond eyes and arched brows, as well as the light-hearted attitude toward the subject matter, also appeared in works by Americans who were influenced by the Viennese style. A number of American artists went to Vienna to study, including Viktor Schreckengost, Russell Barnett Aitken and Edward Winter, the enamelist who was to become the husband of ceramist Thelma Frazier Winter. In turn Viennese artists, notably Vally Wieselthier and Susy Singer came to America to work, bringing with them the Viennese style and techniques.

Taming the Unicorn. Vally Wieselthier; c. 1941. Earthenware. Height: 20½ in (52.5 cm). Width: 14½ in (37.5 cm). Diameter: 14½ in (37.5 cm). Syracuse, N.Y., Everson Museum of Art (gift of IBM Corporation).

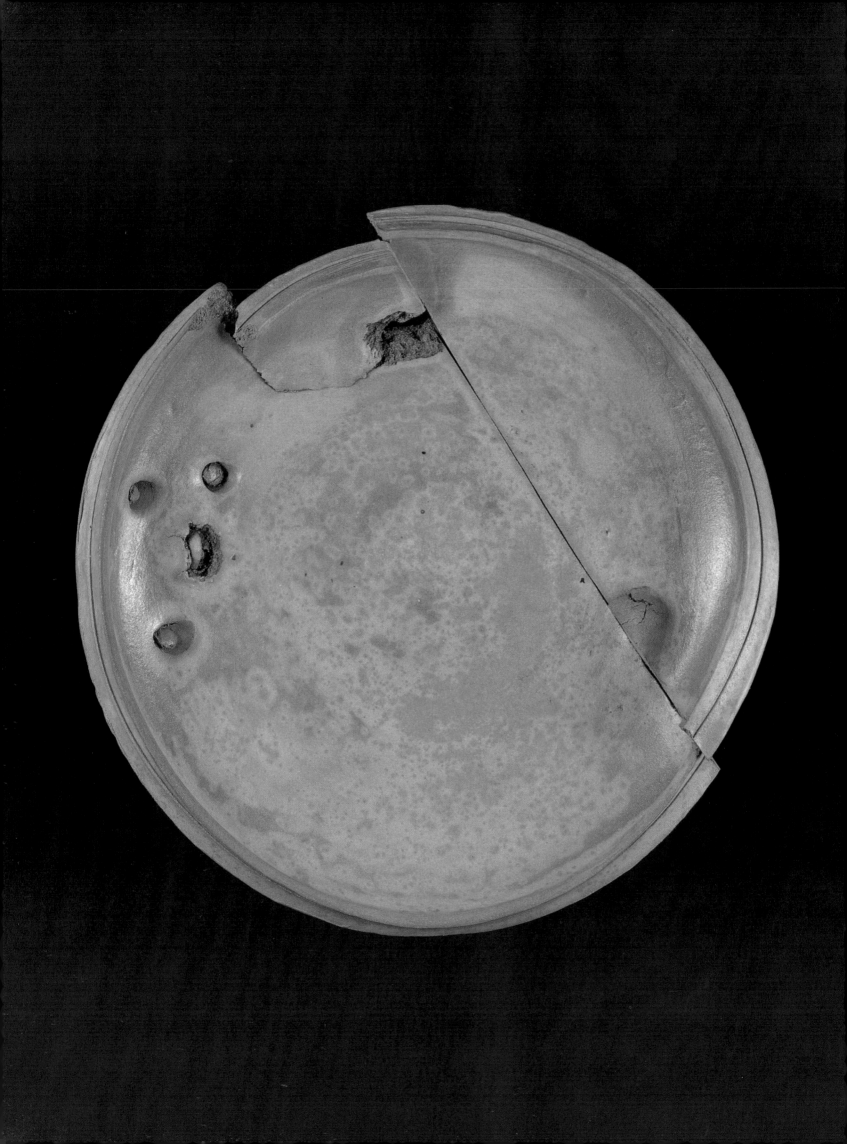

Opposite: Plate. Peter Voulkos; 1978. Stoneware. Diameter: 22½ in (57.5 cm). Syracuse, N.Y., Everson Museum of Art (Museum Purchase with Matching Funds from the National Endowment for the Arts).

Below: George and Mona in the Baths of Coloma. Robert Arneson; 1976. Earthenware. Length: 55½ in (142.5 cm). Amsterdam, Collection Stedelijk Museum.

Under Voulkos, the basic concept of the vessel underwent unrelenting scrutiny and ultimately fundamental change. Voulkos pierced, gouged and tore the walls of his forms, rendering them incapable of containment, and in doing so freed ceramics from the traditional role of function and elevated it to the status of art, although it was many years before this fact was widely recognized or accepted in the art world. In the plate shown opposite, the malleability of the clay is accented by the cut and lifted sections of the plate and by the tear that contrasts the smooth surface with the grittier inner texture of the clay. Punctured and torn, the plate ceases to be functional and becomes instead an aesthetic object. Peter Voulkos was a pivotal figure in the history of contemporary ceramics. Masterful on the wheel and charismatic as a teacher and lecturer, he influenced and inspired a generation of American ceramists.

Throughout the 1970s and 1980s Robert Arneson, the doyen of American clay sculptors, created a series of portraits and self-portraits, usually combining them with visual or verbal puns. His portraits range from Van Gogh to Elvis Presley, with particular emphasis on common, banal imagery.

Here, George Washington looks tellingly at Mona Lisa, who wears her characteristic smile. George is portrayed as he appears on the dollar bill – including a greenish cast and the marks of the engraver's burin. Probably no other two archetypal images are more widely recognized. Recently Arneson has used his art in a more serious vein, yet with the same satiric irony, in a series of works decrying nuclear armament. Arneson's importance to contemporary ceramics is incalculable. He reintroduced the use of colour in sculpture and renewed an interest in portraiture, while restoring clay as an acceptable medium for serious sculpture.

The gentle, yet monumental, form of this jar combines with the richness of materials to produce a great sense of dignity. It illustrates clearly the influence of Bernard Leach and the Japanese *mingei* potters on American ceramics. Many young ceramists were attracted to Leach's philosophy, the most important of whom was Warren MacKenzie, who worked with Leach for two years in England and had returned to the United States to promulgate his teachings. MacKenzie continues to produce finely formed functional wares whose honesty and vitality are equal to that of the Japanese counterparts. He was also an influential teacher, although many of his students have not adhered as strictly to the Leach traditions as he has.

For centuries, artists have drawn on the surface of a ceramic form. But during the 1960s a number of ceramists became involved with the idea in new and innovative ways, usually having to do with the juxtaposition of two- and three-dimensional form of painting and sculpture. Some artists played with illusion, others with form. Rudy Autio has combined the vessel form with the female figure in his work for the past thirty years. In the piece opposite, the surface of the form is ambivalent to the figural painting that enlivens it. The vigorous drawing serves more to accent the form than to define it, and yet the two, line and form, meld together into a single unified whole.

Blue and Gold Chalice. Beatrice Wood; 1987. Earthenware. Height: 10¾ in (27.5 cm).
Collection of Mr and Mrs Charles Diamond, Newport Beach, California.

Horse and Rider. Mary Frank; 1982. Stoneware. Height: 23 in (58.75 cm). Width: 46¾ in (120 cm). Diameter: 27¾ (70 cm). Syracuse, N.Y., Everson Museum of Art (Museum Purchase with Funds from the Stanley Coyne Foundation).

Beatrice Wood works with both vessel and sculptural forms. Her richly lusterous glazes and chalice-shaped vessels, such as the example opposite, evoke a sense of ancient, perhaps biblical, cultures. In Western ceramics, lusters have been used almost exclusively as accent decoration, but Wood uses them for their rich patinas, which add an aura of antiquity, and for their iridescence, which adds sumptuousness to the simple but monumental forms. Much of her sculpture carries on the traditions of the 1940s but also relates directly to the figural work of the 1960s and 70s. It is humorous, lively and often subtly suggestive. Wood moved in the Dada circles of Marcel Duchamp, and her work continues to exhibit his influence in its exoticism and disregard for convention.

Mary Frank's figurative sculpture is indicative of the renewed interest in ceramic sculpture during the past thirty years, but her work is uniquely personal and inventive. Eschewing glazes in order to capitalize on the sensuousness of the clay surfaces, Frank has created figures full of passion, earthiness and intimacy. Like the material from which they are made, the figures seem to be in a state of metamorphosis or transformation. This horseman, perhaps drawn from the Apocalypse, struggles to stay astride his horse, which has split and threatens to dissolve beneath him. The plasticity of the unglazed clay accents the sense of transformation and change that is occurring here.

Below: Untitled Jar (Golden Arches). Adrian Saxe; 1986. Porcelain and earthenware. Height: 21 in (53.7 cm). Syracuse, N.Y., Everson Museum of Art (gift of Mr and Mrs John Dietz).

Opposite: Untitled (Standing Man, Yellow Tie). Viola Frey; 1989–90. Earthenware. Height: 117 in (300 cm). Courtesy Rena Bransten Gallery.

Dubbed by critic Peter Schjeldahl "the smart pot," the vessel has recently become the subject of intense interest and investigation by contemporary ceramists who have focused on decoration, imagery, historicism, assemblage, illusion, or other aesthetic issues in relation to this most ancient of forms. Ken Price, Ralph Bacerra, Ruth Duckworth, Betty Woodman, Akio Takamori, Elsa Rady and Wayne Higby have pursued individual concerns with the vessel. The works of Adrian Saxe are self-consciously ambiguous in that they juxtapose function with decadent opulence and refinement with sharp satire. Influenced by the courtly porcelains of Sèvres, Saxe creates elegant, richly decorated forms which he often gives a personal or ironic twist and places on a raku base. In the example opposite, the stately and finely wrought vessel is topped by lustrous "golden arches" and sits upon an earthy dais of raku.

Frey's monumental figures, often over ten feet tall, have been influential in the direction of contemporary ceramic sculpture. Her modern "heroes," often menacing businessmen or housewives in brightly floral housedresses, echo the psychological concerns focused upon by contemporary clay sculptors such as Robert Brady, Judy Moonelis, Michael Lucero and Arthur Gonzales. Frey tempers the powerful monumentality of her figures by adding slashes of primary colour, which she uses less in a sculptural sense and more as a painter. The result is a complex relationship between surface and form. Clay sculpture presently reflects the diversification found in contemporary vessels. Colour, rich and full blown, has returned, and the line between painting and sculpture continues to be blurred. There is a renewed interest in the malleability of the material, but this is focused on the modelling of the figure rather than on abstract form.

Chinese Ceramics

Asia, defined by one great historical philosopher as "the continent of origins *par excellence*," has made extraordinary contributions to the civilization of humanity. It is difficult to make any sort of list or establish just which contributions were the most important, but, setting aside its great religious and moral ideas and taking into consideration only material products, it can be safely said that, apart from silk, nothing aroused such lively and widespread admiration in the West as the porcelain from the Far East, and from China in particular.

During the course of the sixteenth century, vases, dishes and other wares, whose workmanship and rich decoration had completely captivated Europeans, were already arriving from the Far East via Goa, aboard Portuguese merchantmen, or even via Mexico, on board Spanish vessels. During the seventeenth century these imports became part of a trading programme organized on a vast scale. Further impetus was provided by a lucky act of piracy, when the Dutch captured two Portuguese carracks, one near the island of St. Helena (1602) and the other off Johore (1603), laden with Chinese porcelain. The success of these cargoes at auction in Amsterdam led to the term *kraak-porcelein* (carrack porcelain) being used to describe Ming and blue-and-white wares, and, during the decades that followed, the Dutch East India Company imported millions of pieces of Oriental porcelain. But this was something more than just a reflection of demand and fashion: it was a contact that educated European tastes, in some cases stimulating cultural curiosity and later also encouraging collectors. The tableware and vases arriving from China and also, as we shall see later, from Japan, were appreciated not just for practical, utilitarian reasons and for their relatively low cost. Their

Three-colour glazed court lady sitting on a stool. T'ang dynasty; late seventh–early eighth century A.D. Height: 17¼ in (44.2 cm). Boston, Museum of Fine Arts (no. 50.1807, Charles B. Hoyt Collection). Representing the courtly fashion of the high T'ang period, the aristocratic figure is shown sitting in the Western style.

Marks of Chinese Ceramics

Mark of the T'ang dynasty (618–906 A.D.). In China, the custom of marking wares dates back to the Han dynasty (206 B.C.–220 A.D.). The marks, examples of which are shown here and in the following pages, take a variety of forms.

delicacy and aesthetic harmony also had a certain impact on Europeans, making people aware that these objects reflected a way of life, an artistic tradition.

Major archaeological researches during this century have cast new light on the earliest stages of Chinese ceramic production, and it is the Neolithic period that has produced the greatest surprises, with pieces of extraordinary beauty. The discoveries made during the 1920s by the Swede J. Gunnar Andersson, first at Henan, in the village of Yang-shao (the site from which the name of the culture is derived), and later farther to the west, in eastern Kansu, revealed a very interesting type of pottery, produced by farming communities. Some of the most outstanding wares are of the Pan-shan type, which were made of very fine clay, elegantly modelled without the use of a proper wheel, very deftly decorated and with thin walls and a smooth, compact surface. Their surprisingly sophisticated decoration displays crisscross lines, chequerboard motifs, jagged outlines and whorls converging on a central eye (page 296). As for date, they probably originate from the third or second millennium B.C. Another, undoubtedly later type of pottery, even though in some areas it occurs alongside wares of the Yang-shao culture, is the black pottery named after a village in Shantung province, Lung-shan, which is found throughout both eastern and central-northern China and also further to the south, in the Yangtze basin. These wares, which represent the first examples of Chinese turned pottery and have no painted decoration, are distinguished by their black colour, obtained by firing in a reducing atmosphere.

Although less striking than Pan-shan wares, Lung-shan pottery is equally important. On the one hand, its surprising variety of shapes anticipates the many different developments in Chinese ceramics, while, on the other, its sharply defined silhouettes recall the typical lines of contemporary bronzes. This link with metalware is also a distinctive trait of much of the grey earthenware excavated in the regions that saw the rise of the first historical dynasty in northern China, that of the Shang (eighteenth–eleventh century B.C.). The later ceramics of the Chou dynasty (1028–221 B.C.), whether made for domestic or funerary use, would also display the same quality. In other words, from the earliest beginnings in the Bronze Age, and for many centuries to come, ceramic styles developed in tandem with their metal equivalents. This constant made its mark, and one of its earliest consequences was to encourage potters to try and discover a type of paste that would fulfil the demands, in terms of both shape and decoration, imposed by the bronze models. In fact, in as early as the Shang period there did exist a type of very tough pottery obtained by using pure kaolin, the basic material, it should be remembered, of porcelain paste. The same period also saw the creation of stoneware bearing a glaze based on wood ash. This shows that high temperatures and long firing times entered the technical repertoire of Chinese potters at a very early date.

The final period (481–221 B.C.) of the Chou dynasty is known as the era of the "Warring States." The old feudal structure had dissolved and the power of the Chou had weakened, with a variety of other independent kingdoms and principalities now fighting for hegemony. Some of these states developed to the south of the Yangtze, in lands previously untouched by the more advanced Chinese civilization. The Warring States period was one of wars and disruption,

Above, a mark of the Northern Sung dynasty (660–1127 A.D.) and, below, a mark of the Yüan dynasty (1260–1368 A.D.). The marking of pieces did not become standard practice until the beginning of the fifteenth century.

Reign mark of the Ming emperor Yung Lo (1403–1424 A.D.) in archaic characters. Reign marks refer to the period of a particular emperor; the characters, four or six in number, also indicate the dynasty.

although it was also a time of great cultural and spiritual development, which saw, for example, the birth of Confucianism, Taoism and the Yin-Yang philosophy, all of them innovations that would have a lasting influence on Chinese art and thinking. A splendid, three-legged ewer of the fourth century, from an area south of the Yangtze, bears witness both to the inclusion of new territories within the orbit of Chinese civilization and also to the enduring influence of bronze prototypes on ceramic wares, which were in many cases destined for funerary purposes (page 297).

The unification of the country under a single king, who for the first time in history assumed the title of emperor, was achieved by the Ch'in dynasty in 221 B.C. The excavations at Sian, the ancient Ch'ang-an, which revealed the "terra cotta army" of the Emperor Shih Huang Ti, the dynasty's founder, show clearly how the art of war was the foremost consideration at the time. As it is, Shih Huang Ti ought not to be remembered for any particular love of culture, given the fact that it was he who gave the order for the confiscation and destruction of large numbers of ancient texts on the grounds that they were contrary to the interests of the state. The Ch'in dynasty was short lived, unlike the Han (206 B.C. – 220 A.D.), which inherited the important political advances. The Han not only prevented the break up of the empire, but also strengthened national unity through the creation, in accordance with Confucian ideology, of a highly centralized bureaucracy, making their strength felt beyond the frontiers of China as well. Korea and Vietnam now came under the influence and, in part, the control of the Chinese, while the second century B.C. saw the opening across Asia of the great Silk Road, which acted as a conduit for endless contacts, and not just commercial ones. On a cultural level, a historic invention was made, that of paper.

The items of Han ceramics discovered in northern China include unglazed wares as well as a beautiful red pottery covered in a lead oxide-based glaze, sometimes coloured green or, more rarely, brown. The unglazed wares were painted with colours of which few traces now remain, but the workmanship, in particular on the female figures, is of an extraordinary high quality. The grey clay, modelled with outstanding skill, was covered with a slip after firing and then painted. The detached but very real feeling of composure conveyed by one tall figure of a woman (page 298) reveals something else about these wares, in that the intensity of her expression suggests that decorative values were not the modeller's main concern. Above all, objects of this sort provide invaluable testimony to Chinese plastic sensibilities before the advent of monumental sculpture, which would appear later, following the spread of Buddhism. Ch'in and Han funerary pottery also includes earthenware with a rich, banded decoration that is in clear imitation of bronze vessels inlaid with glass paste (page 299). The motifs on other pieces, however, appear to have been inspired by the lavish lacquer wares made during the same period, which reveal extraordinary imaginative decoration and were a highly prized luxury item.

The end of the Han dynasty in 220 A.D. marked an almost four-centuries long period during which the empire fragmented, a split developed between north and south, feudalism fell prey to the pressures of disintegration, there were barbarian invasions and the country broke up into large numbers of competing and conflicting local dynasties. It was not until 589

Two versions of the reign mark of the Ming emperor Chêng Hua (1465–1487 A.D.); above, the six-character mark and, below, the seal mark.

Another two versions of a reign mark: that of the emperor Ch'ien Lung (1736–1795 A.D.) of the Ch'ing or Manchu dynasty (the last of the Chinese Imperial dynasties); above, the six-character mark and, below, the seal mark.

that China was again reunited, under the Sui dynasty and, later, the T'ang, who soon displaced them and consolidated the work they had begun. The period from the third to the sixth century represents a sort of Middle Ages, a period rich in cultural advancement: the political polycentrism that characterized it coincided with the development of a flourishing artistic life. Painting emerged from the artisanal world to which it had previously been confined and came to the forefront of the figurative arts; sculpture was born; calligraphy became transformed into a great spiritual art form; literature witnessed the creation of excellent poetry. Buddhism and Taoism pervaded the Chinese religious consciousness, also making their mark on other areas of life: the birth of landscape painting, for example, is linked to Taoism.

This was in many respects a crucial phase in the history of ceramics. For more than three centuries, following the fall of the Han, lead-glazed pottery appears to have vanished. In the south, however, which had been spared foreign invasions, hard-bodied wares grew more and more important, and many glazed stoneware pieces have been discovered, most especially in the eastern areas on the right bank of the Yangtze, where, for several centuries, the kilns of the Yüeh kingdom produced an increasingly varied range of stoneware pieces with an olive-green or grey-green glaze. Although there is no precise confirmation of the fact, these kilns were almost certainly the model for the characteristic "dragon" kilns of the Sung period, which took the form of a long series of contiguous chambers. At the end of the fifth century, after a period of undecorated wares, incised or carved bands of lotus petals and swirls began to appear, which may be taken as an indication

of the rapidly growing acceptance of Buddhism by every level of society.

This period also saw a certain return to prosperity in the north, which is reflected in the richness of its tomb furniture. The burials of important dignitaries now contain painted grey earthenware figures of foot soldiers or horsemen, while others contain animals, such as the duck (page 301), which reveals a much greater degree of realism and liveliness than its Han counterparts. Occasionally, some of the terra-cotta figures of camels or horses from this period display greater realism and more skilful modelling than the better-known examples from the later T'ang period. By the end of the fifth century lead-glazed wares had begun to reappear, a revival confirmed by a number of slightly later vessels decorated with moulded patterns. A significant example of this genre is provided by a pilgrim gourd (page 300), whose red body bears a green glaze and whose fine decoration once again brings to mind motifs associated with the advent of Buddhism.

Simplicity and elegance are the hallmarks of Sui ceramics, which saw the revival of white clay as a key material for potters (page 302). The white Sui wares also include pieces that were fired until they became as hard as stoneware. Still in the north, the technique of firing at high temperatures became widely used during the sixth century, with some kilns starting to produce a type of celadon-glazed stoneware. In other examples this type of glaze became almost colourless, while later, even before the T'ang period, an under-glaze white slip was used in order to improve the appearance of the ceramic body. One magnificent Sui camel from the beginning of the seventh century (page 303) has an ivory-coloured glaze.

White slips and very sparse decoration, the result

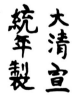

The six-character mark, above, and the four-character mark, below, relating to the reign of the last Chinese emperor, Hsüan T'ung (1909–1911 A.D.).

The marks that include special characters such as the ones signifying pavilion, hall or studio, indicate the place in which the pieces were made or the one for which they were commissioned. Reproduced here are a seventeenth-century "hall-mark" and a potter's mark from around 1724.

of a conscious decision to emphasize the austere beauty of the whiteness, are famous characteristics of some of the high-quality earthenware that continued to be produced in northern kilns during the T'ang period. In the ninth century there emerged a particular type of white ceramic. Translucent, resonant, with a totally impervious body, covered in a felspathic glaze, it represents one of the greatest achievements in the entire history of ceramics, namely porcelain. But the fine "tea wares," for which special praise is reserved in eighth-century documents, cannot have been substantially different. T'ang ceramics were not, however, restricted just to these highly sophisticated wares. They also included a wide variety of stoneware items, decorated with a brown or black glaze and sometimes with splashes of colour, and another type characterized by yellow glazes. The marbled wares provide further proof of the levels of extreme sophistication achieved by T'ang potters.

The T'ang era is justly celebrated as one of the most glorious episodes in China's history. For roughly two hundred years the country opened its frontiers to foreign influences with good effect and it can be safely said that China's international fame dates from this period. Her contacts with the Asiatic world soon revealed themselves as a source of great prosperity, and in the Yellow River valley the metropolitan areas of Ch'ang-an, the capital, and Lo-yang became hives of cosmopolitan activity. From an artistic, literary and cultural point of view, the zenith of the T'ang dynasty lay during the first half of the eighth century, the same period that also saw the birth of the art of printing. T'ang wares were exported to places as disparate as Indonesia and Japan, Korea and Mesopotamia, Sri Lanka and Persia. These trading activities also involved the introduction into China of influences from very remote lands, as is shown by T'ang pottery. The result was that certain ancient decorative motifs, of the impressed rosette type, re-emerged in the Far East after appearing on Sassanian and Arab wares.

By far the most characteristic type of T'ang ceramics are "three-colour" wares, even though the range of colours is somewhat broader than that suggested by the definition. It includes, in fact, a delicate shade of green derived from copper oxide, an amber-yellow iron oxide shading into brown, a transparent white, a blue derived from cobalt oxide and probably imported from the West, manganese purple and also other colours, amongst them a rich, very dark brown. Nor did the wares include just practical items, since the same painted decoration was used with similar success on large numbers of funerary statuettes (*mingki*). The heyday of this magnificent technique lay between the end of the seventh century and the middle of the eighth. On an aesthetic level, its most obvious merits are, on the one hand, the pure brilliance of the enamels, much of which results from their being normally applied over a white slip and, on the other, the extreme skill and sensitivity with which they were applied, generally in splashes. Sometimes the decoration was applied in *cloisons*, so as to isolate the colours and keep them separate, while on other occasions they were allowed to intermingle and flow freely and randomly down the sides of the piece. In other words, the fluidity of the colours was exploited to obtain unexpected smears and drips. The effect is one of astonishing modernity (page 304).

The same refined use of colour also played a decisive part in funerary furniture, which includes figures of both people and animals. The number and

Symbolic marks, used mainly during the reign of the Emperor K'ang Hsi (1662–1722 A.D.), bear emblems taken from the popular iconography of Buddhism or Taoism. These two examples depict the artemisia leaf and the hare.

Another type of mark is the mark of commendation or good wishes, most common at the end of the Ming dynasty. The top example denotes "elegant vessel for the rich and highly placed," the one below, a mark of good wishes, displays the character for "double joy."

height of these statuettes would appear to have been governed by a rigid protocol that reflected the social standing of the departed. There are mythical beasts and other animals, both wild and domestic; there are soldiers, grooms, servants and strangely-adorned figures of foreigners with an almost caricature-like quality, such as the terra cotta of a dark-skinned, curly-headed boy, painted using only unfired pigments (page 305). The female figures, of particular interest for their hairstyles, their clothing and their footwear, are especially fascinating and highly detailed (page 284). One of the most outstanding features of the elegant T'ang three-colour ware is its skilful combination of incised and painted decoration and, in the latter, the effortless juxtaposition of predetermined shapes and more random effects (pages 306, 307).

The collapse of the T'ang dynasty once again plunged China into disarray and opened the way for the Five Dynasties period (906–960). As had already happened in the past, this division led to a rise in the prosperity of the south: for the Yüeh kilns, which already had many centuries of experience behind them, it was a particularly active period. During the T'ang period they had been one of the main centers of stoneware production in southern China, but now, under the patronage of the local princes of Wu-Yüeh, their output reached even greater heights, with very elegantly carved decorations of flowers (page 308), dragons and phoenixes, sometimes reminiscent of the embossed patterns found on silverware, appearing beneath a clear glaze.

The Sung dynasty (960–1279), which reunited the country and revived the empire, marked the opening of an important new chapter in Chinese history. A spirit of rationalism pervaded the country and it is no coincidence that this period saw a powerful resurgence of Confucianism, the development of a naturalistic and scientific culture, the triumph of civil bureaucracy over its military counterpart, a downturn in expansionism and, as far as possible, a prudent return towards forms of peaceful coexistence with the surrounding states that had been founded by nomad invaders from the north. Under the Liao dynasty, for example, the Kitan had established a state in Manchuria. The Northern Sung disappeared in 1127 following the successful invasion of the Jürchen, who, having also overrun the Kitan, founded the Chin dynasty and ruled the lands lying to the north of the Huai river up until the Mongol invasions a century later. The regions to the south of the Huai, which during this period became the most populous area of the country, remained under the control of the Southern Sung until 1279 when they were absorbed into the Mongol empire.

The spirit of rationalism that pervaded so many different aspects of life during the Sung period is also reflected in its ceramics, which reveal a clear striving for harmony, solidity, clarity, strength and a precise balance between pattern and form, with a significant preference for monochrome wares. Production was initially inspired by Yüeh wares, which, given the general trends in taste, were understandably adopted as models (page 309). To the north, in the Shensi region, late Yao-chou celadonware possesses a thick, olive-green glaze covering the grey stoneware body and congealing within the deeply incised patterns (page 310): its shapes are strong and pure, its decoration highly original (page 311). No less famous is Ting ware, produced at Chuyang, in the north-eastern province of Hopei. Ivory in colour, translucent and resonant, with a high kaolin content,

Styles and decoration of Chinese ceramics

Funerary urn of the Pan-shan type, decorated with patterns painted in black and purple. Neolithic Kansu period; Yang-shao culture. Stockholm, Östasiatiska Museet.

and a thin glaze tending towards the brownish and glutinous "tear-drops" that betray its oxidizing firing, Ting ware is normally regarded as a type of porcelain. As well as having rims covered by a band of copper, it is also characterized by decorative patterns delineated in unusually thin carving. The twelfth century saw the adoption of moulded decoration, a different means of achieving particularly finely drawn patterns (page 312).

In the northern provinces a type of glazed stoneware was produced which was particularly prized by Japanese masters of the tea ceremony (a ritual developed in China): the glaze, known as "oil spot," creates silvery reflections on a black ground (page 313). Another type of northern stoneware, known as Tz'ŭ-chou ware, derives its name from the place in Hopei where it was first produced. Characterized by a rather coarse, grey, cream or brown paste, it is generally covered in an under-glaze slip, with the decoration painted over the glaze. A late and highly sophisticated manifestation of this style was based on the contrast between black and white slip, as exemplified in certain magnificent pillows (page 314). The harsh Manchuria of the Liao, on the other hand, produced tall, slim vases with a cup-shaped mouth. In one particularly fine example the swift, strong lines of the decoration appear to be incised in colour in the slip (page 315). Ju wares take us into a completely different dimension. The rarest and most refined of all Northern Sung wares, they were produced for the Imperial court for only a few years during the opening decades of the twelfth century: they have an opaque, pale lavender-blue glaze, shading gently into green, and slender shapes, of classic simplicity, which are generally undecorated (page 316).

In the north, now ruled by the Chin, tastes changed, at least partially. The most outstanding feature of certain bottle-shaped vases, characterized by a very swollen shoulder and low neck, is their silhouette (page 317). Other wares, reminiscent of the Tz'ŭ-chou type, are enveloped in a beautifully painted decoration that conveys a remarkable sense of spontaneity (page 318), while the style of the pillows developed with a markedly more decorative quality (page 319). All in all, the emphasis was on the figurative, on expressivity, accessibility and greater decorative facility. It was the opposite course to that taken by the rarefied, aristocratic Ju wares.

One type of ware that emerged during the Northern Sung period, but whose production continued, with certain specific characteristics, during the Southern Sung period, is known as ying-ch'ing (shadowy blue) porcelain, a term recently introduced by Chinese antiquarians, or ch'ing-pai (blueish white), the name used in ancient texts. Under the Northern Sung dynasty it was widely used as tableware, when it rivalled Ting ware in elegance (page 320). Some Southern Sung ying-ch'ing wares are completely covered in raised floral motifs (page 321).

When, in the mid twelfth century, the Southern Sung capital was moved to Hangchow, new attempts were made to produce Ju wares. Contemporary chronicles mention two kilns built near the Imperial palace, one of which has been located and has yielded fragments of a very beautiful black stoneware with several layers of thick, coloured glaze. An example of Imperial Kuan (official) ware is provided by a vase whose geometric shape imitates certain jade vases and which has a translucent blue glaze (page 322). Another, equally attractive variant has a creamy-grey glaze and a dark craquelure (page 323), which, from the twelfth century onwards, was intentionally

Jar. Shape inspired by contemporary bronzes. Grey earthenware covered with slip and with decoration painted over the slip after firing. Early Han dynasty; 206 B.C.–8 A.D. Paris, Musée Guimet.

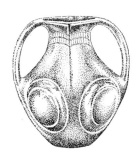

Jar. Black earthenware with rounded body and rectangular opening. Szechuan; Han dynasty (206 B.C.–220 A.D.). London, British Museum.

created during the firing and cooling of the piece. Celadon ware of classical perfection was produced during the Southern Sung period in the kilns at Lung-ch'üan in Chekiang province. The thick, shiny glaze, a pure and rich shade of pale blueish green, was of particularly high quality, while the shapes often imitated antique bronzes.

The Yüan period (1260–1368), which saw the subjugation of China by a Mongol dynasty, swept away the old world of the Sung and marked the resumption and proliferation of trading contacts with the outside world. The positive effects of this were also felt on a commercial level, when porcelain exports doubled, a process in which the kilns of the coastal provinces played an important part. Demand came mainly from Japan, but also from the countries of South-East Asia and the Indonesian archipelago. Ceramics were also carried by sea to India, Persia and the Red Sea ports.

Lung-ch'üan wares, which extended the range of porcelain shapes, as well as introducing new motifs, both impressed and applied, continued to set the tone. White still reigned supreme, as can be seen in porcelain with a *ying-ch'ing* glaze, which was used in around 1300 for Buddhist statuettes made in imitation of sculpture (page 324), as well as for wares with applied decoration in the Lung-ch'üan manner (page 325). One highly important center of porcelain production was located at Ching-tê-chên, in the northern part of Kiangsi province: its production, which would appear to date back to the Han period, received a particular boost during the Yüan period. It was, in fact, at the beginning of the fourteenth century that production began in China of the beautiful porcelain wares with an under-glaze decoration in cobalt blue, using a totally new technique. This

marked a radical advance on Sung thinking, according to which decoration was secondary to glaze and shape. The emphasis was now on delightful visual, rather than tactile effects, thus marking the birth of modern ceramics. The new blue-and-white wares were in great demand in overseas markets. Their decoration was strong, precise, usually fairly copious, with borders and panels that followed conventional layouts which were also popular with Indian and Middle Eastern buyers. A rather unusual variation is represented by porcelain wares with a blue-glazed ground and a reserve decoration of dragons or other animals (page 326). More common are large dishes decorated with floral scrolls, symbols of prosperity and so on, with white motifs on a blue ground alternating with dark blue ones on a white ground (page 327). In the rare examples of Yüan porcelain on which the difficult under-glaze red decoration was attempted, the style is similar to that of blue-and-white wares (pages 328, 329).

The Mongol domination was finally ended by the Ming dynasty (1368–1644), which established a highly centralized state in which the Emperor wielded despotic powers with the help of a complex administrative apparatus. It was a period that saw the building of the Great Wall and also the inauguration of the first direct contacts with Europe. Trade flourished, with a large Chinese fleet taking to the waters, as did agriculture, with new crops being introduced and new areas of land being brought into cultivation.

The manufacture of porcelain attained technical perfection under the Ming, to the detriment of factories specializing in stoneware, such as Tz'ŭ-chou wares, and to the benefit of the Imperial factory at Ching-tê-chên, with even Lung-ch'üan beginning to

Ovoid bottle with long, narrow neck and cup-shaped mouth. Pottery with dark brown glaze. Northern ware; Sui dynasty, early seventh century. Boston, Museum of Fine Arts.

Pitcher with bulbous body, tall, ridged neck and phoenix-head pourer. Reddish stoneware with very blue-tinged glaze. Northern Sung dynasty; eleventh–early twelfth century. Paris, Musée Guimet.

go into a decline. It is no coincidence that the ceramic production of Kiangsi province, a region very rich in kaolin and felspar, the two basic ingredients of porcelain, enjoyed its greatest period of expansion. The rise of Ching-tê-chên was basically determined by radical changes in taste and also, from the reign of Yung Lo (1403–1429), the formidable patronage of the Imperial court. Ming ceramics are characterized not only by the classic blue decoration, but also by the masterly use of polychrome enamels and glazes. The different eras into which the period is divided are identified by the names and years of the emperors' reigns, which is highly relevant, given the fact that a considerable amount of ceramics bear a "reign mark." During one period of the sixteenth century the Imperial court ordered almost one hundred thousand pieces.

The production of blue-and-white Yüan wares continued, but it soon becomes clear that this did not just involve making careful copies of earlier products, an impression that could be gained from the first Ming wares (page 330), made during the reign of the Emperor Hung Wu. The workmanship improved, with tough pastes skilfully modelled into well-balanced shapes and thick, brilliant glazes. The decoration began to reveal such elements as an unusual "pictorial" style, in which pictures appear within real settings rather than against an abstract ground (page 331): in many cases, therefore, ornamentation becomes synonymous with representation. Another innovation was the very thin "eggshell" porcelain, sometimes with a "secret decoration," an-hua, obtained by making very faint incisions in the paste or by sparing applications of under-glaze slip, which is visible solely when lit from behind. In order to heighten the intensity of the blue and white there

was also a technique known as "heaped and piled." There are some pieces, at the same time both simple and sophisticated, which would certainly have been made for the court and whose motifs, in white reserve against a blue ground, exemplified a new synthetic way of representing plants and flowers (page 332). There is another style, called fa-hua, which anticipates the taste for colour that characterizes the Chêng Hua period (1465–1487). In order to prevent the glazes on polychrome-decorated wares from streaking and smudging, the outlines of the patterns were clearly delineated by means of lines and dots in relief or incised lines. This technical device, which became a distinctive stylistic element, was used on a variety of mei-p'ing vases, a type of vase with a swelling, elongated body, tapering towards the base, and a short, narrow neck and small mouth (page 333).

In order to fix the glazes used on the ceramic body, a second, low-temperature firing was required. The term san-ts'ai (three colour) is used to indicate the glazes used in the fa-hua style.

The success enjoyed by polychrome porcelain did not stop blue-and-white wares continuing to be made. One box from the Chêng Tê period, painted in blue and designed to contain writing material, reveals an interesting decorative addition in the form of inscriptions in Persian and Arabic (page 334), perhaps indicating that it was made for one of the Muslim eunuchs who formed a powerful clique at the Imperial court. A second, no less beautiful box, from the Chêng Hua period, adorned with incised dragons, reveals another aspect of Ming sensibilities (page 335): here the decoration displays a completely different rhythm, with the usual contrast between blue and white replaced by an elegant combination of turquoise and dark blue.

Flask. Lead-glazed earthenware, decorated with two nomadic horsemen, its shape in imitation of the leather version used by Liao Tartar nomads. Liao dynasty; early eleventh century. Boston, Museum of Fine Arts.

Tea bowl with decoration of scattered flowers over a brown- and black-veined glaze. Chi-chou ware; Southern Sung dynasty, twelfth–thirteenth century. Boston, Museum of Fine Arts.

In the *tou-ts'ai* (contrasted colour) style, different enamels are painted over the transparent glaze, filling in the outlines created in under-glaze cobalt blue. The enamel colours were, naturally enough, fixed by refiring the piece at a low heat. *Wu-ts'ai* (five colour) porcelain, whose decoration uses over-glaze polychrome enamels and under-glaze blue, is another creation of this period. The Sung love of elegant monochrome wares was replaced by the Ming love of colour. It is possible, for example, to find a combination of green, yellow, red and turquoise on a single piece (page 336). On wares of the Chia Ching period (1522–1566) the "under-glaze blue and enamels" technique is also used to great effect in decorations composed of broad horizontal bands (page 337). The decoration on one particular type of ware from the second half of the sixteenth century exploited the contrast between monochrome and painted areas (page 338), with the monochrome sections, in glowing red or green, embellished by the addition of gold-painted floral motifs. These "enamelled and gilded" wares, whose imagery was derived in particular from books and textiles, were highly prized by the Japanese. During the Ming period printing developed to an extraordinary degree, and it thus comes as no surprise to find vases decorated with figures and scenes mentioned in history books, romances or plays (page 339).

During the Wan Li period (1573–1619) *wu-ts'ai* decoration was popular, with the combination of enamels and blue on a white ground giving rise to scenes of extraordinary beauty, as can be seen on a splendid jar decorated with the so-called "Thousand Deer" motif (page 340). The freshness and richness of its colours are enhanced by the combination with a very crisp and lively design, qualities that are skilfully exploited in the composition.

Apart from Ching-tê-chên, there were many other Ming factories working to satisfy the demands of both the local and export market. In Kuan-tong province, for example, a rather coarse, but very attractive type of porcelain was produced (page 341), known as "Swatow ware" after the nearby port where it was loaded onto ships. Direct trade between China and Europe began in 1517, when the first Portuguese ships reached Canton, and from that moment on there was a constant growth in the export of porcelain to the West. Towards the end of the sixteenth century the main European traders were the Dutch, whose ships were based at Batavia (modern Jakarta).

During the mid seventeenth century China was overrun by the Manchu, who invaded from the north and imposed a new dynasty, that of the Ch'ing (1644–1912). For the porcelain factories, the decades between the death of the Emperor Wan Li and the total reorganization of output under the aegis of an administrator appointed by the court (1683) were a period of difficult transition. But there was a spectacular recovery during the reign of K'ang Hsi (1622–1722), and during the subsequent reigns of Yung Chêng (1723–1735) and Ch'ien Lung (1736–1795) Chinese porcelain production reached extraordinary levels. At Ching-tê-chên work was reorganized along new lines, and we know that, before reaching the kiln, a piece would pass through some seventy hands. This division of labour emphasized the practice of specialist skills: preparation of materials, turning and modelling, finishing, decoration and firing were all important stages in the search for perfection.

During the K'ang Hsi period both the quantity and

Blue-and-white altar vase. Modelled on the wheel in several sections, which were placed one on top of the other to achieve the desired columnar shape. Yüan dynasty; 1351. London, Percival David Foundation of Chinese Art.

Stem cup in under-glaze blue and red. Ming dynasty; early fifteenth century. London, Percival David Foundation of Chinese Art.

quality of output increased, and great care was even taken over the shape and decoration of pieces destined for everyday use. Blue-and-white wares continued to enjoy enormous popularity, but there was an even more marked growth in polychrome wares. Colours became more delicate and translucent, with particular emphasis on a combination of green, yellow and red, whereas turquoise was abandoned and under-glaze blue was widely replaced by an overglaze blue, which was sparingly used, and a purple colour. A dense black was introduced and used extensively for outlines. It is this range of colours that make up the famous *famille verte* palette (a term coined by a French antiquarian), which reigned supreme from the late seventeenth century until 1720 or slightly beyond. Enamelled porcelain wares of this sort display a marked preference for such decorative subjects as flowers, plants, reeds, birds and butterflies, lovingly observed in nature and then translated into airy, dream-like images (pages 342, 343, 344). The *san-ts'ai* style of Ming ceramics also acted as a source of inspiration for Ch'ing decorators (page 345).

The brief reign of Yung Chêng, on the other hand, saw a revival of Sung types, with an increase in monochrome glazes, the production of celadon ware and ceramics of an extraordinarily delicate pale blue, and the return of Ju and Ting wares. One outstanding novelty is represented by the so-called *famille rose* porcelain, which comprised wares with an overglaze decoration characterized by the presence of a pink that had already been seen in the West in inlays of glass and metalwork. It was derived from gold and known to the Chinese as *yang-ts'ai* (foreign colour). All the *famille rose* enamels were rendered opaque by being mixed with white, which allowed for the dilu-

tion of the colour and also for the creation of shaded effects. Having perfected the use of this range of enamels, the craftsmen-painters used them for specially selected subjects: one of the most suitable was believed to be the pattern known to the Chinese as "with bird and flower" (page 346).

The porcelain used at Tê-hua, in Fukien province, to create extremely beautiful statuettes, generally without any decoration, was white or ivory in colour (page 347). To the factories at Ching-tê-chên, however, must go the credit for having produced certain very fine pieces of porcelain with an exceptional sepia decoration, which would appear to have been reserved for the court (page 348).

The eighteenth century was the period during which the greatest amounts of Chinese ceramics were exported to the West. Large quantities of *famille rose* wares, called *fên-ts'ai* (powdery colour) by the Chinese, were destined for the European market, where they were highly prized both for their material quality and for their decoration. As can be seen in numerous examples, these wares combine soft colouring with precise drawing and pleasing decorative subjects (pages 349, 350, 351).

The wares of the long and very productive Ch'ien Lung period reveal a great variety in terms of both quality and typology. There was still the same desire for experimentation and research, as well as a vogue for creating pieces in the archaic style. Every level of the market was catered for. The enamelled decoration found space for landscapes "in the Chinese taste," accompanied by poems in the Taoist manner (page 352), and also for elaborate souvenirs, painted with meticulous attention to detail and bearing cartouches with carefully executed inscriptions (page 353).

Incense burner with figures of dragons. Central element of a ceramic altar group. Porcelain with carved and gilded biscuit decoration. Ming dynasty; Chia Ching period (1522–1566 A.D.). Paris, Musée Guimet.

Four-lobed teapot with handle of woven malacca. Porcelain with enamelled decoration of flowers and birds. Ch'ing dynasty; K'ang Hsi period (1662–1722 A.D.). Stockholm, Östasiatiska Museet.

In the urn opposite the spiral pattern so common on the Pan-shan urns has here changed into a whorl pattern. The shiny black surface is traversed by the unpainted buff-coloured lines, giving intense movement around the central eye patterns, one on each side. The two whorls are separated by the loop handles and are framed by horizontal lines above and below.

A stamped pattern of S-shaped "thunder" motifs is repeated in orderly rows around the upper body: the same motif reduced in size is stamped on the cover. At the top of each of the three slightly flared legs is a *t'ao-t'ieh* mask. This is quite clearly a proto-Yüeh piece produced in Chekiang province. Most of these, made for burial purposes, were copies of bronzes, providing an economical substitution for the rarer metal vessels. This ewer follows the bronze prototype known as *ho* in nearly every detail. The discovery of works like this in Warring States period tombs in south-eastern China makes it possible now to date them to that period.

The hands of this standing figure of a woman appear to have originally held something which is missing now. The face bent slightly downward seems to convey suppressed sorrow. The hair is parted in the middle and bundled at the back. Made as a funerary figure, it probably represents a woman who attends the dead in the afterworld. No funerary figure of a similar appearance has ever been unearthed from a clearly identified site. However, judging from the numerous funerary figures recently discovered in the vicinity of the tomb of the emperor of the Ch'in dynasty, Shih Huang Ti, and those from near that of Chou Ya Fu, the celebrated vassal of a Former Han emperor, the age of such figures is probably earlier than considered heretofore and can likely be ascribed to about the Former Han. The figure was fashioned with grey clay, fired, and subsequently coloured with white slip and red and black pigments. Only traces of the colouring remain.

There are only four jars of the type opposite known to exist in the world, each being slightly different from the others in shape as well as decoration. The Boston jar has somewhat deteriorated and the colours of the glass paste have lost their original brilliance, but it is still undoubtedly a very rare example from a very rare group of Ch'in ceramic works. The shape of this covered jar is similar to the Nelson Gallery's famous *p'ou*-type covered jar reportedly from Chin-tz'un in Honan. But, while the latter is almost completely under the influence of contemporary bronze work, the potter of this jar is concerned mainly with the decoration and the material for achieving such decoration.

Opposite: Standing woman. Painted pottery. Han dynasty; second–first century B.C. Height: 22½ in (57 cm). Tokyo, National Museum (gift of Mr Matsushige Hirota).

Below: Covered jar with pearl medallion design in glass paste. Reddish earthenware. Ch'in or Western Han dynasty; third century B.C. Height: 4½ in (11.6 cm). Diameter of body: 5½ in (13.9 cm). Boston, Museum of Fine Arts (no. 50.1841, Charles B. Hoyt Collection).

Flask-type objects already existed in Han bronzes. In respect to its shape, the piece opposite is still close to those ancient models, with its high oblong foot, its square loop handles and its decoration arranged in a heart-shaped motif. On each side are three acanthus leaves moulded in high relief, and around them are placed cabochons ringed with pearls. This decoration is reminiscent of the motifs introduced into China with Buddhism. We note the same ornamentation, though less developed, above the dancer on gourds dating to the Northern Ch'i dynasty recently discovered in a tomb at Hong-ho ts'un, near Anyang in Honan.

Partly covered with a white slip and without doubt at one time more brightly pigmented, this duck belongs to that numerous class of farm animal models which were placed in tombs from the Han period onwards. In this instance, however, the treatment is one of exceptional elegance, the tense curve of the bird's neck and its alert head finding an echo in the fine upward tilt of the tail feathers and wings picked out by incision. Such products of the Northern Wei in many ways foreshadow the coming sculptural versatility of the T'ang.

*Below: Porcelain bowl with very light greenish-white glaze. From North Lampung, Sumatra.
Sui dynasty; seventh century. Diameter: 4½ in (11.5 cm). Height: 3¼ in (8 cm). Jakarta,
Museum Pusat (no. 726).*

———

*Opposite: Glazed camel with applied decoration. Northern white earthenware. Sui dynasty;
early seventh century. Height: 13½ in (34.7 cm). Length: 16¾ in (42.5 cm). Boston, Museum of
Fine Arts (no. 50.397, Charles B. Hoyt Collection).*

This relatively deep bowl has a slightly flaring mouth, a rounded waist, and a small, short foot. The foot spreads slightly and has a flat base. It is a fine grey-white ware, thinly potted, the mouth being especially thin walled. A beautiful transparent glaze covers the surface down to the waist. At the interior center the glaze has collected to present a faint green tinge. The glaze is crackled all over. The unglazed area is yellowish and is stained with reddish rust.

Several features of the Sui camel are noteworthy, first of all the two musical instruments on its back. The one visible in the illustration is the four-stringed *p'i-p'a*; on the opposite side is a smaller five-stringed *p'i-p'a*, which, in the opinion of some Japanese scholars, originated in India. Between the two humps of the camel is a water bag that has, at the top, lacings probably of rope with a naturalistically modelled lock. Not shown in the illustration are two

pilgrim flasks, hanging from the rear hump by ropes, decorated with the familiar Sui "maple leaf" surrounded by a pearl-string motif. The elegant elongated shape of this ivory-white glazed camel standing on a carved flat geometric base, distinctly different from the well-known three-colour variety of the T'ang period, reflects the influence of the earlier Northern Ch'i, particularly in the style of modelling and decoration.

Among the many excellent pieces of T'ang three-colour glazed ware, this is particularly famous as a representative masterpiece. Dragon-handled vases are relatively abundant among white stoneware, black-glazed pottery, and three-colour wares. The shape is believed to be of Western origin probably traceable to the Greek amphora. It is likely that in the late Northern and Southern dynasties the shape was absorbed in China. It seems that vessels of this form were made frequently during the Sui and early T'ang periods, eventually developing into the Chinese-style norm of dragon-handled vases. This vase, following the tradition, was made during the High T'ang in the first half of the eighth century and displays the utmost employment of three-colour techniques that were fashionable at the time. The florid moulded and applied medallions on three spots on the sides, the impressive form shown typically by the firmly built dragon handles, and the luxurious effect of glazes of three colours running down and merging make it an unrivalled masterwork of its kind.

The flesh parts of the dhoti-clad figure are painted black, indicating one of the dark-skinned races, and this tomb model is thought to represent one of the "K'unlun boys" of contemporary records, a vaguely-defined group coming from South-East Asia and ultimately perhaps from Hindu or even African lands. The clothing is in coloured pigments with effective use of green, red and blue and with gilt necklace and bracelets, contributing further to the interest and movement of the modelling. The boy may have been a groom or a drummer heading a procession.

Dish of pinkish white clay covered with polychrome over white slip. T'ang dynasty; eighth century. Diameter: 12¼ (31 cm). Height: 3¼ in (8 cm). Paris, Musée Guimet (no. 202, Michel Calmann Collection).

This round dish rests on three feet ornamented with a leaf design. The interior has an incised decoration consisting of a central medallion in which a wild goose with outstretched wings is drawn flying amid clouds. The predominantly cobalt-blue and yellow motif stands out against the cream background. Around the medallion four blue lotus stems alternate with four yellow stems to form a rosette pattern. Between the blue-glazed rim and this rosette were eight small flowers with four blue and yellow petals, but in the firing they have almost merged with the glaze of the rim. The outside of the rim is covered with yellow glaze. The feet are highlighted with green. On the inside of the dish three very small spur marks can be seen. The shape of the feet seems inspired by gold- and silverwork models. In tombs and also perhaps on Buddhist altars, this sort of dish must have replaced the stands intended for the presentation of offerings.

On the interior, the incised decoration is composed of a central medallion with a green background. In the middle of this a blue-headed wild goose flies among three white clouds, with outstretched wings highlighted in green and white. Around this medallion eight blue lotus leaves with green stalks alternate with eight blue stems highlighted in yellow. Both the interior and the exterior of the rim are covered with cream glaze. The dish rests on three horseshoe-shaped feet, a traditional form in China since the Han dynasty. Inside the dish three very small spur marks may be noticed. The presence of these brings up the problem of the firing technique of this type of three-colour ware. We might presume that they were piled up in the kiln, but this would mean that the feet of pieces stacked in this way would also bear the same marks. No such marks have been noted to date. In fact, the technique used for applying the colour and for firing them remains an enigma.

Yüeh ware, named after the old principality at the mouth of the Yangtze, has a history reaching back to the third or fourth century B.C. During the T'ang period the ware was much refined and production continued into the earlier part of the Sung. This box has an everted foot, and the grey, hard body is covered with a greyish-green celadon-type glaze. There are six elongated spur marks on the glazed base. The cover is ornamented with an all-over design of three flowers carved in low relief. The piece was probably made at Shang-lin hu, a kiln center in northern Chekiang about seventy kilometers east of Shao-hsing.

The urn opposite has an unusual shape with steps around the body and five slender faceted pipe spouts on the shoulder. The spouts have mouths carved in the shape of flowers, and at their bases are small, applied goblin masks. The four steps on the lower part of the body are incised with alternate bands of lotus petals and scrolls. The surface decoration is quite prominent. The domed cover has a large, bud-shaped knop, its rounded sides being ornamented with oblique incised lines. The ware is grey, covered with a light olive-green glaze. The glaze on the lower half was roughened while it was buried, with soil rust infiltrating into it to produce a reddish colour. While it is a piece of Yüeh type celadon, its provenance is not known for sure.

Among the most treasured possessions of the Percival David Foundation is this Yao-chou type celadon box, the only one of its kind. The box has a very fine-grained grey body of dark tone, which has burned dull brown where exposed to the neatly cut foot ring. While the glaze on the outside is very evenly applied, that on the inside is rather uneven, and where it is thin it has fired to a warm brown colour instead of green. The carving of the floral decoration, the scroll border and feather pattern round the sides is exceptionally fluent and clean. The piece is rightly regarded as one of the supreme examples of a particularly popular class of ceramic ware.

This piece has a deep, conical shape with a rim that curves inwards, and it rests on a flat base. The exterior is decorated with lotus petals arranged in a slightly oblique manner. The interior bears a design of waves accentuated with lines and dots made with a bamboo spatula. The center is formed by one four-petalled flower. This treatment is rare because in the center of waves of this type it is usual to see a fish. The

motif of this piece may be an allusion to the very popular poetic theme of petals scattered on waves. It might also be related to the representation of a peony (*Peonia moulan*) in beehive shape which appears on many Tz'ǔ-chou pieces. It must be remembered that new shapes and decorative motifs used to spread rapidly among the different pottery centers, which then adapted them to suit their usual manufacturing techniques.

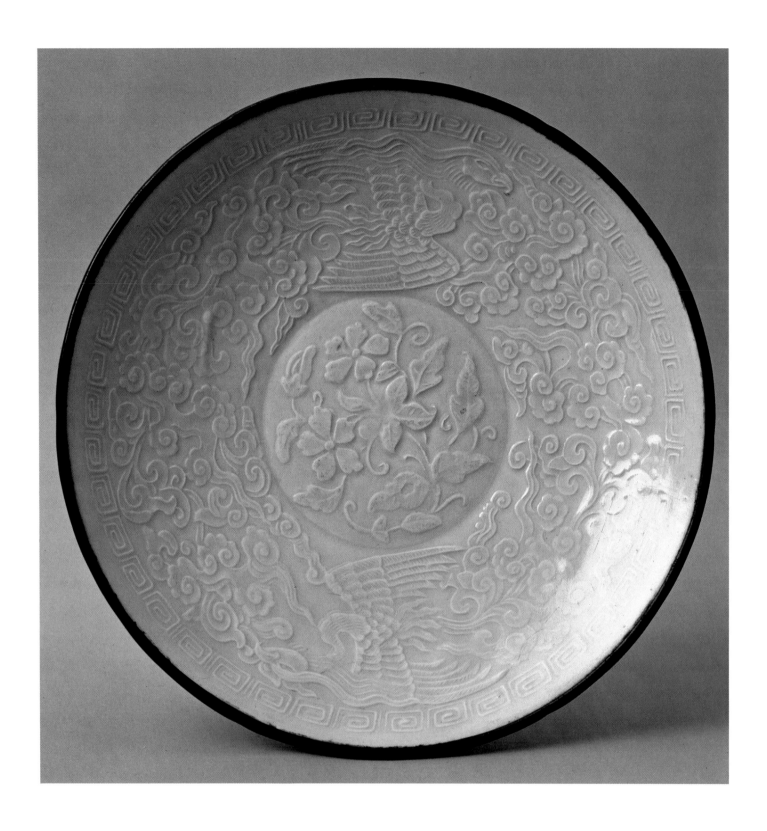

The moulded type of Ting ware decoration is rather different from the incised one. Because of the technique used it was possible to transfer very complicated patterns, as on this shallow bowl. The interior is covered with a design arranged in three sections. In the center is a mallow plant: on the sides two proud phoenixes with volute tails are flying among compact spiral clouds and volutes. Below the copper-covered lip is a key-fret border. This border balances the massiveness of the phoenix pattern. The details are very precise in execution, but their sharp outlines are somewhat hidden under the creamy glaze. Outside, the "tear-drops" are seen.

One of the dark glazes of Sung stoneware, the so-called oil spot, was made in Honan and was mainly used on tea bowls. In this case it covers a ewer of more exceptional shape. The bud shape is accentuated by the conical lid which is fixed to the body and covered by the same thick layer of glaze as encloses most of the vessel; the glaze stops well above the broad foot rim. The ewer has to be filled from underneath through a tube reaching more than half of its height; this makes it suitable only for wine. Stoneware with dark oil spot glaze has always been highly admired by Japanese tea masters.

Tz'ŭ-chou type stonewares were made at a large number of kilns in North China. From excavated fragments it can be argued that the type of pillow opposite consisting of a leaf-shaped bowl on a solid rectangular base was made at the Kuan-t'ai kilns in Hopei province. On this piece the remarkable design of a dancing bear holding a club, tethered to a post, is executed in black against a white slip. Such unusual designs are particularly noted on pillows of this specific shape.

Liao ceramics showed the most florid development in the second half of the eleventh century, when the Liao rule entered its late period. The majority of surviving examples are lead-glazed wares, such as the three-colour, green-, and yellow-glazed pieces. Recent reports state that among them glazed white ware constituted the major part of production. This vase can safely be called a valuable specimen of glazed white pottery from the florescent period. It is a uniquely Liao tall-necked vase, tall, slim and surmounted by a small cup-shaped mouth. The prototype of this shape may perhaps be the dish-mouthed vase that saw a vogue from the tenth to early eleventh centuries, but the modified Liao style is hardly indicative of the original form. The body is a slightly sticky, faint pink clay, coated with white slip except on the base; the surface is decorated with an incised flowering plant, painted in green and covered with a transparent glaze. The plant in deeply incised lines appears to be a weed flowering in spring in barren districts. Echoed by the casually applied touches of green, the decoration is rich in local colour. The vase is thought to be from Kan-wa, the noted Liao ceramic center in Manchuria, though the attribution is not substantiated with material proof.

Below: Ju ware bowl. Northern Sung dynasty; early twelfth century. Diameter of mouth: 6½ in (16.7 cm). London, Percival David Foundation of Chinese Art (no. 3, De Forest Collection).

Opposite: Bottle-shaped vase. Chün ware. Chin dynasty; thirteenth century. Height: 16 in (41 cm). Maximum diameter of body: 6¼ in (16 cm). Diameter of mouth: 2 in (5.4 cm). Diameter of base: 4 in (10 cm). Paris, Musée Guimet (no. 522, Michel Calmann Collection, formerly Schoenlicht Collection).

The simple shape of this bowl with its low spreading foot ring is characteristic of the best of the classic forms of the Sung period. Ju-yao is the only northern ware of the period which was fired on spurs. These leave elegant fire-clay spur marks on the base, which is completely glazed. The soft lavender blue–grey of the glaze has a texture whose sensuous quality was found deeply attractive by Chinese connoisseurs. The rim has been mounted with a gilt metal band to conceal a chip and small crack.

The large bottle vase opposite has a strongly swelling shoulder and thins rapidly towards the base. The neck is low, with a thick rim. On the wide foot rim spur marks can be seen. The concave base has a layer of very pure blue glaze with many crackles through which the brown body appears. The body of this piece bears wheel marks, but one may well wonder if it could have been made in one piece. However, there is no sign of any join. The opaque and opalescent glaze was applied after an initial biscuit

firing and it is thick, with many gas holes and crackles. The shape of this bottle vase is different from those of the Sung dynasty pieces, where the shoulder does not have so pronounced a swell, but its profile is more harmonious than that of the Yüan dynasty examples. It could therefore be attributed to the intermediate period of the Chin dynasty (1115–1234).

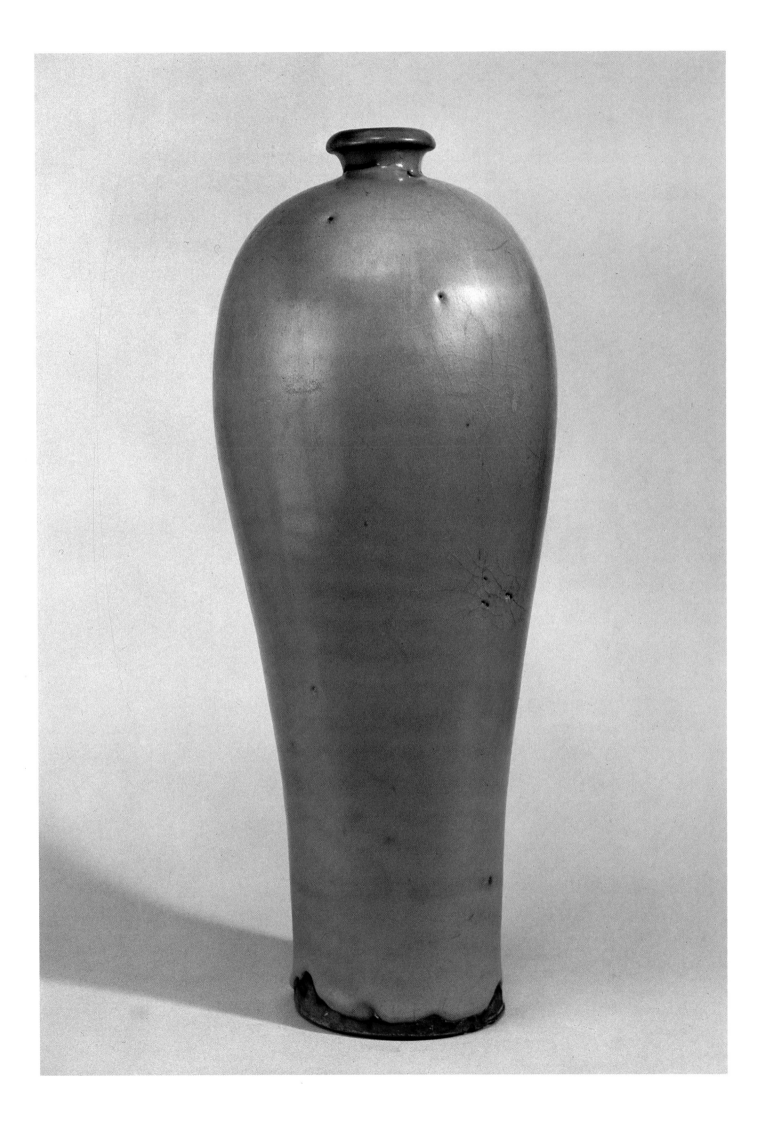

Opposite: Large wine jar of reddish-grey stoneware covered with slip and decorated with a design in iron brown under transparent glaze. Tz'ǔ-chou type. Chin dynasty; 1115–1234. Height: 16¾ in (42.5 cm). Diameter of body: 8 in (20 cm). Diameter of mouth: 1½ in (4 cm). Diameter of base: 4¼ in (11 cm). Paris, Musée Guimet (no. EO. 2063, acquired in 1913).

Below: Pillow with narrative decoration in under-glaze. Black and brown. Tz'ǔ-chou ware type. Chin or Yüan dynasty; thirteenth century. Mark: "Chang-chia tsao" (Made by the Chang family). Maximum height: 5¾ in (14.5 cm). Length: 12½ in (32 cm). Depth: 6½ in (16.4 m). Boston, Museum of Fine Arts (no. 44.619, gift of Charles Sumner Bird in memory of Francis William Bird).

The surface of the wine jar opposite is completely covered with peonies seen from different angles and surrounded with leaves. The vigour and spontaneity of the brushwork are remarkable. Only a few outlines seem to have been sketched in very lightly with a point. Due to an accident in the firing the decoration on one of the sides has a greyish, slightly cloudy tint, which is nevertheless attractive. Mr. Hasebe Gakuji dates a piece of the same type to the twelfth century and suggests that it came from the Pa-ts'un kilns in Yü-hsien, Honan. The shape of the vase cited by him, however, is more elegant. Here the shoulder is fuller and the base is wider. Whether the evolution of shapes depends on location or on differences of period is a problem still to be solved.

The style of pillow decoration in the thirteenth century seems to be under the strong influence of contemporary theatrical and religious illustrations. The main figure painting on the top of the pillow illustrated here is depicted in under-glaze black on a white-slipped body with touches of light red colour. It shows a dramatized female ghost floating freely in mid-air under a new moon and the stars, while an exorcist to the right of her is mercilessly waving his magic sword, trying to force her under his control. A fierce-looking tiger among rocks and grass (which is itself very Yüan in style) is vigorously depicted on the back side of the pillow, while the front has a peaceful deer coloured lightly in brown. In the center of the unglazed greyish body is stamped in low relief the well-known "Chang-chia tsao" mark.

Below: Conical porcelain bowl with incised sketchy design under light blue glaze. Ying-ch'ing ware. Northern Sung dynasty; 960–1127. Diameter of mouth: 5¾ in (14.6 cm). Height: 2 in (5 cm). Stockholm, Östasiatiska Museet (Ö.M. formerly Gustaf VI Adolf Collection, no. 1513).

———

Opposite: Vase with carved peony design, ying-ch'ing glaze. Southern Sung dynasty; twelfth century. From Ibaraki-ken, Japan. Height: 15 in (38 cm). Diameter of mouth: 2 in (5 cm). Diameter of base: 4¾ (11.9 cm). Tokyo, National Museum.

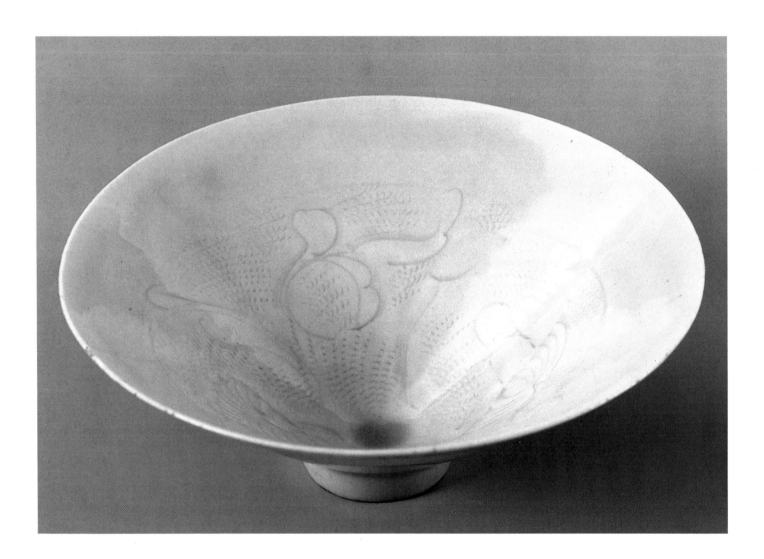

Y*ing-ch'ing* porcelain shows a great variety of shapes and decoration, far more than Ting ware, which proves that it was used all over the country by all categories of people. Even today kilns have been found in many southern provinces where this kind of porcelain was produced. The potters were very conscious of the delicate material and preferred a light and sketchy design for decoration. Most common are the popular flowers, such as lotus, peony, chrysanthemum and mallow, often in combination with sweeping

scrolls. On this conical bowl only four almost abstract waterplants are suggested; the water is hinted at by dotted lines.

Unearthed in the Taisho era (1912–1926) at Ibaraki-machi, Ibaraki-ken, the vase opposite is one of the most excellent oversized pieces of Chinese ceramics excavated in Japan and is unsurpassed among the numerous extant examples of pale white (*ying-ch'ing*, "shadowy blue") porcelain. The

shape with a small mouth and a tall slender body is one known as *mei-p'ing*. *Mei-p'ing* vases like this, with broad shoulders and with a ridged flange beneath the mouth rim, are abundant in the pale white wares of the Southern Sung to Yüan periods and were imported in quantity to Japan. This vase is decorated with large peonies on the shoulder and lotuses on the sides, both carved in accentuated relief as if the entire vessel was wrapped in flowers.

This vase in a shape imitating the ancient jade *tsung* is believed to be a work from the Chiao-t'an *Kuan* kilns of Southern Sung. It was made by preparing the main body in cylinder form, adding the four corners to make it square in shape, and carving five indentations on the corner angles. It is extremely thick walled and heavy in weight. The thick celadon glaze covering it inside and out is a translucent blue colour, partly tinged with opaque white to create delicate changes of colour. The glaze is finely crackled all over. Its *yao* (place of manufacture) is yet to be studied. Be that as it may, the firmly built, impressive form, fully reproducing the dignified jade shape and exhibiting flawless ceramic technique, cannot be credited to the ability of an ordinary *yao*.

The vase reportedly was originally an heirloom in the Daté family, where it was used as a water jar for the tea ceremony. The foot rim, also exposing the black-brown biscuit, encircles a shallow concave, which is glazed inside. The mark "Chung Hou Ch'u" is incised there through the glaze.

Opposite: Stoneware vase with crackled creamy-grey glaze. Kuan ware. Southern Sung dynasty; late twelfth–thirteenth century. Height: 4 in (9.9 cm). Diameter: 5 in (12.4 cm). London, Victoria and Albert Museum (Acc. No. C. 25–1935, Eumorfopoulos Collection).

Below: Vase in the shape of a jade tsung. Celadon. Kuan ware. Southern Sung dynasty; twelfth–thirteenth century. Incised inscription of "Chung Hou Ch'u." Height: 7¾ in (19.7 cm). Diameter of mouth: 3¼ in (8.2 cm). Diameter of base: 5 in (12.7 cm). Tokyo, National Museum (gift of Mr Matsushige Hirota).

Suitably for an official ware of the Southern Sung court the jar exhibits both nobility of form, embodying more than a hint of bronze age style, and a glaze of exquisite subtlety and richness. The body material, a slate-grey stoneware may be seen at the foliated lip where the straight neck spreads outwards and also at the foot, where it is partly exposed. The glaze is of an indefinable creamy-to-pearl grey, applied in numerous layers, and developing a bold pattern of dark-stained crackle. The piece is of a type generally considered as a product of the Chiao-t'an or "Suburban Altar" kiln not far from the palace in Hangchow.

Kuan-yin, the much adored Bodhisattva of compassion is shown seated with one arm resting on a raised knee in the pose of *maharajalila,* or "Royal Ease." Bare to the waist, she is crowned with a jewelled diadem formerly set with a figure of Amida in the center, and also wears bracelets and an elaborate jewelled necklace of strung beads. The figure is related to a series of Buddha and various Bodhisattvas of unusual size for porcelain sculpture, among which is a Kuan-yin figure at Kansas City dated, by inscription to the second or third year of Ta-tê – A.D. 1298 or 1299.

The bottle opposite is of characteristically Yüan octagonal form and made of a harder and more thickly potted porcelain than the Sung ware, thus accentuating the unevenness of the bluish-green tinted glaze; here and there appear unglazed, orange-burnt areas. The applied ornament of flower sprays on each face reveals a new and cruder striving after naturalism. They are framed in strings of pearl beads which are used also in decorative pendants applied above and below. It is a near-historic piece, relating closely to another now in the National Museum, Dublin, with a history of European ownership dating back to the fourteenth century, the oldest such piece surviving. The metal mounts here are probably German work of early eighteenth century date.

Porcelain mei-p'ing *vase with decoration carved in slip under the glaze. Yüan dynasty; fourteenth century. Height: 13¼ in (33.6 cm). Maximum diameter of body: 8 in (20.1 cm). Diameter of mouth: 1¾ in (4.5 cm). Diameter of base: 4 in (10.4 cm). Paris, Musée Guimet (no. G. 1211, Grandidier Collection).*

This broad-shouldered vase with a slightly flaring foot is completely covered with cobalt-blue glaze, except for a three-clawed dragon which encircles the whole body, treated in reserve and accentuated with white slip. The whole piece is covered with transparent glaze. The dragon is finely carved in every detail and appears in delicate relief, while the flames and plain lines are slightly sunken. The interior and the base are bare. This type of dragon is characteristic of the Yüan dynasty, with scales, a dorsal ridge, a slender muzzle and a tail that broadens towards the end and is bejewelled. Also typical is the pearl, which is linked to the flames by a very thin line. Some pieces with similar decoration are known, in particular a large dish from the Ardebil Treasury in the Archaeological Museum in Tehran.

Large dishes such as the one opposite, exported to Persia soon after their manufacture, were also among the first pieces of early Chinese porcelain to enter Western collections in the nineteenth century. Characteristic is the lavish use of cobalt for the blue background and the freedom of the designs which occur in different combinations on every piece. The blue on this dish is particularly brilliant and the successive bands of the design alternate between blue on white and white reserved against blue. The edge of the rim is blue and on the underside a single lotus scroll is enclosed between double concentric lines. The base is unglazed and is cream with orange–brown flecks, shallowly recessed.

Large porcelain dish with floral scroll design reserved in white against a blue background.
Yüan dynasty; fourteenth century. Diameter: 18 in (45.6 cm). Height: 3 in
(7.4 cm). London, British Museum (no. Franks 167).

Below: Foliated porcelain cup stand with a chrysanthemum scroll design in under-glaze red. Yüan dynasty; fourteenth century. Diameter: 3¾ in (9.7 cm). Stockholm, Östasiatiska Museet (Ö.M. formerly Gustaf VI Adolf Collection, no. 1944).

Opposite: Porcelain vase with phoenix design in under-glaze copper red. Yüan dynasty; fourteenth century. From Bali. Height: 10½ in (26.5 cm). Width: 5½ in (14.2 cm). Jakarta, Museum Pusat (no. 3837).

This cup stand with foliated cavetto and rim shows a typical shape used during the Yüan and early Ming dynasties as a base for under-glaze blue and copper-red decoration. The flower patterns are skilfully varied; in the center, within a raised edge, is an open lotus flower and the edge itself bears a petal border. Around the flat base runs a chrysanthemum scroll of rather strict design framed by double lines, while the lobed cavetto is decorated with symmetrical flower sprays of lotus and peony with palmette leaves. The horizontal rim with rolled lip carries an abstract spiral scroll which takes up the rhythm of the chrysanthemum scroll.

The vase opposite has a pear-shaped body narrowing gently towards the top, and rests on a large, firm foot. The mouth, apparently broken, is capped with a metal collar that is decorated with fine engraving. The decoration is painted under the glaze in splashy copper pigment ranging in colour from russet to light pink. The main motifs are the phoenixes in flight, interspersed with clouds, all in linear drawing.

Porcelain dish decorated in under-glaze blue with chrysanthemum patterns. Ming dynasty, Hung Wu period; 1368–1398. Diameter: 18 in (46 cm). Stockholm, Östasiatiska Museet (Ö.M. formerly Gustaf IV Adolf Collection, no. 2621).

In this Ming dynasty dish, the flat center is occupied by a chrysanthemum plant with three main stalks; these split up into several smaller ones which spread freely over the surface. Four flowers in full blossom, buds and leaves give a good impression of plants growing in a garden. Around the cavetto a strong and springy, almost baroque, scroll is depicted with more conventionalized lotus and peony flowers. A tiny scroll on the rim repeats the chrysanthemum pattern. The blue is not very strong, but the design is sensitively executed.

*Large dish with pine and rock design. Blue-and-white. Ming dynasty; early fifteenth century.
Diameter: 25 in (63.5 cm). Height: 3½ in (9 cm). Teheran, Iran Bastan Museum (no. 8848,
Ardebil Collection).*

This is a very large dish without an everted lip. The principle in common in the decoration of such dishes is to paint a naturalistic design of flowering plants, trees and rocks on the flat interior bottom and to scatter six to eight flowering or fruiting sprays on the gently curving cavetto. There are two more similar examples in the Ardebil Collection. In Japan the Nezu Art Museum, the Idemitsu Art Museum and the Umezawa Kinenkan Museum possess one piece each. The last example, in particular, is almost identical in design with the present piece. The main decoration of this dish consists of pine trees with their roots enclosed by rocks, and lily, cycad, azalea and primrose plants around them. The subdued tone of the cobalt blue adds to the quiet mood of the design. A mark of Sah Abbas is incised above the base.

This dish is of very high quality and spectacular in the simplicity of the design, in plain white reserve against an even monochrome blue ground. Four branches of peach and other fruit surround the central spray of pomegranate flowers and leaves. Only the faintest traces of blue appear within the white areas, and the incised modelling lines, if they exist, are so faint as to be invisible.

The decoration of the vase opposite in the *fa-hua* style, with lines and dots in relief, is particularly well suited to the shape. The background is of a very luminous turquoise glaze which is streaked and is of varying thickness. The decoration is in deep violet blue, purple, green, light yellow and black. The principal motif shows a procession of three horsemen, each followed by a servant carrying a parasol.

Box containing two ink trays. Porcelain painted in under-glaze blue. Ming dynasty; first quarter of sixteenth century. Mark of Chêng Tê (1506–1521). Height: 4½ in (11.5 cm). Base: 10 × 6 in (25.8 × 15.5 cm). Cover: 9½ × 5¼ in (24 × 13.5 cm). Paris, Musée Guimet (no. G. 4558, Grandidier Collection).

This rectangular box is composed of two compartments containing two ink trays, and a cover. The lower compartment forms a pedestal wider than the box. On top of the cover and on four sides of the middle compartment, a decoration of stylized leaf scrolls surrounds medallions and lozenges that are enclosed by a double line and contain inscriptions in Arabic and Persian. On the cover the Arabic inscription reads: "Seek perfection in calligraphy, for it is one of the keys to existence." On the sides of the middle compartment, the Persian inscription reads: "Silence is an invaluable elixir. Ignorance is an irremediable ill." On the four sides of the cover is a design of *ju-i* and of small knobs. On the pedestal is a design of extended and scalloped *ju-i*. On the base is a six-character mark of the reign of Chêng Tê (Ta Ming Chêng-tê nien chih) in a double rectangle cartouche. In the reign of the Ming emperor Chêng Tê (1506–1521) a certain number of blue-and-white porcelain pieces appeared that were very carefully made and bore Arabic and Persian inscriptions. For the most part they consist of articles intended for the writing desk, though candlesticks, bowls, vases and dishes also exist. The decoration seems very homogenous, comprising stylized leaves and *ju-i*, as on this box. The inscriptions make one assume a Moslem clientele. Most probably they were intended for the Moslems in the entourage of Chêng Tê, perhaps for the Hui-t'ung kuan (the Foreign Embassy Quarters), where many Moslem envoys stayed under Chêng Tê.

The decoration on this box is an incised design of turquoise dragons on a dark blue ground, interspersed with floral scrolls. The pattern is repeated on the top and shoulder of the lid and on the base, and is bordered by bands of classic scroll. The quality of the piece is said to be better than other examples, and it is the only one to bear the mark of the Chêng Hua period. The six-character mark is well written and enclosed within a double ring on the smooth white base. The interior of the lid is glazed and the interior of the base is unglazed, except for a circular area in the middle. There are several firing cracks in the base.

Below: Porcelain dish painted in enamels with bird and plant design. Ming dynasty. Chêng Tê
mark and period; 1506–1522. Diameter: 8¼ in (21.3 cm). Height: 1½ in (4.1 cm). London,
Victoria and Albert Museum (Acc. No. C. 56–1935, Eumorfopoulos Collection).

Opposite: Porcelain mei-p'ing vase decorated in under-glaze blue and enamels. Ming dynasty.
Chia Ching mark and period (1522–1566). Height: 11½ in (29 cm). Width: 6½ in (16.5 cm).
Stockholm, Östasiatiska Museet (Ö.M. formerly Margot Holmes Collection MHC, no. 2078).

This dish is painted with a sparing and well-composed design of a parrot-like bird perched on a flowering plant growing beside a rock, with a sun overhead. Use of the enamelling technique was greatly extended in the sixteenth century, and in addition to green, yellow and red we find here a bright turquoise blue. The outside is decorated with flowering plant sprays; the reign mark is written on the base in the same red enamel.

The mei-p'ing vase is signed Chia Ching. The body is heavier and the sides are straighter, without the characteristic concave shape of the early Ming vases. The decoration of conventionalized curling lotus scrolls in the under-glaze blue is divided into three borders around the body. Around the neck are petals in blue on a red ground. The Chia Ching mark is painted in blue on the base.

Opposite: Porcelain ewer with ornamental design in enamels. Ming dynasty; sixteenth century. From Sahu, Halmahera island, Maluku. Height: 9½ in (24 cm). Width: 6 in (15.7 cm). Jakarta, Museum Pusat (no. 2366).

_____

Below: Porcelain dish with figural and floral design in enamels. Ming dynasty; sixteenth century. From North Lampung, Sumatra. Diameter: 12 in (30 cm). Height: 2½ in (6.3 cm). Jakarta, Museum Pusat (no. 3171).

The ewer opposite has a pear-shaped body with two flattened sides, a tall neck and a tall spreading foot. On the front side is a long, slender spout, and on the rest is a curving handle. The neck and the spout are connected by an S-shaped support. It appears that originally there was a small ring attached to the top of the handle. The decoration is painted mainly in red and touched with yellowish green and light sky blue. Gold was originally applied to the red areas of the inverted heart-shaped panels on the flattened sides, the four-foiled ogee panels on the fore and rear of the neck, as well as to the spout and the handle, but it has disappeared.

This white porcelain dish with gently curving sides is decorated in red, green and yellow over-glaze. The approximately flat center medallion shows a judge clad in a red robe and a crown, a half-naked criminal with his hands tied behind him, an officer behind him brandishing a club, and a soldier holding a banner by the judge. It seems to illustrate a scene from some story or drama.

The porcelain of the jar opposite is thick, heavy and greyish. The decoration combines under-glaze blue and green, iron red, light brown and yellow enamels. The design is outlined in iron red. The so-called Thousand Deer theme seems to have appeared for the first time in the Wan Li period, but it was unusual. Here the motif is spread over the whole piece, with the exception of the neck, which is decorated with six separate flowers. The deer are in groups: in a watchful stance, at rest, bathing or running, all in very realistic attitudes painted from life.

This dish has a greyish-white body dressed with a thin coat of iron pigment, painted over with a design in white slip, and subsequently covered with a transparent glaze. It is decorated, in the center medallion, with a sitting lion, a pine tree, flowering grasses and clouds; surrounding it are dragons, fishes and waves; and on the everted, flat lip are blossoming sprays of various kinds. The roughly fashioned foot is one characteristic of the so-called *gosu-de*. The dish has been damaged and mended.

This vase of "*rouleau*" shape has a flaring cylindrical neck separated from the shoulder by three adjacent bands in light relief. The decoration uses all the *famille verte* enamels (including blue enamel) in such vivid shades that they stand out strikingly against the white porcelain background. The belly is ornamented with a large tree with green and blue foliage, very stylized perforated rocks, arborescent peonies, clouds and a pond where lotus plants are growing. In this setting are a great many birds, either perched or flying. Pairs of cranes, phoenixes, pheasants, ducks, sparrows, etc., can be picked out, all treated with great delicacy. On the neck are small birds and prunus branches. On the base is an under-glaze blue double circle.

The decoration on the dish opposite is immediately reminiscent of the contemporary designs executed in colour woodblock printing in "The Mustard Seed Garden Painting Manual," especially the prints with insects and flowers in the third part, which was published in 1700. The traditional Chinese ornamental garden rock has been playfully lightened until it is almost weightless, a form far beyond the possibilities of any natural rock from Lake T'ai. So treated, it becomes the perfect complement and setting for a variety of insects, plants, flowers and grasses, with a rich series of greens providing the dominant colouring. On close inspection, the ripening heads of millet are seen to be starred with florets in red and yellow. The underside is left plain, but an artemisia leaf and ribbon within a double ring forms the characteristic mark in under-glaze blue. There is a double foot ring.

Opposite: Vase with the theme of "A Hundred Birds." Porcelain decorated with famille verte *enamels. Ch'ing dynasty. K'ang Hsi period; 1662–1722. Height: 17 in (43.5 cm). Maximum diameter of body: 8 in (20.2 cm). Diameter of mouth: 4½ in (11.3 cm). Diameter of base: 5 in (13.1 cm). Paris, Musée Guimet (no. G. 4979, Grandidier Collection).*

Below: Large porcelain saucer-dish with a design of insects and flowering plants. Over-glaze enamels. Artemisia mark. Ch'ing dynasty. K'ang Hsi period; 1662–1723. Diameter: 13½ in (34.3 cm). Height: 2½ in (6 cm). London, British Museum (no. Franks 511).

Of typically K'ang Hsi form, the four-sided, tall-necked vase with handles in the form of dragon-like branches illustrated opposite is painted on each face with designs of flowering trees growing by rocks. The enamels of the *famille verte* are here applied direct to the unglazed porcelain "biscuit" with a corresponding gain in richness, and the overall effect of the three greens, purple, white and black set against the clear yellow ground – from which such pieces are sometimes classed as the "*famille jaune*" – is altogether sumptuous.

The Ming *san-ts'ai* style of decoration remained popular long after the end of that dynasty, and the example above with its scene of Buddhist worthies strolling in landscape round the outside, and flower sprays inside, is typical in treatment and in colouring of the early Ch'ing use of the technique in this palette. It should be noted that there is a six-character mark of the Chia Ching period (1522–1566) in under-glaze blue on the base, but the piece is clearly not of that period on the basis of its shape, style of drawing and the wider range of tones in which the painting is executed.

Below: Porcelain dish painted in famille rose *enamels with design of quail. Ch'ing dynasty. Yung Chêng mark and period; 1723–1736. Diameter: 8 in (20.3 cm). Height: 1¼ in (3.2 cm). London, Victoria and Albert Museum (Acc. No. C. 646–1903, gift of W. G. Gulland).*

Opposite: Kuan-yin statuette of white porcelain from Tê-hua (Fukien). So-called blanc de chine. *Ch'ing dynasty; second half of seventeenth century. Height: 12¼ in (31.2 cm). Maximum width: 7 in (18 cm). Length of base: 6 in (15.5 cm). Width at base: 4½ in (11.5 cm). Paris, Musée Guimet (G. 535, Grandidier Collection).*

A single pink flowering spray and a few green reeds provide the foil to the picture of a quail asymmetrically disposed on this saucer-shaped dish. A crimson pink and thick white are telling ingredients of the new palette of enamels introduced at this time, which allowed for opaque and shaded tints as well as sweet and pretty colouring. On account of their European inspiration they were known as "*yang-ts'ai,*" or "foreign colours."

The white porcelain of the statuette opposite is very heavy with a particularly fine grain and an unctuous glaze of pure white verging on grey, which takes on bluish tints where it is thick. The hollow interior is completely covered with the same glaze which is very crackled, and the head joint is apparent. The foot rim is bare. The goddess is seated on an oval ribbed pedestal with her hands hidden by the folds of her robe. She is wearing a diadem decorated with a small figure of Amitabha in front of an aureole. On her breast a lotus flower in relief hangs from a pearl necklace. At the back is the seal of the potter.

Porcelain brush holder with landscape decoration in sepia. Ching-tê-chên ware. Ch'ing dynasty. Yung Chêng period; 1723–1735. Mark: "Yung-cheng nien chih." Height: 5 in (13.1 cm). Diameter of mouth: 6¾ in (17.2 cm). Boston, Museum of Fine Arts (no. 57.748, gift of Mr and Mrs Paul Bernat).

Pieces decorated in sepia are very rare, reportedly made only for the court. The overall aesthetic impression is comparable to a fine etching in Western art. Illustrated here is a refined example which shows a landscape executed in a continuous handscroll-like composition. The brushwork has a painterly quality which is different from mere decorations by craftsman-potters. Spatial arrangement and style of the painting reflect the characteristic compositional flavour of the period. The brush holder has thickly potted straight sides with a thickened mouth rim on the interior side. It is glazed white inside and out.

Plate with narcissus design. Porcelain decorated with famille rose *enamels. Ch'ing dynasty. Yung Chêng mark and period; 1723–1735. Diameter: 8¼ in (20.9 cm). Height: 1½ in (3.9 cm). Diameter of base: 5 in (12.5 cm). Paris, Musée Guimet (no. G. 586, Grandidier Collection).*

This bowl-shaped plate is of translucent white porcelain. The *famille rose* enamels are simultaneously strong and delicate and the composition of the decoration is completely in harmony with the shape of the piece. The firm contour lines are drawn in black, except for the flowers – brown is used for the narcissi, carmine for the rose. The entire narcissus plant is represented – roots, bulb, leaves and flowers – while the rose bush branch just has leaves, one flower in bloom and another in bud. The narcissus is the flower of the twelfth month, blooming in the new year and bringing happiness for the coming year. The rose is an auspicious spring flower. Two *ling-chih* fungi, symbols of longevity, complete the good wishes contained in the design. The red enamel of one of the fungi is used together with the whole range of the *famille rose.*

Below: Large vase with peony design. Famille rose *enamels. Ching-tê-chên ware. Ch'ing dynasty. Yung Chêng mark and period; 1723–1735. Height: 20 in (51.1 cm). Diameter of mouth: 5 in (12 cm). Diameter of base: 6¼ in (16.2 cm). Tokyo, National Museum (gift of Dr Tamisuke Yokogawa).*

Opposite: Large white porcelain vase with "Thousand Flower" design, decorated in enamels. Ch'ing dynasty. Ch'ien Lung mark; end of the period. Height: 18¾ in (48 cm). Maximum diameter of body: 14 in (36 cm). Diameter of mouth: 8½ in (21.5 cm). Diameter of base: 10 in (25.8 cm). Paris, Musée Guimet (no. G. 3444, formerly Camondo Collection [sold in 1893], Grandidier Collection).

The shape of this vase, with a round, almost globular body and a thick, tall neck, is one popularly known as *t'ien-ch'iu-p'ing*. A thick growth of peony plants and their large flowers are painted in naturalistic manner on its body to the neck. The *fên-ts'ai* enamels are used effectively to depict the shaded flower petals and the yellowish ends of the leaves. The decoration cannot be by an ordinary ceramic decorator but must have been the work of an experienced, expert artist.

The porcelain of the "Thousand Flower" vase opposite is thick and heavy and is decorated on the outside with a rich and varied spectrum of the *famille rose* enamels and iron red. The base and the interior are turquoise: the rounded lip of the mouth is gilt. This decoration appeared under Ch'ien Lung and continued under Chia Ching (1796–1820), but it is seldom of this outstanding quality as regards the vividness of the colours and the harmonious arrangement of the flowers.

The decoration of this vase consists of a finely painted landscape and a poem accompanied by three red seals. The whole is executed with the delicacy that has become known as "in the Chinese taste" to distinguish it from the over-decorated enamel wares made for the European market. The poem may be translated, "The water pavilion beside the waves is a structure rare, the autumn pond a myriad *mou* of jade-green glass. Whoever it is who idly leans on the high rail gazing, 'tis just the time when the distant peaks seem floating in the mist." The six-character mark of Ch'ien Lung is written in seal style in under-glaze blue on the base.

The export porcelain plate opposite has a greyish white glaze that is dotted with small holes. The enamelled decoration of a Dutch ship seems to be the work of two different people: the rigging and the sails are painted with extraordinary precision and must be the work of a specialist, while the sea and the clouds are clumsily painted. It is possible that the inside circle of gilt spearheads was painted in advance, while waiting for a European order for it to be decorated on the spot (in Canton). On the rim of a cartouche surmounted by a crown reads in Dutch: "The ship *Vrijburg* under the command of Captain Jacob Rijzik, in China in 1756." It was the custom in Holland for a captain to have a picture of his ship painted. Examples of this in Delft faïence are known, as well as others in Chinese porcelain. There are a certain number of plates with a border decoration that is identical, though sometimes inverted, and where the text contained in the cartouche is different.

Opposite: Vase with over-glaze enamel decoration. Ch'ing dynasty. Ch'ien Lung mark and period; 1736–1795. Height: 9½ in (24.4 cm). Width: 5 in (13.2 cm). Washington D.C., Freer Gallery of Art (no. 38.10).

Below: Plate decorated with a sailing ship. Porcelain with enamelled and gilt decoration. Ch'ing dynasty. Ch'ien Lung period; 1756. Diameter: 15 in (38.1 cm). Height: 1¾ in (4.5 cm). Diameter of base: 9 in (23 cm). Paris, Musée Guimet (no. G. 106, Grandidier Collection).

Korean Ceramics

The beauty of Korean ceramics was recognized relatively late in the West, during the early years of the twentieth century, even though it had long been acknowledged in the Far East. At several points in history, whether in the fifth or the sixteenth century, Japanese potters had had good reason to draw inspiration from Korean wares, and even the Chinese had paid tribute to them in as early as the Sung dynasty. It cannot be denied that in its ceramics, as in other areas, Korea owed a debt to the neighbouring civilization of China, but this did not take the form of a purely repetitive transposition of Chinese ideas. Quite the opposite is true, for the Koreans imparted a new, inspirational quality to Chinese models that gives them a feeling of great freshness and spontaneity.

The earliest Korean pottery, fragments of which have been discovered among piles of shells, is coarsely textured and has no decoration. Radiocarbon analysis suggests that it was made during the early part of the fourth millennium B.C., while the third millennium saw the emergence of jars decorated with "combed" patterns that are comparable to Siberian wares of the same period. During the first millennium B.C., under the influence of Chinese settlers in Mongolia, farming made its appearance in northwest Korea in the form of millet cultivation. At this period the "combed" linear decoration on pottery was replaced by patterns of dots and geometric motifs. When nomadic horsemen from the Eurasian steppes penetrated Korea around 600 B.C. and introduced bronze working to the area, bottle-shaped jars covered in a shiny red slip that were almost certainly destined for funerary purposes began to appear. Rice farming spread along the western seaboard during the third century B.C., a period that also saw the

Vase with inlaid design of prunus tree, bamboos and swimming birds. Celadon. Koryŏ dynasty; twelfth–thirteenth century A.D. Height: 13 in (33.7 cm). Diameter of the mouth: 2¼ in (5.9 cm). Width: 8 in (20.5 cm). Diameter of base: 5 in (12.9 cm). Tokyo, National Museum.

Styles and decoration of Korean ceramics

Funerary urn with impressed decorative motifs and green glaze. Namsam, near Kyŏngju; unified Silla kingdom, eighth–ninth century. Seoul, National Museum of Korea.

production of a wide variety of smooth-surfaced wares, whose origins may perhaps lie in China, that were blackened with smoke at the end of the firing. China began to play a decisive role in Korean history at the end of the second century B.C., when it occupied the north of the country and established four military settlements, the most important of which, Lo-lang, was retained until 313 A.D.; during the same period the skills of silk working, lacquer ware, impressed tiles, ceramics and lead glazes were introduced to Korea, as well as the art of writing. Other elements of Chinese civilization entered Korea via the Koguryo dynasty, whose rulers arrived from Manchuria and established a kingdom in the north of the country, while further to the south the territory was divided between the two kingdoms of Paekche, to the east, and Silla, to the west. Buddhism, an important part of Korean civilization, spread through the country during the fourth century.

A ray of light is shed on this distant world by the grey stoneware figures of horsemen, dating from the fifth–fourth century, found in the Gold Bell Tomb at Kyŏngju, the capital of the Silla kingdom. Perhaps inspired by Chinese *mingki*, they display a powerful and, in certain details, minute realism which gives them a remarkable originality (page 359).

The unification of the country, achieved under the Silla kingdom in 688 A.D. with Chinese support, signalled the start of a long period of growth in Korean art, which now reflected T'ang influences. As far as funerary wares are concerned, the most notable items are earthenware jars with a characteristically globular body, a splayed foot, a cover surmounted by a tiny knop and decorated with a frieze pattern reminiscent of the designs found on Chinese silk. At the beginning of the tenth century power passed from the

Silla kingdom to the Koryŏ dynasty, which established its own capital at Kaesŏng in the north. The Koryŏ dynasty maintained good relations with the succession of different dynasties that now emerged in China and also with the small independent kingdoms that existed alongside them during this particular period of Chinese history. One of these was the Wu-Yüeh kingdom, whose ambassadors presented the Koreans with examples of celadon ware, which became adopted as models by local potters. Inspired by these Wu-Yüeh wares, the Koreans perfected their technique during the course of the eleventh century. The kilns, large numbers of which have survived, are concentrated in the south-western provinces, an area with rich supplies of excellent white clay. Excavations in the tomb of King Injong, who died in 1147, have revealed a vase with a flower-shaped mouth, tall neck, lobed body and broad "pleated" foot (page 358), which gives a good idea of the heights of excellence reached by Korean ceramics. Contemporary Chinese sources speak in awed tones of the results achieved by Korean potters.

It was not only in their glaze that Korean celadon wares achieved a high degree of perfection, but also in their decoration. The incised patterns were joined by beautifully modelled openwork designs, often in the form of arabesques or geometrical shapes, as well as an inlaid decoration of similar technical perfection. This highly original technique, known as *sanggam*, which was first introduced around the middle of the twelfth century, involved highlighting the incised motifs by means of a brown or white slip and then, after drying and a first firing, covering them with a layer of celadon glaze. The hexagonal decoration on the sides and lid of one rectangular cosmetic box (page 360), discovered in a tomb, exemplifies the

Gourd-shaped pitcher and cup with decoration of youths amidst vine tendrils. Celadon ware with inlay partially painted in underglaze copper red. Koryŏ dynasty; second half twelfth century. Seoul, National Museum of Korea.

Cup. Celadon ware with inlaid decoration of swirling hosoge, *imaginary flowers similar to peonies. Discovered in a tomb; Koryŏ dynasty, mid twelfth century. Seoul, National Museum of Korea.*

skilful use of openwork decoration that characterizes so many of the lavish ceramic objects made in Korea at the time. On inlaid pieces the glaze normally has a slight craquelure, as can be seen on a *maebyŏng* vase (the Korean equivalent of the Chinese *mei-p'ing*) from the second half of the twelfth century (page 361). The Korean "willow and swimming bird" pattern provides the extremely elegant decoration on another, slightly later *maebyŏng* with inlaid plants, water fowl, insects and geometric motifs (page 354).

At the beginning of the thirteenth century the influence of Chinese Tz'u-chou ceramics can be detected in the graphic sobriety of Korean decoration, while during the final stages of the Koryŏ period the trauma of the Mongols' arrival is reflected in a decline in the quality of the clays and glazes, as well as in less accurate firing techniques. However, a less sophisticated technique is matched by a very aesthetically pleasing decoration. An example of this is provided by a celadon vase which has a painted willow decoration of great elegance and simplicity (page 363).

In 1392 General Yi Song-ye expelled the Mongols, declared himself a vassal of the Ming Chinese, proclaimed himself king and established his capital at Seoul. Confucianism began to spread throughout the country, while the Yi dynasty also took advantage of the very long period of peace to promote the development of Korean art, with a committee being set up under the supervision of the Office of Painting to control and encourage the manufacture of ceramics. The traditional techniques were retained, while the shapes began to reflect those found in Ming porcelain. An example of this can be seen in a vase made of white stoneware, with flattened sides and a relatively tall foot (page 362).

There were many kilns scattered throughout the southern provinces, and it was perhaps the Zen monks working in them who were responsible for a particular style of decoration, appreciated purely as an exercise in intellectual pleasure, which exploited a few, rapidly executed brushstrokes to create a brief flutter of bamboo fronds or the sketchy outline of a fish. But the most famous examples of Yi porcelain are to be found amongst the more "rustic" wares. Nothing matches the fame enjoyed by the rough bowls, crudely potted on a wheel, which in Japan are known as *ido*. They exercised a strong fascination on the masters of the Japanese tea ceremony and were preserved with all the care accorded to precious objects. There is one which is particularly famous because it belonged to a great master of this ceremony (page 364).

At the end of the seventeenth century Korea was subjected to a two-fold invasion by the Japanese, when it suffered, among other indignities, the deportation of its potters. A few decades later it fell under the domination of the Manchus, who founded the Ch'ing dynasty in China. Despite the harsh conditions of vassalage, the Yi remained faithful to the Ming culture, and both the seventeenth and eighteenth centuries saw the introduction of new and original ideas by the Koreans in the areas of literature, painting and ceramics. Under the patronage of the court the ancient kilns were revived in several places and at Kwanju, not far from Seoul, an official ceramics center was opened. Another type of Yi ware has a copper-red decoration executed in a style reminiscent of that found in India-ink painting, as can be seen on a white porcelain jar, whose body portrays a growing lotus stem (page 365). Once again, the decoration underlines the Korean desire to convey a feeling of directness and immediacy.

Jar with flattened sides. Inlaid decoration of peonies that reflects a style of popular art. Yi dynasty; fifteenth century. Seoul, National Museum of Korea.

Tall-necked wine jar. Decorated in under-glaze blue with the ten "symbols of longevity" (including the crane and the tortoise). Yi dynasty; nineteenth century. Seoul, National Museum of Korea.

The vase opposite is an eight-lobed example with a foot not unlike a spreading pleated skirt. The mouth is in an exaggerated melon-flower shape. The glaze has little crackle, is light greenish grey, and shows very quiet gloss. Lobed vases of this sort are thought to have been inspired by Chinese ones of the Sung dynasty and modified by native Korean taste. Characteristic are the ample, graceful curves and the beautifully balanced form. The refined paste and flawless glaze make it a noble masterpiece of Koryŏ celadon at the height of its development. Shards of excellent lobed vases, similar to this in quality and form, were excavated during field research on the Koryŏ celadon kiln sites at Sadang-ri, Taegu-myŏn, Kangjin-gun, Chŏlla-namdo.

These vessels were excavated in 1924, along with a golden crown, from the Gold Bell Tomb at Rotong-dong, Kyŏngju-si, Kyŏngsang-pukdo. They are unusual examples in the shape of mounted figures with the horses' trappings represented in precise detail. The semiglobular and apricot leaf-shaped ornaments attached to the croup straps, the shapes of the stirrups and blankets, as well as the costumes of the riders, all show the style of the time clearly. The horses, each with a hollow trunk, a spout at the front and a handle at the rear, serve as water-pouring vessels, but are ceremonial and cannot be used practically. On the rump is a cup-shaped projection serving as a mouth, by which water was poured into the cavity of the body through a hole in its bottom. The differences between the costumes of the figures and the trappings of the horses suggest that the elaborately dressed figure on the right represents a dignitary while the one on the left in a simpler robe is his attendant. The attendant is ringing a bell in his right hand to clear the way. They are of a hard, high-fired ware.

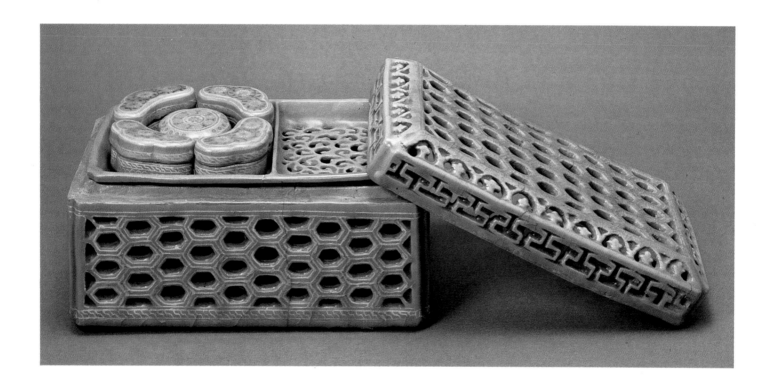

This box was excavated in 1939 from an old tomb at Mosan-ri, Nam-myŏn, Changhung-gun, Chŏlla-namdo. Apparently for use by a lady, it contained a rectangular bronze mirror, a gilt silver needle case with lotus scroll design, an oil bottle of inlaid celadon and some other objects. Inside, supported by the mouth of the box, is a rectangular tray with an openwork arabesque design which holds a set of five covered vessels. The top of the cover has bevelled edges. The shape is one found among Chinese cosmetic boxes of the Han dynasty and

Korean sutra (Buddhist scripture) boxes of lacquered and nacre-inlaid work of the Koryŏ dynasty; among such boxes, this shape is one of the more antique.

We seldom find examples of *maebyŏng* (Korean equivalent of the Chinese *mei-p'ing*) vases which still retain their original cup-shaped covers. In the example opposite, the shape of the cover leads us to suppose that a piece of silk or lace cloth was placed over the mouth reaching to the shoulder, over which the

cover was put. The cover is decorated with inlaid white clay with a crane on the top and clouds on the sides. The mouth of the base is ornamented with a band of clouds around the rim, the shoulders with a band of *ju-i* heads, and the area above the vase with a band of frets, all in white inlay, while the sides of the body are inlaid with sparse clouds in white and cranes in white and black. The spacious arrangement of the decoration saves it from appearing cluttered. The glaze is thin and glossy, of "kingfisher" colour, with crackle appearing around the inlays.

Below: Vase with flattened sides with inlaid peony and butterfly design. White porcelain. Yi dynasty; fifteenth century. Height: 9½ in (24 cm). Diameter of body: 9 in (22.7 cm). Seoul, National Museum of Korea (no. Tŏk 5464).

Opposite: Cylindrical vase with willow design painted in iron brown under celadon glaze. Koryŏ dynasty; thirteenth century. Height: 12¼ in (31.2 cm). Diameter of mouth: 2¼ in (5.5 cm). Diameter of base: 4¾ in (11.8 cm). Seoul, National Museum of Korea (no. 12419).

A soft, milk-white glaze with fine network crackle covers the bottle opposite. Each flattened side is inlaid in black slip with peony sprays and a butterfly represented in a rough, linear fashion. The foot is relatively tall compared with the neck. Glaze of this texture is seen frequently on ware from Kyŏngsang-namdo, and together with the shape and decoration, it clearly exhibits the characteristics of Yi white porcelain which followed in the wake of Koryŏ white porcelain. Somewhat different in glaze, paste and technique from Yi iron-glazed wares of the so-called *kugibori* ("nail-scratcher") type, it retains lingering traces of Koryŏ inlaid white porcelain.

Tall cylindrical vases are found occasionally among Koryŏ celadon wares with iron-brown painting. This one is a typical example. The mouth has a dignified form recalling that of a *maebyŏng* vase. The edge of the shoulder is bevelled generously to eliminate a rigid, angular appearance. Lofty elegance characterizes the spacing and style of the willow design painted with simple brushwork. Both the glaze and the paste are coarse. The glaze is almost a greyish green and in parts shows kiln transmutation effects due to oxidization. Conscious technical elaboration is absent from the shape as well as from the decoration, the only ornamentation being the willow tree painted on each of the front and rear sides. The unostentatious decoration typifies the liberal creative mode that prevailed in Koryŏ art in general at the time.

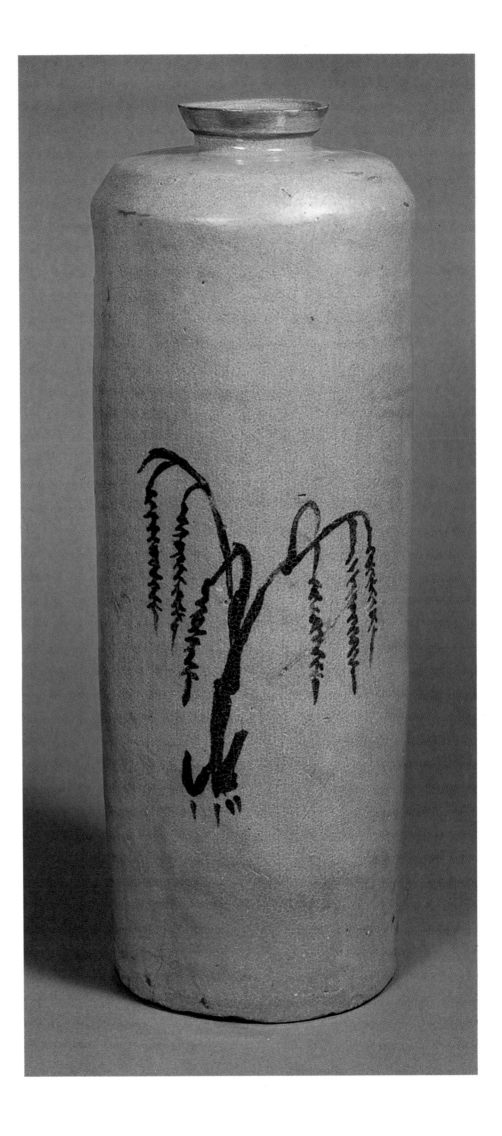

Korean tea bowls began to be favoured by tea ceremony masters in the late Muromachi period, replacing the Chinese ones. *Ido*-type tea bowls, along with *mishima*, were celebrated among the Korean wares from an early date. The term *ido* appears in records of tea ceremony parties in the early part of the Tenshŏ era (1573–1592 A.D.). This bowl, believed to have been used by Oda Uraku (1547–1621 A.D.), is only next in fame to the ŏ ("great")-*ido* tea bowls named Kizaemon, Tsutsu-izutsu, and Hosokawa. It is a relatively thick-walled bowl of an impressive form, with a small, turned foot. Around the foot remains a clear mark of the tool with which it was turned. The bowl is covered thickly with the glaze characteristic of *ido* known as the *biwa* (loquat yellow) glaze, which has formed granulations (*kairagi*, "shark-skin granules") around the foot.

The Yi dynasty potters of Korea made good use of copper-red pigments as they did also of iron brown and cobalt blue, and achieved notable successes with this fugitive medium. Their porcelain is less highly fired than the Chinese and is prone also to crazing and other surface defects; as in the case of this jar, however, the forms are ample, strong and filled with a peculiar sense of repose. The design of a growing lotus stem and its two curving projections here is executed with a Zen-like directness and economy, and achieves an impression of monumental stillness.

Japanese Ceramics

The manufacture of ceramics in Japan dates from before the eighth millennium B.C., according to recent carbon-dating results, and it is thought to have been introduced by a population of nomadic hunter-gatherers arriving from the Asian mainland. The earliest Japanese wares in their use of unrefined clay, their hand modelling and the way in which they were baked in open fires, sometimes in direct contact with the flames, can be linked to similar ones found in northern Asia. Their decoration, however, of surprising accuracy and exuberance, would appear to be uniquely Japanese. This characteristic decoration takes the form of interlaced and angular patterns, executed on unfired clay and composed of incised and impressed motifs and of raised elements. *Jōmon*, which in Japanese means "cord mark," is the name given to these prehistoric wares (page 372) and also to the culture that produced them, the first to emerge in the archipelago.

The next culture, the Yayoi, which was apparently introduced by a new population, soon made its mark, from the third century B.C. onwards, with a more advanced type of pottery. Not only was it made of denser, more refined clay, but it also had thinner walls and more regular shapes, achieved by the use of the wheel; what it lacks, however, is the decorative originality of *Jōmon* wares. This new cultural environment also witnessed the spread of farming and the introduction of metal working; rice appeared for the first time and funerary practices changed, with burials now taking place in necropolises situated far from the villages. During the fourth century B.C. some members of the ruling class began to be buried in chambers covered by mounds of earth. This era, which lasted from the fourth to the sixth century, is known as the Tumulus (Kofun) period. Tomb

Haniwa figure of a man in keikŏ *armour. Fired clay. From Gumma-ken; Tumulus period (Kofun), sixth century A.D. Height: 51¼ in (131.5 cm). Tokyo, National Museum. This man is protected by a suit of armour of* keikŏ *(scale armour) type, with shoulder pieces, cuisses, jambeaus and gauntlets.*

Styles and decoration of Japanese ceramics

Oval jar with flat base and funnel-shaped mouth. Yayoi pottery of the Ise district type. Aichi-ken; late Yayoi period. Tokyo, National Museum.

furniture, including pottery, was deposited in the cells and chambers, but the most interesting items were the *haniwa*, which were placed as sentries outside the tumuli: these lively examples of burial goods consist of human (page 366) and animal (page 373) figures, as well as miniature reproductions of buildings, boats and tools. Following the Korean example, kilns were also tunnelled into the sides of hills during the Tumulus period, and the high temperatures achieved in them had the effect of melting the grains of silica contained in the clay and creating a glazed effect. Sometimes a luster-like patina was obtained by ashes accidentally falling on the piece during firing.

This period also saw the early beginnings of the Japanese state, which was established in the third century under the leadership of a powerful group of noble families from Yamato. The fifth century saw a rise in the Chinese influence, which became particularly strong in the seventh and eighth centuries. Buddhism penetrated Japan, competing with Shintoism as a religious and cultural force and acquiring enormous political strength. During the eighth century, in order to escape interference by the local Buddhist monasteries, the Imperial court was obliged to move from Nara and establish its capital at Heian (modern Kyoto).

The first lead-glaze ceramics arrived from China during the seventh century, and over the next century a type of soft-paste, three-colour pottery was produced at Nara, using the same lead glazes as those used by the Chinese. During the Heian period (794–1185) other kilns were established near the new capital. A type of pottery slightly reminiscent of Korean and Chinese celadon ware also occurs, during the Late Heian period, amongst the pieces made in the so-called "six ancient kilns" and would continue to be made for many years to come. The "six ancient kilns" (the number six clearly refers to their locations and not to the actual kilns, of which there were hundreds) were, in order: Seto, Tokoname, Echizen, Tamba, Shigaraki and Bizen. Simple, rustic wares, with no decoration, were common, but each center had its own speciality. The kilns of Shigaraki, a village near Kyoto, which were spread over a hill, became renowned for cups and bowls with characteristic, white, granular flaws resulting from impurities in the local clay, whose effects were skilfully exploited by the potters. Tamba became particularly famous for its tea containers.

Chinese wares provided a continual source of reference, even after the Heian period. Toshiro, the man regarded as the father of Japanese ceramics, travelled to China in 1223, where he spent four years perfecting his skills at various kilns before working at Seto. On his return to Japan he began making glazed stoneware based on Sung models. Even towards the end of the Kamakura period (1185–1333) pieces were made at Seto in imitation of Chinese celadon ware, with an under-glaze decoration of swirls and floral motifs (page 374). This seems particularly significant when one considers that the Kamakura period was the one in which Japan freed itself, in other areas, from its cultural subservience to China and "discovered" its own independence. During the twelfth century Kamakura became the seat of the shogunate, which represented the apex of the new military and administrative apparatus that had been established in every Japanese province by the local aristocracy. The old organs of state, overseen by the court, were replaced and instead of the civil officials, similar to those found in the Chinese bureaucracy, there

Two mukozuke *cups. White-glazed stoneware with brown painted decoration. Shino ware; Momoyama or Edo period, late sixteenth–early seventeenth century. London, Victoria and Albert Museum.*

Dish. Porcelain painted in underglaze blue and enamels with a shakunage (mountain rose) *design. Produced at Okawachi in a factory founded by the prince of Nabeshima for his own personal use; Edo period, seventeenth century. London, Victoria and Albert Museum.*

emerged the new *samurai* class. Spiritually, the most salient feature of the Kamakura period was the spread of Zen, which now became the favourite mental discipline of the new warrior aristocracy, and which had been introduced to Japan from China centuries earlier.

The newly emerging Japanese taste, which was characterized by rather sophisticated preferences, did not favour the technical perfection and formal splendour of the Chinese, but instead tended towards the simple and the rustic. The Japanese appreciated sparse decoration, randomly spontaneous effects, natural irregularities and signs of hand working and they also liked the qualities of the raw materials to be reflected in the piece's appearance. One particularly famous type of pottery was made at the Mino kilns in Owari province, founded towards the end of the fifteenth century by craftsmen who had been forced to flee from Seto, which had been plunged into a constant state of war in the wake of the disintegration that followed the decline in central power. Trays, dishes, water jars and tea bowls were turned on the wheel and then worked by hand with the specific intention of giving them a feeling of irregularity. One typical product was the cylindrical tea bowl, whose misshapen nature made them comfortable to hold. A similarly skilful and intentional distortion of pieces, after they had been turned on the wheel, can also be seen in the important wares from Karatsu, on Kyushu island, the production of which began either in the late sixteenth century or during the seventeenth century. A similar phenomenon is represented by a Chinese or Korean potter, recorded under the name of Ameya Yakichi or Tanaka Sokei, who settled in Kyoto around the end of the sixteenth century and reverted to making pottery by hand, completely abandoning the wheel. These are all indications of how pottery was regarded as an art form in Japan at that time.

A brief anthology of pieces made during the Momoyama period (1573–1615) confirms this in several ways. The first example is provided by a Mino bowl (page 375), whose interior contains a white decoration of a few lines and touches depicting rocks and a wagtail, and whose roughly square shape and unequal sides seem to represent a conscious desire to obliterate any hint of serial uniformity. An even clearer message is conveyed by a Mino-Karatsu water jar (page 376), whose irregular body prominently displays the ridges left by the potter's fingers, as well as revealing a very cursory decoration and an intentionally imperfect glaze. One stoneware dish, salmon pink in colour, reveals a decoration of emblematic simplicity, achieved by means of a few deft brushstrokes, beneath its milky glaze (page 377). Two types of pottery produced during this period in the Mino kilns were subsequently named after two ancient and very famous masters of the tea ceremony, Shino and Oribe. One Motoyashiki piece that combines the characteristics of both types is a gourd-shaped vase (page 378) with a fresh and, to all appearances, very elementary decoration. Another example of Shino stoneware, with a white glaze, takes the form of a wine pot, its solidity emphasized by profuse and deliberately artless decoration (page 379).

During the Momoyama period the Japanese had their first contacts with Western civilization, when Portuguese traders landed on the small island of Tanegashima in 1543; the port of Nagasaki was opened to them in 1571 and in as early as 1549 the first Jesuit missionaries had appeared. This was a period of great openness in the history of Japan,

Flask in the shape of a gourd, painted in enamels with a bearded poet seeking inspiration beneath a tree. Arita, Kakiemon style; Edo period, c. 1660–1680. London, Victoria and Albert Museum.

Portable tier of boxes with decoration of dragons and waves. Work of the artist Aoki Mokubei; Edo period, eighteenth–nineteenth century. Tokyo, National Museum.

destined to end in 1640, when a completely opposite policy of strict isolation was adopted, heralding an era in which the country's sense of national unity was reinforced. One of the main protagonists of this historic operation, which reduced the numerous chiefs and local feudal lords (daimyo) to the status of dependent vassals, was the great warlord Hideyoshi, who, at the end of the sixteenth century, invaded Korea. Although his expeditions failed, many Korean potters were taken prisoner and deported to Japan, while others emigrated there of their own free will in the decades to come. All the destruction and deportations resulting from these wars, combined with the voluntary emigrations, led to more than 300 kilns being dismantled in Korea. It would also appear that the manufacture of porcelain in Japan had its foundations in these events.

In 1616 a deposit of kaolin was discovered near Arita on the island of Kyushu. The technique of porcelain manufacture had been known for some time, and now that the Japanese had access to the necessary raw material they were able to start practicing it immediately. The first wares to be produced, at Arita, were examples of the classic blue-and-white porcelain with an under-glaze cobalt decoration, but ceramists were soon experimenting with polychrome decoration which was applied over the glaze and then fixed by means of a second firing. Credit for this advance is traditionally given to Sakaida Kizaemon, later known as Kakiemon I, descendant of a family of Karatsu potters and founder of a dynasty of masters destined to last for many centuries. Examples of Arita ware reached Europe during the second half of the seventeenth century through the Dutch East India Company.

The Dutch were the only Westerners who had been granted permission to establish a trading post in Japan, situated on the small island of Dejima in Nagasaki harbour, and the first examples of Japanese blue-and-white porcelain arrived in Holland in around 1630. Some 20 years later the European market also demanded polychrome wares. This expansion in trade must be seen against the background of the Manchu invasion of China and the crisis in Chinese porcelain production that followed the fall of the Ming dynasty, which meant that for a certain period of time Japan found itself in the position of being almost the only source of Oriental porcelain. Later, partly as a result of the very high prices of Japanese wares, Chinese porcelain reverted to being the most popular type, but at that point the Chinese were on occasion obliged to copy the designs of their Japanese pupils. At the end of the seventeenth century Japanese Kakiemon wares were particularly highly prized in Europe for their elegance and refinement.

All this happened during the Edo period (1615–1868), at a time when Japan, under the rule of the Tokugawa shoguns, had already closed its frontiers to outsiders. Its commercial contacts were restricted to Nagasaki, the only port open to foreign trade. In 1658 seven junks laden with porcelain left Japan for Hsiamen; in 1659 the number of pieces imported into Holland was 5,548; the following year there were more than 70,000. Japanese porcelain, in quantities that are not easy to estimate, were later imported into Europe by the East India Companies of England, Denmark and France, who loaded their ships in China or even in India and the Arabian peninsula.

Japanese porcelain was known as Imari ware, after the name of the only port of embarcation in the Arita area, where ceramics destined for both the

Marks of Japanese Ceramics

Seal mark used from the seventeenth century onwards by a long dynasty of potters. Japanese potters bequeathed their sons and pupils the right to use their personal mark.

domestic and international markets were assembled; the export wares were then transported to Nagasaki. Imari was the term used to describe a type of porcelain with a relatively crowded decoration in a variety of colours, including an under-glaze blackish blue and a dark red, sometimes embellished with gold. Because these wares were copied by the Chinese they had to compete with a type of porcelain known as "Chinese Imari." Japanese craftsmen, in turn, skilfully copied Chinese wares, such as fake Ming porcelain, particularly of the Chêng Hua period.

Over the years, commercial success proved detrimental to maintaining a consistent technical quality, at least as far as the finest wares were concerned: Kakiemon wares, for example, only succeeded in preserving the pristine purity of their paste, the delicacy of their polychrome colours and the original transparency of their glaze until the opening decades of the eighteenth century. The decline in quality of Japanese porcelain was, however, a relatively late phenomenon.

The seventeenth century saw a flowering of artists and schools that were completely unaffected by commercial considerations. At Kyoto a type of ceramics known as Kyōyaki was produced, which is linked to the name of Nonomura Ninsei, a past master in the creation both of monochrome glazes and also brilliant over-glaze enamelling. This tradition was continued in the wares made at Takamatsu on the island of Shikoku: the decorative elegance and precision found on a covered container (page 380), thought to be the work of Morishima Shigetoshi, better known as Rihei, offers a fine example of this phenomenon. The virtuoso skills of Ninsei can also be admired in an exceptional vase decorated with a prunus tree beneath the moon and a pattern of gold-painted clouds (page 381). One type of porcelain, known as Ko Kutani ("old Kutani"), derives from a center located in the western part of Honshu, where it was produced from around 1639. Its characteristic floral decoration, as fluid as it is graphic, exploits a palette of rare beauty and elegance (page 382).

The wares of greatest artistic merit were not, understandably, those made for the open market, but were created, for example, in kilns set up in the parks and gardens surrounding the residences of the nobility, who commissioned them for their own private use. This was the case with Nabeshima wares, which were made at Okawachi, not far from Arita, exclusively for the princely family of the same name, either for themselves or as gifts to be presented to their fellow nobles. These wares, made either of stoneware or porcelain, are mainly in the form of dishes, some of which are true masterpieces (page 383), decorated with landscapes, flowers, birds, fruit and patterns reminiscent of the richly woven designs found on kimonos. A similar artistry is to be found in the works of Ogata Kenzan, the most famous of the Kyoto potters, which reveal a clear surge in quality. Images such as those that appear on one of his famous, signed trays (page 384), possess an extraordinary delicacy and intensity.

One particular type of porcelain developed during the Ming period, with gold decoration on a red or green ground, became very popular in Japan, where it was known as *kinrande*. An influence on, amongst others, the style of Ninsei, it was just one of the many strands which go to make up the great ceramic art of the Orient and which was readopted to brilliant effect by a highly talented artist at the beginning of the nineteenth century, Aoki Mokubei (page 387).

Mark with signature of the painter and potter Ogata Kenzan (1663–1743).

九 大
谷 日
造 本

Mark on nineteenth-century Kutani porcelain. The six characters proclaim "made at Kutani in the great Japan."

Ewer. Jōmon pottery. From Aomori-ken; late Jōmon period. Height: 8½ in (21.8 cm). Diameter of mouth: 3¾ in (9.5 cm). Width: 10 in (25.6 cm). Tokyo, National Museum (gift of Mrs Misao Takamatsu).

Vessels of this form, with an oval body, ascending spout, and rounded base, since early times were referred to as earthenware teapot shapes. The upright neck is decorated with small raised and incised dots; around its base are two parallel bands. The body is decorated with *surikeshi* (erased) *jōmon*: the surface was first decorated all over with a *jōmon* (cord mark) pattern, then curved borders were drawn, and subsequently the *jōmon* pattern inside the borders was removed by burnishing. The erased areas are a glossy black, probably the result of a special technique. Incised dots like those on the neck ornament the zones between double border curves. Small raised dots like protuberances within the borders serve to mitigate the sharp appearance of the projecting spout.

Haniwa figure of a horse. Fired clay. Tumulus (Kofun) period; sixth century A.D. From Saitama-ken. Height: 34½ in (87.5 cm). Tokyo, National Museum.

Figures of horses are the most numerous among *haniwa* animals. The majority of them are decorative horses in full trappings. This horse is a typical example. It has a saddle placed over an *aori* (blanket) on the back. A pair of ring stirrups hang from the saddle. Four large pendent *bataku* (horse bells) are fastened to the breast strap. Bell ornaments are attached also to the cheek plates of the bit and to the three *guŏyŏ* (apricot leaf-shaped metal ornaments) on the hip straps. Curb chains and reins are fastened to the bit. *Tsuji-kanagu* (metalwork ornaments at crossings) are attached where the head straps cross.

The figure is outstanding in workmanship among *haniwa* horses. Unfortunately its cylindrical legs are rather too short for the smart appearance of the steed. The mane and saddle have been replaced.

This is a representative piece of Old Seto from the late Kamakura period. Its shape and decoration reflect influence of Chinese celadon and white porcelain of the Sung and Yüan dynasties, which were imported to Japan at the time. This trend, noted in Old Seto in general, was an important characteristic of the ware. It is a yellowish white ware of considerably fine quality; the forming technique is coil and throw. The short, relatively wide and slightly tapering neck characterizes this jar. The base is flat. The peony scrolls executed in thick line incising all over the exterior are patterned after Sung and Yüan ceramic designs, but are modified into a Japanized modest expression. The ash glaze covering the entire exterior surface, of a yellowish dead-leaf colour, has fused well.

Shallow bowl with wagtail design. Grey Shino type. Mino ware. Momoyama period; sixteenth century. Height: 4¼ in (11 cm). Diameter of mouth: 11¼ in (28.5 cm). Tokyo, National Museum.

Of the many outstanding Shino bowls, this is one of the best. The bowl swells out sharply in step fashion from the foot, and from above it is roughly square in shape, though the sides are unequal. The interior design of rocks and a wagtail is depicted with incised lines and white slip. The flowing water, also rendered with lines, is suggestive of a mountain stream running through a valley, and the whole design bears the stamp of an assured artist. In the opinion of Toyozō Arakawa, the white slip was applied judiciously and with great care, thus revealing superb artistic sensibility on the part of the potter-artist.

Below: Mino-Karatsu water jar. Momoyama period; late sixteenth–early seventeenth century.
Height: 7½ in (19 cm). Width: 9¼ in (23.6 cm). Washington D.C., Freer Gallery of Art
(no. 67.17).

———

Opposite: Red Shino ware dish. Momoyama period; late sixteenth–early seventeenth century.
Diameter: 8¼ in (21.3 cm). Height: ¾ in (2.2 cm). Washington D.C., Freer Gallery of Art
(no. 62.22).

Karatsu-type *nobori-gama* were introduced in Mino by Kagenobu, presumably under the influence of the tea master Furuta Oribe, who had spent some time in the Karatsu region. The tea ceremony water jar (*mizusashi*) opposite shows the relationship between two great stoneware types produced over six hundred kilometers apart. The body is greyish Mino clay fired brown on the unglazed areas. The jar is wheel-thrown with the finger ridges studiously retained and two vertical grooves added. The shape, seen in both Mino and Karatsu water jars, has slumped into the desired irregularity. The uneven and scarred glaze covers iron-oxide sketches in the Karatsu manner. The base is string cut.

Beni Shino, which may be a delicate salmon pink as in this dish, simply means Red Shino and evidently was made at one Mino kiln, Takane. Essentially it is made of the same materials and in the same way as other Shino. The glowing colour effect is created by the use of a red slip on the greyish-white stoneware body and under the milky felspar glaze. The dish is almost flat with a slightly recessed foot. The raw red slip can be seen on the unglazed portions of the back. Bamboo grass has been simply and surely painted in black under the glaze.

This gourd-shaped vase is of a type made at Motoyashiki, perhaps the most important Mino kiln of the Momoyama period. The site has been carefully excavated and preserved. Shards and wasters of both Shino and Oribe wares were found, as well as examples combining features of both types. The mixed type is pleasingly represented in this vase with angular trellis and hanging grapevine painted in iron brown on stoneware under a typical Shino glaze. The glaze, however, is somewhat thinner than in many purely Shino types of the same period. There are minor restorations of the lip.

Vessels such as *mukōzuke* food bowls and the covered wine pot shown opposite were made for use in the light meal that preceded the tea ceremony, and were based on ideals of simplicity and rusticity. The material is painted in iron brown, with basketwork trellis patterns round the sides; on the small lid are a tree, grasses and plants. The apparent artlessness of the designs on such wares conceals a deliberate and economical touch and truthful observation of nature.

Opposite: Shino-Oribe vase. Momoyama period; late sixteenth–early seventeenth century. Height: 8½ in (21.5 cm). Width: 4 in (10.5 cm). Washington D.C., Freer Gallery of Art (no. 64.4).

———————

Below: Stoneware wine pot with white glaze painted in brown. Shino ware. Momoyama or Edo period; early seventeenth century. Length: 7 in (17.8 cm). London, Victoria and Albert Museum (Acc. No. C. 648-1923).

This large wheel-thrown vessel is thought to be by the potter Rihei, who worked on the island of Shikoku at Takamatsu from about 1649 until his death in 1678. It is believed that he came from Kyoto and that he used Kyoto clay and glaze materials, which explains the resemblance of this ware to types of Kyōyaki. The shape is formal and clean, the over-glaze enamels precisely and thickly applied in a formal scroll pattern with gold discreetly used. Barely recessed within the slightly stepped-in foot, the base is flat and unglazed. Lining the inside of the vessel is a thin reddish-brown coating overlaid by a silvery layer which has some blackened areas.

The shape of the jar opposite is patterned after that of the tea storage jars known as Luzon jars, which were valued highly by tea masters since the Muromachi period, but here it is decorated with an elegant over-glaze design characteristic of Ninsei. The design, applied over a thick, opaque white glaze, is that of a blossoming prunus tree under the moon. The red blossoms are bordered in gold, and the silver ones in red; the branches are in black and green; and the moon in silver on the shoulder. The silver has tarnished. The cloud patterns around the shoulders and belly are painted in gold as if done in bits of applied gold leaf, a technique frequently noted on Ninsei's works. A large "Ninsei" mark is stamped on the left side of the base. The jar has been in the Tokyo National Museum since 1878.

This is a large and relatively deep porcelain dish with a profile showing gentle curves, supported by a short foot. It is a greyish-white ware, covered with a transparent glaze, fired, then decorated over the glaze with large-flowered peony scrolls rendered in black lines with small flower motifs in between, and painted all over in transparent yellow, green and purple enamels. The underside is likewise ornamented with conventionalized scrolls drawn in black and covered all over with a yellow enamel. The foot rim is exposed, but the base inside it is glazed. A small square mark, hardly decipherable, is written in black and green enamels at about the center of the base. Among the wares collectively classified as Ko (Old) Kutani, this dish belongs to a variety known as Ao (Green) Kutani.

Large dish with design of bamboo fences and vines. Under-glaze blue and over-glaze enamels.
Nabeshima ware. Edo period; seventeenth–eighteenth century. Diameter: 12 in (30.8 cm).
Height: 3¾ in (8.2 cm). Diameter of base: 6½ in (16.3 cm). Tokyo, National Museum.

This dish is a masterpiece from the prime of Okōchi kiln, that is, the period between the Genroku and Shōtoku eras (1688–1716). It is an *ō-zara* ("large dish") about 11¾ in (30 cm) in diameter. The shape is basically an ordinary wooden wine-cup form, but is exceptional in the treatment of the mouth rim, which is rolled inward. The interior is decorated with a design of finely drawn bamboo fences, one on the upper left and the other on the lower right, and with washes of under-glaze blue, entwined by autumnal vines in over-glaze red enamel. The subtle representation of the seasonal subject well exhibits the features of enamelled Nabeshima porcelain. The reverse side is painted with peony scrolls, and the outside of the foot with a sequence of interlocking circles, both in under-glaze blue.

Below: Rectangular tray by Kenzan. Edo period; early eighteenth century. Length: 6½ (16.9 cm). Height: 1 in (2.4 cm). Washington D.C., Freer Gallery of Art (no. 05.58).

Opposite: Porcelain saké bottle painted in polychrome enamels. Kakiemon, Arita. Edo period; late seventeenth–early eighteenth century. Height: 7¼ in (18.6 cm). Diameter of neck: 1 in (2.6 cm). Diameter of base: 3¾ in (9.5 cm). Paris, Musée Guimet (no. MG. 8194, Original Collection of the Musée Guimet).

In the tray opposite, the artist-potter Ogata Kenzan, in a novel technique of colour painted in white slip under the transparent low-fired glaze, is able to create the freshness, softness, and nuances of watercolour painting, an effect impossible to duplicate in over-glaze enamels, which by nature must have sharp, distinct edges. The mandarin ducks in snow painted on the dish opposite symbolize the twelfth month. Kenzan's signature with a poem is painted on the back. Kenzan is among the Kyoto potters best known in the West, and his tradition continues to the present day. A similar dish in the Hakone Museum is dated Genroku fifteenth year (1702 A.D.).

This saké bottle is in the shape of a bamboo shoot on which, a little above the flat base, two green-tinted buds are sprouting. It is made of milky (*nigoshide*) porcelain characteristic of Kakiemon pieces. The design of trees and plum blossom is painted in polychrome enamels. On the upper part a neck emerges from flower petals in light relief. This decoration, from which under-glaze blue has disappeared, is probably dateable to the end of the seventeenth century. The milky effect of the porcelain was imitated at Saint-Cloud toward 1720. The shape is specifically Japanese and we have not found anything similar in Western repertoires. The bottle comes from the collection of Emile Guimet, and we do not know where it was acquired. It may have been during his stay in Japan in 1876. During a lecture on his travels there, he did in fact mention his many conversations with potters.

The design of the bottle-shaped vase opposite, with its globular body surmounted by a slender neck, possesses a rare elegance, and the quality of the smooth, white, fine porcelain is excellent. On the belly is a landscape with the background painted in washes, while in the foreground more distinct clumps of pine trees lend the composition balance. This sort of landscape is reminiscent of the *suiboki-ga* of the Muromachi period. The kilns at Hirado are traditionally attributed to Keichō 3 (1598), when Korean potters settled on the island. They were to progress swiftly from

pottery to porcelain, but their initial production was clumsy. In 1712 good-quality kaolin clay was discovered on Amakusa island and this encouraged studios to be set up at Mikawachi. Between 1751 and 1843 these were under the patronage of the Matsuura family, the daimyo of the area. This well-balanced piece may be attributed to that period.

Aoki Mokubei was among the most able and versatile of the many individual potters of the early nineteenth century in

Japan. At Kyoto he produced wares after the Chinese manner, including the Ming *kinrande* enamelled type, a development of which is seen in this sweetmeat box. Every surface excepting the bases is painted with inventive designs which spread freely across the tomato-red ground; on the lid *shou-lao* holds informal court among Immortals and admirers, while the lower tier, divided in five compartments like a jewel symbol, is decorated with the five fruits, peach, pomegranate, persimmon, loquat and lychee. The box is perhaps incomplete, and no signature is discernible.

GLOSSARY

Alabastron. Slim vessel of very elongated body, with flared mouth, narrow opening and flat or everted rim, used in Graeco-Roman Antiquity as a container for oils and perfumes. Very common throughout the fifth–fourth century B.C.

Albarello. Drug jar of cylindrical body, similar in shape to a section of bamboo cane, used by apothecaries and chemists. The first albarellos were produced in Persia and the shape was then spread throughout Western Europe by Hispano-Moresque potters.

Amphora. Two-handled vessel for the storage of wine and oil. The first decorated examples appear in Greece in as early as the Geometric period. During the sixth and fifth centuries B.C. the dominant type was of globular shape with a metope-like decoration and flat or rounded handles; from around the mid sixth century this was joined by the type with an ovoid body and continuous band of decoration. The same period also saw changes in the shape of the neck, the lip, the shoulders and the foot, as well as the handles, providing potters with new and different decorative possibilities.

Arabesque. Decorative motif formed of stylized, abstract floral designs, which can be continuously repeated. The arabesque has always occupied an important place in the decorative repertoire of Islamic art.

Armenian bole. Red clay with a high percentage of iron, famous in Europe during the Middle Ages and the Renaissance for its excellent medicinal properties as an astringent. Its original source was, as implied in its name, Anatolia (although it also seems to occur in France). Because of its bright, sealing-wax red, it was used by Ottoman potters, at the same time as the Italians, for the under-glaze painting of pottery. Iznik wares are characterized by the use of Armenian bole, which appears on the surface in gentle relief.

Arretine ware. Type of ware modelled in a very refined clay and covered with a glossy red glaze. It was used normally for tablewares, especially dishes, but also bowls and pitchers, in shapes imitating contemporary metalware. Arretine wares, which derive their name from Arezzo, Italy, were turned on the wheel. They come in a variety of different types: some have a smooth surface, with the addition of a few manually executed reeded or milled patterns, while others are decorated using the *à la barbotine* technique or have pre-moulded relief elements applied to the body. There is also the vast category of vases with relief decoration, which were moulded after being turned on the wheel. This technique had the undoubted advantage of allowing low-cost mass production so that these wares were able to penetrate every level of society and every province and region of the Classical world. The production of Arretine wares, which lasted for little more than 50 years, began in around 30 B.C.

Artemisia leaf. In China, one of the Eight Precious Things and a symbol of good luck. It appears frequently in decoration, particularly on *kraak* porcelain of the late Ming dynasty (1368–1644) and was often used as a mark during the Kang Hsi period (1662–1722).

Aryballos. Small Greek vase used for oils and perfumes, characterized by a broad body, narrow neck and sometimes, a single handle, used extensively by Greek athletes to contain the oil with which they anointed their bodies during contests. They first became widespread at the end of the ninth century, when the potters of Corinth began to produce them in large quantities for export as well as for the domestic market.

Askos. Type of Greek vessel with a shape resembling that of a wineskin. It exists in various versions: the most common has a swollen body, slightly flattened at the sides and with an off-center opening. Also frequent is the animal-shaped *askos* with a cylindrical pourer on the back. Although not very common, this type was made in Greece during the sixth–fifth century B.C. and at a later date, with certain variations, by potters in southern Italy.

Baidunzi. More commonly known as *petuntse*, from the term adopted by the Jesuits during the eighteenth century, which soon became common in Europe. It is a non-plastic, felspathic rock that is added to kaolin to produce porcelain. Ground into a powder, it was sent to porcelain manufacturers in little white blocks ("*baidunzi*" in Chinese).

Bamboo. A symbol of longevity in Chinese iconography because it remains green during the winter. The bamboo bends with the wind and does not break so it also symbolizes the scholar who remains faithful even in the face of poverty. Together with the plum and the pine, it is one of the Three Friends of Winter.

Barbotine, à la. Technique of relief decoration involving the application of semi-liquid clay, by means of a brush, reed or syringe, to the surface of a piece.

Bell crater. So called because its shape resembles that of an inverted bell. It has a very broad body, with no neck, and small, horizontal handles positioned near the rim.

Bellarmine. A type of flagon or pitcher, produced mainly in the Rhineland, with a bearded mask on the neck or below the pourer. During the sixteenth century this face was believed to be a caricature of Cardinal Bellarmine, a figure of hate in Protestant countries because of his Counter-Reformation beliefs.

Berrettino or *Berettino.* Grey-blue or dark blue glaze on which arabesques, trophies, grotesques, flowers and fruit etc. were painted in white or polychrome. It was used in particular by the potters of Faenza during the sixteenth century.

Bianchi di Faenza. Majolica wares, made at Faenza and characterized by a milky white glaze that gave particular prominence to the surfaces and shapes of the pieces. Produced at Faenza from the mid sixteenth to the beginning of the eighteenth century, these wares were widely copied by factories in Northern Europe.

Biscuit. Term applied to ceramic wares that have been fired but not glazed. The temperature of this first firing can range from 1472°F (800°C) to 2372°F (1300°C), depending on the structure of the piece and the type of glaze to be used.

Bisque or *Biscuit porcelain*. Name given to unglazed white porcelain, which is similar in appearance to marble and has a matt surface. Biscuit porcelain was used, particularly during the nineteenth century, to model figures. The Sèvres factory was the first to use it.

Blue-and-white (Chêng Hua). The technique of under-glaze painting in cobalt blue was introduced in China at the beginning of the fourteenth century. In China the cobalt oxide was mixed with the material used for the felspathic glaze, ground, mixed with water and then painted directly on to the unfired body. After this last operation a felspathic glaze was applied, which by being baked in a reducing atmosphere at the same high temperature as the body (2336–2372°F [1280–1300°C]) became bonded to it. The colour of the blue depends mainly on the purity of the cobalt; iron or manganese impurities will produce a greyish or blackish colour. Initially the Chinese almost always used cobalt imported from the Middle East, which, although untainted by manganese, did contain traces of iron. This produced an intense, dark colour, but, if not accurately diluted, its high concentration of iron tended to make it break out of the glazed surface and create a black or reddish-brown oxidization. At the beginning of the fifteenth century local cobalt began to be used, but always mixed with the imported product. The heyday of blue-and-white wares were the Hsüan Tê (1426–35) and Chêng Hua (1465–87) periods, which is why the reign marks of these eras were the ones most widely reproduced in later centuries.

Bucchero ware. Special type of shiny black pottery, turned on the wheel and first produced in Etruria during the seventh century B.C. The characteristically glossy black seems to derive from a special process of firing in a reducing atmosphere (one low in oxygen). A distinction is normally made between thin bucchero, dating from the beginning of the seventh century B.C., with thin walls and mainly incised decoration, and heavy bucchero with thicker walls and high-relief decoration; which was created separately and then applied to the surface (fifth century B.C.). Amphoras, craters, *oinochoes*, *rhytons*

and *kantharoi* are common, but there are also numerous vases. The word derives from the Spanish *bucaro*, a term used to describe certain vases made in South America that became popular in Italy at virtually the same time as the first Etruscan tombs and necropolises were discovered.

Butterfly. Symbol of joy, summer and marital happiness.

Calyx-crater. Very common from the sixth to the end of the fourth century B.C., it was one of the favourite shapes of Attic black-figure and red-figure potters. It is characterized by a flared vase with no neck and with two, often oblique handles emerging from the base.

Camaïeu. Type of monochrome decoration, generally executed on porcelain, exploiting the *chiaroscuro* effects obtainable from shaded gradations of the same colour. Blue *camaïeu* decoration was particularly widespread during the eighteenth century.

Celadon. Name applied to stoneware and porcelain whose surface colour varies from pale to olive green because of the presence of iron oxide that has been fired in a reducing atmosphere. The name "celadon," by which these wares are known in Europe, was first coined by the French because of the colour's similarity to that of the ribbons worn by the shepherd boy Celadon, protagonist of the novel *Celadon* by Honoré d'Urfé (1568–1626).

Chevrette. Pharmacy jar, used for oils and syrups, with a short neck, spout and handle.

Chinoiserie. Decoration in the Chinese taste introduced into Europe by the potters of Delft during the second half of the seventeenth century. It consisted of Oriental motifs reinterpreted in accordance with European stylistic concepts. Dragons, fantastic birds, small Chinese figures in exotic clothes, landscapes with pagodas and dwarf trees are recurrent subjects. The fashion for chinoiserie, which continued throughout the eighteenth century, declined with the advent of Neo-Classicism.

Chintamani motif. From the Sanskrit. Decorative motif composed of a group of three closed half moons and short wavy lines, widespread in Anatolia from the early Middle Ages, but characteristic of the Ottoman wares of Iznik. Another frequent element on the latter is the single closed half moon, similar to a pearl, an ancient Central Asiatic and Far Eastern motif linked to the concept of water-born fertility, the equivalent of the Indian *chintamani*: the jewel of the Naga (a water spirit in Hindu Mythology, half human and half serpent, said to augur prosperity).

Chrysanthemum. In Far Eastern iconography a symbol of Autumn and of joviality. It is associated with a life of comfort, far from public office.

Coiling. Method of modelling pottery vessels by hand, by piling up coils of clay and then pressing them together with the fingers.

Coloured and/or liquid clay. Very dilute clay used as a fixative, which was mixed with metallic colourants and used to decorate ceramic wares, generally those covered in a slip, in order to prevent the colours from running beneath the glaze. It was first used by the potters of Eastern Persia at the end of the ninth century.

Column crater. A variant of the classic Greek crater, characterized by the particular shape of the handles, in the form of small, vertical columns on which there rests a horizontal attached directly to the rim of the vase. Very widespread during the Late Corinthian era and throughout the seventh–sixth century B.C.

Compendiario style. Decorative style created by the potters of Faenza during the second half of the sixteenth century, with barely sketched drawings of female figures, busts, cherubs and coats of arms, all executed in a very sober palette of blue and yellow. It was used, above all, on the *bianchi di Faenza* (q.v.).

Craquelure. Technical term to describe the crazing and crackling effects caused to the surface by the different rates of expansion in the ceramic body and the glaze during the firing and cooling process. From the twelfth century onwards these "flaws" were exploited by the Chinese for decorative purposes.

Crater. Vessel widely used in Greek and Roman Antiquity for holding and mixing liquids, particularly wine and water. It has numerous variants, but the basic shape is characterized by a large bowl on a small support, a large mouth and generally small handles. Frequently mentioned and described by Homer, it would appear to have been brought to Greece from Assyria by the Phoenicians. (See *Bell crater, Calyx-crater, Column crater* and *Volute crater.*)

Creamware. Typical English product of the eighteenth–nineteenth century, which spread rapidly to France, where it was known as *faïence fine,* and Italy, where it was sometimes known as *terraglia all'inglese.* It has a hard paste, with an ivory-coloured body covered in a lead glaze. Being light, strong, translucent and, most especially, cheap, it became very popular throughout Europe, where it competed with faïence and majolica.

Cuerda seca. Technique of ceramic decoration consisting of outlining the shapes of the motifs in a mixture of grease and manganese so as to separate the different coloured glazes that form the decoration. The *cuerda seca* technique was first used in Spain and the Maghreb (North Africa) during the fourteenth century, although it also enjoyed limited popularity in other Islamic areas, for example Central Asia during the period of Timurid domination (1369–1500).

Deer. Because of its very long life, a symbol of longevity in Chinese iconography. It is also the only animal able to find the sacred mushroom of immortality.

Delftware. Term used to describe English pottery made in imitation of that manufactured at Delft. It is also used in a broader sense to describe all tin-glazed earthenware.

Dragon. Mythical creature, lord of the seas and the skies, emblem of the East. In China it symbolizes strength, authority

and goodness. There are said to be three types of dragon: one lives in the sky, one in the ocean and another in the marshes and mountains. A dragon may have three, four or five claws. The five-clawed version, which represents the emperor, is often accompanied by the phoenix, the symbol of the empress. Over the centuries the dragon has been portrayed in different ways: in the fourteenth century with branching horns, during the first half of the fifteenth century with a lion's mane and of terrifying appearance, while the fifteenth century saw the introduction of a sea dragon with a forked fish tail. During the Ming (1368–1644) and Ch'ing (1644–1912) dynasties the five-clawed dragon often appears on official wares made for the court, almost always amidst clouds or waves and in pursuit of the flaming pearl, probably a symbol of thunder or the sun.

Ducks. Together with geese, ducks are Oriental symbols of marital fidelity and happiness because they mate for life. They were often adopted as decorative motifs on fourteenth- and early fifteenth-century ceramics, together with lotus flowers.

Eight Precious Things. Often adopted as decorative motifs on Far Eastern ceramics and occasionally also as marks. They are: 1) the mirror, sometimes regarded as a jewel that encourages conjugal happiness and neutralizes malevolent influences; 2) the coin, a symbol of riches; 3) the solid lozenge, a symbol of victory and used in ancient times as a hair ornament; 4) the open lozenge, like its solid equivalent a symbol of victory and a hair ornament; 5) the musical stone, a ministerial emblem; 6) the pair of books, a symbol of wisdom; 7) the pair of rhinoceros horn cups, a symbol of plenty; 8) the artemisia leaf, a symbol of happiness. The latter was often adopted as a mark on wares of the K'ang Hsi period (1662–1722).

Elephant. Symbol of strength, sagacity and prudence. It is an animal sacred to the Buddhists, sometimes portrayed in the act of offering flowers to the Buddha or, more frequently, as the conveyance of Samantabhadra, one of the Buddha's disciples.

Faïence. French term used to denote tin-glazed earthenware. It derives from the

Italian city of Faenza, which was famous for the production of such wares.

Famille jaune. Term coined during the nineteenth century by the Frenchman Albert Jacquemart to describe a type of Chinese enamelled porcelain whose dominant ground colour is yellow. It was first produced during the K'ang Hsi period (1662–1722).

Famille rose. Term coined during the nineteenth century by the Frenchman Albert Jacquemart to describe a type of porcelain characterized by the use of an opaque enamel, whose colour varies from pink to purplish pink, which was imported into China from Europe, where it was known as "purple of Cassius" after the Dutchman Andreas Cassius of Leyden who had discovered it in 1670. First produced in the Yung Chêng period (1723–35), it was extensively exported. Pink, an opaque colour derived from colloidal gold and called by the Chinese *fen-ts'ai* (powdery colour) or *yang-ts'ai* (foreign colour), was used in conjunction with other opaque colours (pale green, yellow, mauve etc.) which stand out in greater relief than those of the *famille verte* palette. The decoration, which is of great precision and elegance, takes the form of floral and zoomorphic motifs, with Western subjects introduced during the mid thirteenth century.

Famille verte. Term coined by the Frenchman Albert Jacquemart and used to indicate a type of Chinese enamelled porcelain whose dominant colour is green. The other colours are iron red, blue, yellow and purple. The earliest pieces also used underglaze blue, which in later examples was replaced by blue enamelling. The finest examples were made during the K'ang Hsi period (1662–1722); the porcelain is purest white, of good quality and with a clear, uniform glaze. The decoration, initially somewhat simple and generally with birds and flowers, later became more complicated and more detailed. One unique type of *famille verte* ware are the "birthday plates," made in 1713 to mark the 60th birthday of the Emperor K'ang Hsi.

Felspar. Refectory mineral composed of silica and alumina in conjunction with potassium (orthoclase) or lime (anorthite).

The basic component of porcelain and stoneware.

Flowers of the Four Seasons. Symbols of the four seasons in Chinese iconography: the peony represents Spring, the lotus Summer, the chrysanthemum Autumn and the plum Winter.

Frit. Special ceramic glaze material which, because of its high percentage of silica (80–90%), is often described as "artificial" or "composite." Very ancient in origin and sometimes also known as "Egyptian faïence," this paste is characterized by its colour, which ranges from white to greyish white. It must be rested before being shaped. Not being very malleable, it was hard to work and in order to turn it on the wheel an organic binding agent, perhaps gum, would probably need to have been added. Some pieces with a ceramic body made of frit are very hard and sometimes translucent in appearance: the same qualities as those displayed by European soft-paste porcelain.

Glaze. The vitreous layer with which a ceramic body is covered, both to make it impervious and also for decorative purposes. Obtained from silica and an alkaline or more often lead-based flux, it is coloured with metal oxides. It may be of two types: high- and low-temperature. The low-temperature variety is normally fused with lead, but it may also be alkaline (in the case of porcelain it is always alkaline). Lead glazes produce glowing colours: green, from copper oxide; brown and amber, from iron oxide; purple, from manganese oxide; blue, from cobalt oxide. High-temperature glazes are usually characterized by darker colours: iron oxide in different concentrations and under different baking conditions will produce pale grey, lavender blue, brown, rust, yellowish brown and black. A combination of iron and manganese gives a shiny black, cobalt produces blue, while copper produces red in a range of shades that depends on the firing technique used, one of the most intense being ox-blood red (sang-de-boeuf).

Greek vase painters. During Classical and Hellenistic Antiquity very few Greek vase painters signed their works. As a result, the names used by modern scholars are inspired by a particular masterpiece, by the name of the museum or collection in which a work is located, by the inscription on a piece, by the name of the site, necropolis or tomb where it was discovered or, alternatively, by some particular stylistic peculiarity.

Grisaille. Chiaroscuro decoration in shades of grey.

Grotesques. Renaissance decorative elements consisting of swags, helmets, shields, cornucopias, putti, real and imaginary animals, masks and sphinxes. The word derives from the Italian *grotte* (grottoes), underground chambers discovered during the excavations of ancient Roman buildings, where many wall paintings displaying these decorations were found.

Heaped and piled. A very common effect on Chinese blue-and-white porcelain of the fourteenth and fifteenth centuries. It resulted from the difficulties encountered by potters in grinding the imported cobalt, which often led to small particles of unground cobalt sticking to the brush. In areas where large numbers of these particles were applied they often burned through the glaze and formed tiny rust marks.

High-temperature decoration. Decoration using pigments that are resistant to high temperatures 1650–1740°F (900–950°C). During firing, these colours combine with the transparent glaze which melts and fixes the colours, as well as making the object impervious. The range of high-temperature colours is not very extensive, the main ones being cobalt blue, manganese purple, antimony yellow and iron orange.

Hydria. Greek vessel normally used for drawing and carrying water or for mixing liquids, particularly during ritual libations, although it also occurs as a cinerary urn. It is characterized by a large body, a broad mouth and two horizontal handles, with a third, vertical one for pouring. It is found in Greece in as early as the seventh century B.C., remaining part of the potters' repertoire until the end of the fourth century. It later became particularly popular amongst Italic potters. The decoration, initially restricted to the middle of the body, later tended to cover the shoulders as well, with particular areas picked out and treated in different ways (frieze decoration for the shoulder and foot, or for the lower part of the body; metope decoration for the central area).

Istoriato. Decoration typical of sixteenth-century Italian ceramics. The pattern covers the entire surface, which bears figured scenes, both religious and profane, painted in a rich polychrome.

Jasper ware. Hard, translucent white stoneware, obtained by adding barium sulphate to the clay. Created by the English potter Josiah Wedgwood in 1774–5, it comes in a variety of colours (black, brown, lilac, green), the best known of which is pale blue.

Kantharos. One of the most common Greek pottery shapes, also found in Late Neolithic sites on Crete, which later became widespread during the Classical era in Etruria and in the Roman Empire. A drinking cup, it has a deep bowl resting on a tall foot and large handles rising above the rim to which they are attached.

Kaolin. White clay, composed mainly of silica (50%) and alumina (30%), with other components in lesser proportions. Together with *baidunzi* (q.v.), it is the vital ingredient in the manufacture of porcelain. It takes its name from the Gaoling mountains to the east of Ching-tê-chên, one of the most important centers of Chinese porcelain production.

Kendi. A water vessel (the name is derived from the Sanskrit *kundika*, meaning a water vessel used in India for Buddhist rituals), it was produced from at least the fourteenth century for export to South-East Asia. Of globular form, it has a small, breast-shaped pourer. Zoomorphic *kendis*, normally in the shape of elephants or toads, appeared in the sixteenth century.

Kraak porcelain (kraakporselein). This term refers to a particular type of Chinese blue-and-white export ware produced during the Wan Li period (1573–1619) and throughout the seventeenth century. It derives from the Dutch version of the Portuguese word "caracca" (carrack). The description was introduced following the capture, in 1602 and 1604, of two Portuguese carracks, the *San Jago* and the *Santa Caterina*, whose cargo, consisting mainly of blue-and-white porcelain of various qualities and with decoration enclosed in radial panels, was sold in Amsterdam and so penetrated the European market. In Japan it is known as *fuyo-de*.

Kufic inscriptions. The oldest form of Arabic script, Kufic owes its name to Kufa, the Iraqi city in which it was invented. In the eighth century Kutba laid down its dimensions and during the following century Ustad Ahwal Sistani formulated a calligraphic canon in Baghdad. Already used on coins and monuments, at the end of the ninth century it was also adopted for textiles, ceramics and metalware, with the stroke letters accentuated. The development of Kufic ended in the twelfth century, although it still continued to be used in architectural inscriptions.

Kundika. Vase of Indian origin used in Buddhist rituals with a long neck and a long, tapering pourer leading out of a broad lip. On the back it has another, small pourer through which it is filled.

Kwaart. Term used to indicate the coating of lead-based glaze spread on the decorated surface of the majolica in order to obtain a more glossy effect. It was used by Italian majolica manufacturers, who called it *coperta*, but especially by the potters of Delft. The term is also used to refer to the ceramic coating in general, whether lead- or tin-based.

Kylix. Greek vessel, very common in every period and found even during the Late Neolithic. Characterized by a splayed cup on a tall foot and decoration covering the entire surface, both inside and out, it has two horizontal handles that disappeared in its Roman version. Its typical shape gave rise to the modern chalice.

Lebes. Bowl, probably made of bronze originally and very similar to a cauldron, used for heating water and for washing. Over the centuries its shape gradually changed until it passed into the Greek ceramic repertoire as a vase with a deep bowl, broad mouth and no handles, which was often used for ritual ablutions or as a prize for athletes in sporting contests. Common from the seventh century until the end of the fifth century B.C.

Lekythos. Greek vessel used for holding oils, perfumes and unguents, mainly for athletes. It is nevertheless often associated with funerary offerings, and as such enjoyed widespread popularity in the ancient world. The shape, already known in Corinth since the sixth century B.C., spread rapidly to Attica, where it continued to be made until the end of the fourth century, and then to the potters of southern Italy. Partly for this reason there are numerous variants, both formal and decorative. The most common type is of slender form, with a single handle, tall neck and broad mouth, a flat shoulder distinct from the body, and a small foot.

Lotus. A symbol of purity and perfection because it grows untainted by the mud, it is also an emblem of summer, of fertility, of Buddhism and Taoism. One of the most common Oriental decorative motifs of all time, it appears by itself, in ponds with other water plants or within volutes and panels.

Low-temperature decoration. Executed on a pre-fired glaze, it is characterized by a wide range of colours that are fixed by means of a third firing in a muffle kiln at a low temperature 1380°F (750°C).

Majolica. Ceramic, made of a porous paste and covered with a tin-based glaze or enamel. The biscuit was immersed in a bath, from which it emerged with a white coating that completely masked the colour of the underlying clay; this was the white ground on which the decoration was painted. The name was originally used to designate the luster pottery imported from Majorca or Malaga. It then came to be applied specifically to Italian tin-glazed wares, especially those produced during the sixteenth century at Faenza, which in turn gave its name to a type of tin-glazed ware made in France during the seventeenth–eighteenth century (faïence).

Metal oxides. Colouring agents mixed in powdered form with glazes and enamels. The most common are oxides of iron, cobalt, copper, manganese and antimony. The colours obtained depend on the firing technique (reducing or oxidizing atmosphere) and the constituent elements of the ceramic covering.

Mina'i or haft-rangi (seven-coloured) wares. Glazed wares, whose name derives from the Persian word *mina'i* (enamel), produced in Seljuk and post-Seljuk Iran (twelfth–thirteenth century), whose decorative technique is described in an ancient treatise on Persian ceramics. The ceramic body was composed of a frit paste covered in a white or blue glaze, either lead- or tin-based. After baking, the colours (seven in number and often in different shades of the same colour), were painted by brush on the glazed surface, with the sole exception of cobalt blue and sometimes also green, which were painted beneath the glaze. The piece, protected from direct contact with the flame, was fired once or several times at a temperature lower than 1110°F (600°C) so that all the colours of the decoration were fixed in several stages.

Muffle or covered kiln. Kiln made of refractory material in order to protect the wares from the heat of the flame.

Oxidizing firing. Method of firing that takes place in an oxidizing atmosphere (one containing a very high oxygen content), produced by a dry fuel and a strong flow of air. During firing, the oxygen may combine with the metallic trace elements contained in the clay or the glaze and so produce metal oxides.

Nashki inscriptions. From the Arabic. Cursive character of Arabic script in use from the tenth century (the Vizier Ibn Mukla has been credited with its introduction into the chancellery of the caliphs of Baghdad). Of soft, rounded form, it marked a new development in calligraphy. It was also adopted for use on ceramics and, from the twelfth century, on monuments as well. The twelfth century witnessed its spread throughout the Islamic world, with the partial exception of North Africa and Spain.

Oinochoe. Vessel used very widely in Antiquity to hold and pour wine or water. Its shape is similar to that of the modern pitcher, with globular body, circular or trilobate mouth and, on the whole, a single handle. It also became popular with Italic potters, with certain variations in the shape of the body and the neck, which tended to become more elongated.

Olpe. Jug regarded as a variant of the *oinochoe.* It differs in its body, which tends to broaden near the foot, in its poorly defined, cylindrical neck and circular or trilobate mouth. The majority of examples were made by Attic potters during the sixth century.

Over-glaze decoration. Type of decoration painted on the surface of a piece that has already been glazed and fired, which is fixed by a second, low-temperature firing in a muffle kiln.

Pelike. Type of Greek vase comparable to the amphora, characterized by a rounded body, broad mouth, extended lip, neck indistinct from the body and generally fitted with two handles modelled in a variety of shapes. Used by Attic red-figure and black-figure decorators.

Phiale. Shallow, flared cup, fitted with a central boss to make it easier to grasp. Rare in the Greek repertoire, it occurs during the third–second century B.C. among the wares made by Campanian potters. It was also known by the Latin name *patera* and was used by the Romans for sacrificial libations.

Phoenix. In China, the emblem of the empress and said to appear in times of peace and prosperity. It represents the South, being, together with the dragon, the tiger and the tortoise, one of the creatures symbolizing the Four Quadrants. It is also a symbol of the sun's heat and of the summer harvest.

Porcelain. Type of ceramic characterized by a dense, tough, translucent white paste. It comes in various types:

Hard paste: obtained by mixing kaolin with *baidunzi* (q.v.), which represents the vitrifying component of the porcelain. The paste, after being modelled, is baked at a low temperature 1470–1650°F (800–900°C) to obtain the biscuit, which is then covered in a felspathic glaze and baked at a high temperature 2370–2550°F (1300–1400°C). This creates a tough, compact body of a characteristic mother-of-pearl colour.

Soft paste: produced before the discovery of the formula for the manufacture of hard-paste porcelain, of which it is in reality an imitation. It can be composed of different elements. The most common form of soft-paste porcelain is formed of a paste of white clay and ground glass, fired at a low temperature. Not being very tough, it is easily scratched and therefore much rarer than hard-paste porcelain.

Bone china: type of porcelain paste containing a high percentage of bone ash (calcium phosphate), which bakes at a lower temperature than hard-paste porcelain. It was first produced by the Bow factory in England.

Posset pot. Cylindrical vessel with handles, spout and cover used in England during the seventeenth and eighteenth centuries to hold posset, a drink made of ale or wine, curdled milk and spices.

Pot-à-oille. Type of soup tureen very common in eighteenth-century France. Its shape, derived from silverware, is globular, with two handles and often with a single foot, although it sometimes rests on four small feet.

Pot-pourri vase. Vase with pierced cover used to perfume rooms. Fashionable in the eighteenth and nineteeth centuries, it contained water, flower petals and aromatic herbs.

Pouncing. Tracing technique used for the decoration of glazed wares. A piece of paper with perforations outlining the desired pattern is placed upside-down on the surface to be decorated. Very finely powdered charcoal or "pounce" is then passed through the perforations on to the glazed surface, thus producing an exact outline of the design.

Psykter. Greek vessel used for keeping wine cool. Several shapes are known, the most common being the amphora type with a body divided into two parts, the inner one acting as a container for the wine and the outer one acting as a cooler. There are examples with both black- and red-figure decoration.

Puzzle jug. Pitcher with a pierced neck, of a type produced from the Middle Ages up until the nineteenth century. It is modelled in such a way that the drink can be sipped through a tube that runs from the spout to the base.

Pyxis. From the Greek word for "box," it is a small container for cosmetics, perfumes and other toilet items, of cylindrical shape, with low foot, generally concave walls and surmounted by a cover with or without knop. The decoration generally covers the entire surface of the body and lid. Its shape, common in Attica from the sixth to the seventh century B.C., was copied by Italic and Roman potters and then passed, with certain variations, into the medieval repertoire.

Raphaelesque. Descriptive of ornamental motif found on Italian majolica of the sixteenth century and inspired by the grotesques in Raphael's Vatican *Loggie.* Characteristic elements include swags, volutes, mermaids and monsters, all depicted with great imaginative freedom and painted in rich polychrome.

Reducing firing. Method of firing that takes place in a reducing atmosphere (one containing soot and carbon monoxide), produced by damp fuel or a restricted airflow. In this oxygen-poor atmosphere the carbon monoxide combines with the oxygen present in the ceramic body or the glaze, triggering a chemical reaction that produces carbon dioxide and provokes colour changes in the coloured oxides.

Reserve. Undecorated area in a piece of pottery which retains the original colour of the surface.

Resist. Wax or varnish covering the original colour of certain areas of the porcelain surface when a piece is glazed.

Rhyton. Vessel in the shape of an animal, whose modelled head is surmounted by a low cylinder that acts as a spout and on which there is generally painted decoration. Part of the Greek repertoire during the fifth–sixth century, *rhytons* were also made in the Roman Empire.

Rocaille. Generic term used to describe the decorative caprices found in garden pavilions and nymphaeums. In ceramics it defines a type of decoration characterized by volutes, shells, curls and flowering sprays, typical of the rococo period.

Salt-glazed stoneware. Special type of ware with a glaze obtained by adding a certain amount of common salt (sodium chloride) to the kiln. By combining with the silica in the body, this forms a thin, colourless and very tough vitreous film (sodium silicate). The earliest wares are German and date from the end of the fourteenth century.

San-ts'ai. Chinese term, meaning "three colours" and referring to the technique rather than the number of colours, which are not so strictly limited. It was a technique that involved the application of a lead silicate glaze to two types of wares. The first are the polychrome wares of the T'ang dynasty (618–906), characterized by colours ranging from pale yellow to amber (obtained from iron oxide), from pale to dark green (obtained from copper oxide) and from pale to dark blue (obtained from cobalt oxide). The body, covered in a white slip, is re-covered with green, brown and yellow glazes, which, being very liquid, run and mix together, forming brown, yellow, green, blue and white splashes and drips. The second type is a porcelain with a lead-silicate enamel glaze, characteristic of the Ming period, more commonly known as *fa-hua*.

Sigillated ware. Particular type of pottery modelled in a specially refined clay rich in iron oxides, very widespread in Greece and particularly in Italy from the Hellenistic Age onwards. At the dawn of the Christian era the Romans produced a type of sigillated ware characterized by a shiny red surface, which proved popular in even the most remote provinces of the empire. As a result, during the first century A.D., flourishing manufacturing centers sprang up in Gaul, the Rhineland, Britain and North Africa. It occurs mainly in the form of tablewares, whose shape and decoration recall similar wares made of metal. Pieces were made mainly using moulds, with relief decoration. The name derives from *sigillum* (seal), since many of these vessels bear the impressed name of the maker or the owner of the workshop. The most famous sigillated wares are the so-called "Arretine wares" (q.v.).

Skyphos. Type of vase, common in both the Greek and Roman repertoire, characterized by a broad, deep cup, small foot and two handles placed either roughly halfway down the body or just beneath the rim. It is the ancient version of the modern two-handled cup or bowl.

Slip. Liquid clay, sometimes coloured, or, in the case of the Ottoman Iznik wares, a siliceous quartz composition, into which ceramics were dipped in order to modify the colour of the ceramic surface and make it homogenous. Because it is applied before firing, the slip must contract at the same rate as the paste, it must bake at the same temperature and it must have the same expansion coefficient.

Smaltino. Italian term indicating a tin-based glaze, grey blue in colour, similar to *berrettino* (q.v.).

Spur marks. Small circular or elliptical marks of unglazed clay, whitish or blackish in colour, found in the glaze, generally on the base of a piece, but sometimes in the interior. They are made by the refractory clay supports on which the piece is baked in order to prevent it from adhering to the floor of the kiln in the event of the glaze running during firing.

Stamnos. Type of Greek vase considered in its original form to be a variant of the amphora or, perhaps more correctly, of the two- rather than three-handled hydria. It has a large body, small horizontal handles and decoration covering its entire surface. Favoured by Attic black-figure, and particularly red-figure decorators, it was used for storing wine, oil and sometimes even money.

Stoneware. Ceramic ware characterized by a hard, coloured, compact, opaque and impervious body. It is made of a special clay paste fired at very high temperatures 2190–2370°F (1200–1300°C). The first stoneware was produced in China during the fourth century and later exported to the Middle East. The most important European manufacturing center was the Rhineland.

Terra cotta. Modelled clay, left to dry and then fired in the kiln at 1650–1740°F (900–950°C). It has a porous body, of reddish colour because the paste is rich in ferrous elements. Terra cotta has been used by every civilization for building materials and for the manufacture of pottery.

Three Friends of Winter. In Chinese iconography these are the pine, the prunus and the bamboo: emblems of longevity and of the Winter, and also symbols of gentlemanly qualities. The prunus symbolizes good luck and independence because it flowers at a time when almost nothing else is growing; the pine symbolizes the constancy of friendship in times of adversity; the bamboo, symbolizes the integrity of the scholar and the gentleman, loyal in adversity. They are also symbols of Taoism, Buddhism and Confucianism, or of the scholar, the poet and the painter. They were introduced as decorative motifs at the beginning of the fifteenth century.

Trompe l'oeil. Form of painting that literally "deceives the eye" and creates an illusion of reality, used in ceramic decoration during the eighteenth and nineteenth centuries.

Trophies. Decorative elements in the form of arms, shields and musical instruments, generally placed on the rims of dishes and vases. Used in particular by the decorators of Casteldurante during the sixteenth century.

Under-glaze decoration. Type of decoration painted on the biscuit before glazing. It is achieved using low-temperature colours, meaning pigments (metallic ones) that resist the high temperatures to which the piece is subjected after being glazed.

Volute crater. The distinguishing feature of this crater are the handles, which stretch upwards from near the rim in a scroll shape. It was particularly popular among Italic potters.

Select Bibliography

G. Ballardini, *Corpus della maiolica italiana*, Rome 1933–38.

G. Ballardini, *Le ceramiche di Faenza*, Rome 1933.

M. Gonzales Marti, *Céramica del levante español*, Barcelona 1944.

A. Lane, *Early Islamic Pottery*, London 1947.

W. B. Honey, *French Porcelain of the Eighteenth Century*, London 1950.

R. Soame Jenyns, *Later Chinese Porcelain*, London 1951.

R. Soame Jenyns, *Ming Pottery and Porcelain*, London 1953.

W. B. Honey, *European Ceramic Art from the end of the Middle Ages to about 1815: a Dictionary of Factories, Artists, Technical Terms . . .*, London 1953.

K. Hüseler, *Deutsche Fayencen*, Stuttgart 1956.

A. Lane, *Later Islamic Pottery*, London 1957.

E. Stazzi, *Porcellane italiane*, Milan 1964.

S. Fisher, *English Ceramics*, London 1966.

H. P. Fourest, J. Giacomotti, *L'Oeuvre des faienciers français du XVI à la fin du XVIII siècle*, Paris 1966.

B. H. Leach, *A Potter's Book*, Levittown, N.Y., 1965.

J. V. Noble, *The Techniques of Painted Attic Pottery*, New York 1960.

E. Köllmann, *Berliner Porzellan*, Brunswick 1966.

R. J. Charleston, *World Ceramics. An Illustrated History*, London 1968.

R. Cleveland, *200 Years of Japanese Porcelain*, Kansas City 1970.

H. P. Fourest, *La céramique française*, Paris 1970.

R. Soame Jenyns, *Japanese Pottery*, London 1971.

R. J. Charleston, *Roman Pottery*, London 1972.

E. Atil, *Ceramics from the World of Islam*, Washington 1973.

T. Mikami, *The Art of Japanese Ceramics*, Tokyo–New York 1973.

J. Boardman, *Attic Black Figure Vases*, London 1974.

J. Boardman, *Attic Red Figure Vases: Archaic Period*, London 1975.

S. Valenstein, *A Handbook of Chinese Ceramics*, New York 1975.

R. Ruckert and J. Wilsberger, *Meissen-Porzellan des 18. Jahrhundert*, Vienna, Munich, Zurich, Innsbruck 1977.

P. Evans, *Art Pottery of the U.S.: An Encyclopedia of Producers and Their Marks*. 2d ed., 1987.

G. Clark, *American Ceramics: 1876 to the Present*, New York 1988.

E. Levin, *The History of American Ceramics: 1607 to the Present*, New York 1988.

B. Perry, ed. *American Ceramics: The Collection of Everson Museum of Art*, New York 1989.

Index